AMERICAN HAZARD

AMERICAN HAZARD

P. W. RAINIER

THE TRAVEL BOOK CLUB
121 CHARING CROSS ROAD
LONDON, W.C.2

This Edition *1943*

BOOK
PRODUCTION
WAR ECONOMY
STANDARD

THE PAPER AND BINDING OF
THIS BOOK CONFORM TO THE
AUTHORISED ECONOMY STANDARD.

Made and Printed in Great Britain by Butler & Tanner Ltd., Frome and London

THIS book is dedicated to—

Bill Bitard, the business partner with whom
    I almost acquired two fortunes.

Gable, the "Desert Rat," with whom I tried
    to find gold.

Jamie Heddleston, the lawbreaker, on whom
    I pinned a deputy sheriff's badge.

Margaret, my wife.

Ruth, a dead game sport.

NOTE

THIS book has been written sketchily during such opportunities as occurred while on active service with the Royal Engineers. Allowances should be made for the distractions of Libyan desert sand-storms, countless flies and occasional mild Italian bombing.

CONTENTS

PART I

THE RAVAGED EAST

PART II

THE GOLDEN WEST

vii

CONTENTS

PART III

THE GLORIOUS SOUTH

PART I

THE RAVAGED EAST

CHAPTER I

A NEW ENVIRONMENT

B-L-O-O-O-O-O bellowed the siren of the Furness
Withy freighter, *Start Point*, every few minutes as she
moved gently ahead. Like some great water animal
she was, swimming slowly about and calling for its mate. In
between blasts I listened. It was 9 a.m. of the thirtieth day of
August, 1919, and the Skipper had told me that about that hour
we should be off the Five Fathom Bank buoy. Soon I heard the
ghostly tolling as the buoy rolled on the greasy swell. The noise
gradually moved astern and the *Start Point* steamed slowly into
the Delaware River. I had arrived in Philadelphia, Pennsylvania, the Quaker City, on my first visit to the U.S.A.

Four months in England I had wandered disconsolate since the
Elder Dempster liner had brought me from West Africa to
Liverpool. A four months interlude. All my life I had dreamed
of seeing England, dreamed as every Colonial does of seeing his
" mother's land." But my soul had too recently been seared
by disaster for me to appreciate England's friendly beauties.
Then I had met my Yankee friend Nick in London. The same
Nick who had once given me a job on the Revue dredge in
Mozambique, the Nick who had stood aghast while I smoked
his drunken ruffians out of their grass hut and " Long Jim "
clubbed them as they stampeded from between its burning walls,
the Nick to whom I had afterwards shipped a gang of gold
thieves to man his tin dredge in the Malay States.

Nick represented a big American company in London now,
the Bucyrus Company. This was the company which had
manufactured the dredges that I had been handling in Mozambique and Nigeria during the past years. A few weeks after our
meeting in London Nick had arranged a job for me in the U.S.A.
I was to spend some months in the great Bucyrus works to learn
the steam shovel branch of their business and then to travel for
them as an Erecting Engineer, setting up machinery in the field

3

—the job had appealed to me because the field was a wide one . . . the Bucyrus machines were used in almost every country of the world. I had taken passage in the *Start Point*, a freighter, because the victorious allied armies were moving home, being demobilised in their millions and every passenger line was booked up months ahead.

Without any of the trouble which my ship friends had prophesied, I passed the customs and immigration authorities, took a taxi through the busy Philadelphia streets to the railway station, expressed my two trunks to Milwaukee, handed my suitcase to the Pullman porter and took my seat in the train. . . . I never did see those two trunks again, although I would have sat on them all the way rather than have lost them, as they contained all my African photos and knick-nacks as well as a lot of good English clothes.

Philadelphia did not impress me much as a city—it seemed much as other cities that I knew. But I was mightily impressed by the raucous bellow of the locomotive whistle as the monster roared imperiously for the right of way when it began to move majestically out of the station. Belligerence was its note. Belligerence and rage. My memory had retained a note of fear in the tinnier toots of the smaller English locomotives. If trains had sex I should have classed the American as the male who pursued and the British as the female who fled, shrieking as she went.

One of the most informal places I know is the smoking-car on a crack American train. The big locomotive ahead was working hard on the up-grade as I seated myself in the only vacant place on the long cushioned bench of the smoker. The man on my right produced a match and courteously lit the cigar I fished from my pocket.

"What state are you from, Neighbour?" he asked conversationally.

"Can't you guess?" I was already beginning to pride myself on the American accent I had acquired during the few hours' journey.

He shook his head slowly. "I can place most folks, but I can't place you."

"I'm from South Africa."

He turned suddenly and stared into my face, his mouth open.

"From Africa! But you weren't born there?"

"Oh, yes, I was. I lived in Africa all my life too, until less than a year ago."

His mouth opened wider. "But you look quite white."

I grinned . . . feebly.

"There are lots of white people in Africa," declaimed the portly gentleman on my left, gazing keenly at the glowing tip of his cigar. "My brother-in-law went down there. Traveller for Goodyear he was. Liked it, but was glad to get back." Then he turned towards me, pointing the red-hot cigar end towards me as though it were a pistol. "How do you like this country?"

"I like it."

He seemed disappointed at my lack of expansiveness. I got the impression that I had barely passed the test. "It's God's country, all right."

I grinned. "That's what we call our country too."

He looked shocked.

"I bet there are lots of snakes down there," remarked the man on my right, he who endorsed my colour.

"Some." I found later this question was always put to me in American gatherings as soon as my neighbours heard that I came from Africa. Snake conscious they were. With reason. I was to see more snakes in my eight years in the States than I had seen in all the twenty-nine years' residence in Africa.

Right across the aisle from us a cadaverous-looking individual was ruminating a large cud of tobacco which bulged out one cheek like a monkey's pouched nuts. "There's more snakes here since prohibition than there used to be before," he remarked solemnly. "Jug snakes," he continued. "The ones that come out of bottles with green and pink stripes on them." Old Cadaver roared at his own joke till he was in danger of swallowing his cud. "If you'll come along with me I've got something to show you," he added in my direction.

I followed him to the lavatory. He closed the door carefully and fished a flat pint bottle out of his hip pocket.

"Sniff that," he whispered, reverently, when he had drawn the cork.

I sniffed dubiously. "Smells almost like whisky."

5

" Almost ! Christ, that is whisky. I've got the best boot-legger in town, bar none. Take a drink."

I swigged a mouthful from the bottle and coughed. " Tastes hot." My throat was on fire.

" You want to keep trying. Your throat gets calloused in time." He removed a quid of apparently semi-digested tobacco from his mouth and deposited it carefully on the edge of the wash-basin. " Now, if you chawed tobacco like me you'd get a real kick out of it. A drink's no drink to me unless I've got my mouth well lined with tobacco juice. In the old days, you know, they'd put tobacco juice in the rum to make it kick." He tipped the bottle to his mouth and gurgled audibly.

There might have been something in what he said about one's throat becoming accustomed to fiery liquor, because each drink burned me less as the whisky shrank in the bottle.

There is nothing like being thrown into strange conditions for reducing one's self-esteem. I was perfectly at home in the con-ditions to which I was used in the more primitive parts of Africa. There I was as much in my element as an elephant or a savage. I knew where to look for what I wanted or how to move from place to place. But here, in a highly industrialised world, I was continually blundering into snares. Twice in the next two days I put my foot into things. True, had conditions been reversed and the inhabitants of the U.S.A. been placed in my own environ-ment they would have done no better than I in theirs. The vast stretches of the African bushveld were as far from their conception as a great teeming city had been from mine before I saw one.

My first blunder was in Chicago, where I had to change from the Pennsylvania railway system to that of the Milwaukee & St. Paul. I stepped out of the Pennsylvania station and hailed a taxi.

" Drive me to the Milwaukee & St. Paul station," I said to the taxi-driver as he took my suitcase.

His gaze travelled speculatively over my new English clothes. " What time's your train leave, mister ? " he queried.

" In an hour."

He slammed my suitcase into the front seat and jumped to the wheel. " We'll make it if I step on it," he cried.

For about fifty minutes he drove me furiously through the city. Then, drawing up to my station with a squeal of brakes, he consulted the astronomical figure on the meter and accepted the fare without remark.

Dashing into the station I took my seat just a minute before the train moved off. I mopped my face and sighed my relief.

"Didn't leave much time to spare, Stranger," remarked the fellow-occupant of my seat sympathetically.

"I can't understand why the deuce they have railway stations so far apart. Took us nearly an hour driving fast to get here from the Pennsylvania station."

"Huh?"

I repeated my complaint.

"Good God! The stations are side by side. All you have to do is to pick up your suitcase and walk across the street."

It was a Saturday afternoon when I arrived in Milwaukee. I knew the factory would not be accessible till Monday morning so I went to the Plankington Hotel, lunched on a huge square of their famous planked steak and wrote letters afterwards. Then I walked down the street looking for a letter-box in which to post them. I walked a long way looking for the familiar pillar-box, which all my life had represented the place in which letters were dropped before being magically transported to the corners of the earth. I had just come to the conclusion that Milwaukee citizens did not write many letters when I caught the gleam of red ahead. A queer looking contraption it was. Like no letter-box I had seen. A patent Yankee contraption evidently. There did seem to be an opening in front, but it was covered with a sheet of glass. I was juggling with the glass to see if it moved when an excited individual rushed up.

"Break the glass. Break the glass," he cried, gazing about the street as though to find something with which to break it. He saw a small stone and dashed for it triumphantly.

"Where's the fire?" he asked as he ran back.

"What fire?"

"The one you're trying to give the alarm for."

"I'm trying to post a letter."

He dropped the stone and eyed me pityingly.

"Do they post letters in fire-alarms where you come from?"

"I thought it was a letter-box. Our letter-boxes are red."

"You poor sap. There's a letter-box on that tree." He

pointed to a small square green box that was quite obvious when one knew what to look for.

After that I wandered to the high bluffs on the lake front. Sitting by the statue of Eric the Red—the Viking who beat Columbus by a good many centuries to the discovery of the New World—I gazed out over the expanse of Lake Michigan. Blue. The same blue that I had seen in the Indian Ocean from the hills of Zululand when I was young.

Monday morning I went to work in the Bucyrus factory. Four months I worked there, one of two thousand men. Clad in overalls we punched a time clock at seven each morning . . . when nature called during the day we punched a time clock going in and another going out and got fined if we loitered. Chipping castings in the foundry. Machining valves in the machine shop. Driving rivets in the structural yard. Setting valves in the engine works. One by one I passed through each department, moving on to the next as soon as I felt that I had mastered what I wanted to know . . . as the medical student studies the ear, the throat or the nose, so I studied the different organs which compose the mechanism of the modern excavating machine. A surgeon of steel, that's what I was becoming.

I liked the American workmen with whom my lot was cast. I liked the staff too. College men the latter were for the most part. Men of every type from the rabid pro-prohibitionist to the chap who claimed to be literary because he had never seduced any woman less educated than a college graduate. The officers of the company were grand fellows who looked after the welfare of their men like fathers. But the great barn-like factory seemed like a jail to me and I was glad when at length I was sent for by the Superintendent of Outside Construction and told that I had gained sufficient experience to be transferred to his department. Erecting Engineer . . . travelling. It meant seeing more of the country each time I moved from one job to another to set up and test those great earth-moving machines of various kinds that the Bucyrus Company manufactured and shipped to the far ends of the earth.

CHAPTER II

THE MEN WHO MINE COAL

THE big car rushed at the narrow Pennsylvania country road like a hog at the barn trail when he hears the feeding call. The fat tires threw a sheet of slush to either side and splintered the forming ice in the puddles. The big headlight beams swung wildly from side to side, throwing into momentary relief sections of gaunt and leafless woods, wooden telephone poles and the irregular zig-zag of "dog-leg" fences, made by the primitive expedient of laying zig-zag logs on the ground, laying another across them with their ends across the ends of the next in line and continuing the process until the fence is the required height. Major Richards hunched over the steering-wheel, the width of his burly shoulders enhanced to Samsonian proportions by the heavy sheepskin coat he wore. Beside him in the comfortable warmth of my own sheepskin, I wondered how fast he would drive if he were really in a hurry instead of merely bringing an Erecting Engineer into camp from the nearest railway station. The Major swung his body over the wheel as a right-angle bend in the road rushed towards us. The car heeled on to two wheels and the headlights swung in a ninety degree arc to peer down the road ahead. I gave a yell of warning and the Major jammed the brakes on hard and skidded the car to a stop. There was a body lying in the road ahead. Clad in blue overalls. Lying on its face with its legs in a puddle.

I reached the body ahead of my companion and turned it over in the glare of the headlights. It grunted as I did so and there was a reek like methylated spirits.

"Good God! He's only tight," I laughed foolishly in my relief.

The Major was standing with his hands in the pockets of his sheepskin coat, his strong square face silhouetted against the lights.

"That's what the damned 'pussy-foots' have done to us," he growled. "Forced a prohibition law through against the wish of the country . . . did it while most of the boys were fighting in France, so that they couldn't vote. Before Prohibition that fellow in the puddle would get tight Saturday nights on honest beer, but he'd work his six-day week like an honest man. Now all he does is to sozzle prohibition rot-gut till he's as full of it as a sponge . . . he and his mates. That's why a man can't get an honest day's work done nowadays."

"You know him, then?"

"He's Jake Hall. Runs the little steam-shovel, grading for the coal-track."

"Why don't you fire him if he's drunk all the time?"

"He's a good man in between spells when he's sober. The next one would probably drink as much and do less in between."

The Major bent over suddenly and felt with experienced fingers in the pocket of Jake's overalls. He extracted a bottle, pulled the cork with strong white teeth, sniffed gingerly, drank a gulp and spat vehemently.

"Filth," he growled. "Try it." He handed me the bottle.

It was half full of liquid which showed a bright pink against the light. Strawberry syrup was the colour. A smell of varnish came from the neck of the bottle. Varnish, methylated spirits and another familiar scent that I couldn't identify.

"Not for me." I was afraid of it. Too many stories about people going blind from cheap bootleg liquor. A man's health —his life even—depended on the ethics of his bootlegger in prohibition America. One chose a bootlegger with almost as much care as one chose a wife.

"Try, damn it," cried the Major. "One swig can't kill you."

But one swallow was enough for me. I gagged and spat as he had done.

He barked a short laugh. "Let's get him home," he said. "We'll pour a purge into him and try to get him fixed to work to-morrow."

That night I lay warm in blankets on a camp-bed in a wooden barn of a workman's dormitory while snow drifted in through the chinks in the walls. How good that country air tasted!

My six months in the Bucyrus factory had been an experience well worth while, but I didn't want any more indoor life for a while.

The camp was a collection of wooden shanties set in a snow flat at the foot of some leafless oak woods. Across a stream was a spur of a railway track on which was shortly expected to arrive the train-load of machinery for the four-hundred-ton monster steam-shovel, which I was here to put together and groom until its dipper was shovelling ten-ton bites of earth and rock to uncover the coal-seam, as a spoon would remove the thick icing from a layer cake. But until the machinery should arrive I was at a loose end. Free to amuse myself.

One afternoon, a few days after my arrival, the Major hunted me up.

" Want some fun ? " he asked.

" I'm game. What is it ? "

" I've found the place in the village where the men get that damned moonshine liquor. Let's raid it."

" Why not let the police do it ? "

" There aren't any police in a jerkwater place like this. Only the Sheriff."

" Why doesn't the Sheriff do it ? "

" The old beaver's a complete zero. We'll do it ourselves."

" That's all right for you. You're in your own country, but I'm a foreigner. I can't afford to get on the wrong side of the law. Let's at least take the Sheriff with us."

" But that old bastard hasn't the guts to raid a hen-roost. Hatching eggs would be about his line."

" Then we'll kidnap him and take him with us."

The Major looked at me keenly and his face split into a grin. An automatic pistol and holster he clipped on to his belt. For me he borrowed a huge Colt .45 without a holster. It was as big as an old-fashioned horse pistol and refused to fit into the pocket of my sheepskin coat, so I slipped it into the waistband of my trousers. As I did so I reflected that this was the first time I had ever worn a revolver to protect myself from my fellow-men. The wilds of Africa did not seem wild now, for all that continent's much maligned savages.

The village was a mean hamlet of one street, lined on either

side by drab wooden houses. Streaks of white snow were showing through the brown churned-up sludge of the street, as though
white cream had been half mixed into a chocolate custard. The
place seemed lifeless. Dead. Only the smoke from the house-
chimneys showed that people were alive inside. The Major
halted his car outside the Sheriff's door. I got out and
knocked.

When the Sheriff came to the door the Major beckoned him
from behind the steering-wheel of the car, where he sat with
the engine still purring.

"We want you to come with us to raid that moonshine
joint." His tone was peremptory.

A small man was the Sheriff, with a large walrus moustache
set in a face like a rabbit's. As he stood, little dewdrops were distilling themselves on the tip of his nose. When a drop was fully
formed a twitch of the nose would shake it on to the moustache,
where it found its way by gravity to the ends and dropped
off.

"There's a tough gang runs that joint," he expostulated.
"We'd need a strong *posse* of men to tackle it."

Major Richards hitched his automatic into sight. "We're
posse enough," he growled. He jerked his thumb at me. "This
guy's a gunman from Africa. He's tough."

The representative of the law glanced uneasily over his shoulder
at me where I stood between him and the security of his own
door. Visibly he gulped and his nose twitched rapidly.

"It's all hunky-dory for you guys to go raiding joints," he
hedged. "But I've got votes to think of and the 'lections ain't
far off, neither."

"To hell with your votes," roared the Major. "You repre-
sent the law and I want that joint cleaned up before they poison
all my men. We'll do the rough stuff but you'll come with us
to make it legal."

The Sheriff suddenly attempted to dive under my arm but I
caught him, heaved him bodily into the seat alongside the Major
and scrambled in beside him. The Major clashed into gear and
the car squelched on down the deserted street.

"Christ, have a heart, you men," wailed the Sheriff. "Where
the hell am I or anyone else going to get a drink if you clean up
the only joint in town?"

The Major eased the car silently to a stop before the last house in the street, a dilapidated looking place that needed a coat of paint even more than the rest of the village. The door of the barn-like structure was closed but its chimney was smoking, and there was a reek in the air like the reek from the neck of that bottle. Unmistakable.

The Major and I jumped into the street simultaneously. The Sheriff followed us but shot down the road past the house and round the corner at a high rate of speed, his head hunched between his shoulders, like the rabbit he was scooting for his burrow.

When I noticed the Major was holding his pistol in his hand I fished my revolver from my waistband.

" If we charge that door together," he instructed, " we'll break it down and be in on the gang before they expect us."

It seemed sound strategy to me, but I was by no means comfortable about the affair. The idea of breaking into other people's houses instead of having the police do it was outside my experience. Someone was likely to be shot over this business, I reflected. That meant that the shooter would get into trouble. I preferred to get into trouble over shooting someone else rather than have anyone get into trouble over shooting me, so I fervently hoped I wouldn't have to do the shooting and hoped still more fervently that no one would do any shooting at me.

The Major and I were both heavy men and when, together, we charged the flimsy wooden door with the points of our shoulders its rusty hinges pulled clear of the door-post and it crashed forward into the room. A big room it was, I had time to notice. We sprang to the middle of it and stood back to back, weapons in hand, like a couple of traditional town marshals cleaning up a joint in a wild west thriller.

There was a slatternly woman in the room and half a dozen dirty children, ranging from half-grown to crawler. This was the Sheriff's " tough gang." At our sudden apparition they all began to howl at the tops of their voices.

" I'll gut that blasted Sheriff for this," I heard the Major growl between his teeth as he slipped his gun into its holster. His face was turkey red with embarrassment, and I felt myself blushing down to my middle. As unobtrusively as possible I eased my revolver into my waistband out of sight—it seemed as big as a fifteen-inch gun on a battleship—but my embarrassment made me clumsy and it slipped down my trouser-leg and clattered on to the floor. As I snatched it up the foul reek of the place caught at my throat and threw me into a fit of coughing, under cover of which I stepped through an open door into the adjoining room, evidently the kitchen.

The smell was even worse here and the heat terrific. There was a roaring fire in the stove on which stood a round galvanised iron bath-tub. Covering the bath-tub was a sweat-stained, thick felt horse-blanket of a violent pink colour. Sodden with steam was the blanket and under it, filling the tub, was a corn-mash infusion which was boiling furiously. Near the stove was a tin bucket partly full of the same pink liquid which we had sampled from Jake's bottle a few nights before. Simple but efficient. A whisky still. When the horse-blanket was saturated it had only to be wrung out into the bucket. The dye from the blanket provided the rich pink colour and the smell of horse sweat had been the familiar odour which I had not been able to identify when I sniffed at Jake's bottle.

We opened the window and heaved bath-tub, contents, bucket and blanket out into the snow. A cloud of evil-smelling steam shot up and the snow was stained pink like a splash of blood.

"You've got to stop selling liquor to my men," then shouted the Major, lifting his voice above the howling chorus as a ship's officer bellows above the screaming of a gale at sea.

The slattern shrieked a reply but it was lost in the hubbub. Gritting her teeth she flung open another door and hustled her farrow into another room, slamming the door on them. Their howling dropped in volume when they lost sight of us, but their moans of terror seeped through the cracks in the wooden partition like a hyena's moaning through the bars of his cage. With one dirty hand trying to straighten her disarranged hair she faced the Major.

"Mine childers hoongry," she screamed. "How I get money?"

"Where's your man?"

"Man dead one year, choost after we come from old country."

" Which country ? "

" Me Slovak."

" Can you wash clothes ? "

" Wash good. Wash clean," she asserted unconvincingly.

" I'll give you the camp washing at ten dollars a week if you swear to sell no more liquor to my men."

" I swear." She crossed herself several times. I also registered an oath . . . . to send my own washing elsewhere.

The Major felt in his pocket and handed her a crumpled five-dollar bill. " To pay for the muck we threw out," he explained to her as we turned to leave.

" I'll bet she's at it again within a month," he remarked as we entered the car. He was right. In considerably less than a month's time the pink liquor began once more to appear in camp.

" Going to raid the gang again ? " I queried, when he showed me a bottle of liquor he had confiscated.

" You go to hell," he replied with a grin as a heave of his powerful arm sent the bottle crashing against a tree-trunk.

The Major's camp was a good one. His army experience enabled him to run it with clockwork precision and his discipline was strict. But to keep a certain type of American workman from his liquor is about as easy as keeping a rutting buck from a doe.

By the time I had been in this camp for six weeks the great stripping shovel was gouging its dipper into the rock covering which nature had laid upon the coal-seam. The great steel structure snorted and rocked on its framework as it tore loose its load of rock and swung its long boom sideways with triumphant puffs of white steam that plumed into the frosty air as the contents of the dipper dropped on to the slope of the hillside below. Behind the great shovel, on the smooth black expanse of coal it had already uncovered, a smaller shovel was gouging mere ton lots of coal with its dipper and loading them into strings of dump cars, hauled by miniature locomotives that shuttled backwards and forwards—they seemed fussy imitations of their larger and more dignified railway brethren—between the shovel and the loading tipple on the railway spur half a mile away. This stripping method was the new kind of coal mining which was just then in its infancy and with the growth of which my next years were to be intimately connected. In stripping we took the mountain off the top of the coal instead of making a hole in the mountain to get at the coal underneath.

My job here was done now. The Major handed me a written acceptance of the machinery on behalf of his company. I mailed it to the Bucyrus Company in far-away South Milwaukee, and in a couple of days received a wire instructing me to set up a similar plant near a town called Osceola Mills in the Alleghany Mountains, some hundreds of miles to the eastward, beyond Altoona.

In Altoona I had to spend the night and catch a local train next morning. A darkey porter showed me the way to an up-stairs bedroom which had attained the atmospheric condition of a Turkish bath under the influence of a large steam radiator which was hissing and bubbling in a corner. The change from the arctic atmosphere outside caught at my throat and staggered me. I dived for the window and threw it open, while the porter eyed me with the pitying, tolerant expression with which the sane usually regard the harmlessly insane.

Inside the window, coupled to a ring in the wooden floor of the room, was a coil of light chain a few yards long. Tied to the end of the chain was a coil of half-inch rope.

"I suppose that's used to hang out of the window on when you want to cool off," said I, attempting a joke.

"No Suh. That's for fire-escaping. Guests don't mostly hang out of windows in this heah hotel. Mos' people wot comes heah has their haids screwed on right."

Pitch dark it was when I boarded the branch line train for the little mountain town of Osceola Mills—a "jerk-water" line the conductor called it when he fell into conversation after punching my ticket. "Jerk-water" was right. The train bumped and rolled as the smoke-belching engine dragged it around the mountain spurs and the water in the full engine tender splashed in spray as the roughness of the track jerked it overboard. Of all the marvels of the U.S.A. (it is a marvellous country even if not quite as marvellous as its inhabitants think it—a trite remark which could be made of almost any country in the world) I found no marvel to compare with the juicy richness of the American slang.

After several hours I stepped out of the Osceola Mills station

16

with a heavy suitcase in my hand. As soon as my feet touched the icy sidewalk they shot out from under me and I skidded several yards on my behind until I fetched up almost against the radiator of a waiting automobile.

" Guess you're the guy I've come to meet," drawled a voice from behind the curtains. As I picked myself up a slender youth in overalls opened the door for me. In beside him I climbed. Dodds, he told me his name was. Timekeeper at the mine for which I was bound.

In low gear we climbed a mountain spur. A pair of snow-filled ruts was the road . . . frozen mud. Through cut-over pine country we climbed continuously until the town of Osceola Mills looked like a yellow chessboard in the valley below. Around us was the scrub which grows when the original pine forest has gone. Here and there among the bushes a solitary hemlock showed black against the snow, only lacking tinsel and candles to make it a Christmas tree. After a couple of hours in low gear we reached the camp. There was one large two-storied building with a tar-paper roof; like a dismal barn it looked from the outside, except that it had windows in it. Nearby was a small wooden bungalow . . . the superintendent's house, Dodds explained.

I was to sample a good many mining camps during the eight years I was to spend in the U.S.A. Some of them I was to find very good. Most were passable, but the one I was now entering was easily the worst I experienced. I picked up my suitcase and followed Dodds inside.

The atmosphere that smote me in the face as I entered was staggering. Stale, breathed air, cheap tobacco smoke and the smell of unwashed bodies were all in it. You could almost have shovelled it out in chunks. A hyena's lair was sweet in comparison.

" My God ! " I ejaculated.

Dodds grinned. " It's a bit thick but you'll get used to it in time. It's worse than usual to-day. Sunday, so all the men are in camp."

Somewhat at the cost of my own self-respect I found that as the days passed I did become somewhat inured to it, although the first impact after entering from the fresh wintry air outside always made me reel.

Now I saw that the whole of the lower floor of the large building was one single room. It was overheated by two great cast-iron stoves which roared through their black stove-pipes till they showed cherry red in spots. Round the stoves were gathered groups of men who chewed tobacco and spat. The stoves were their target and each hit was registered by a hiss and a small puff of steam, while thick spots of fuzzy deposit on the glowing stoves testified to the good marksmanship of past Sundays. At the back of the room one long table between wooden benches stretched from end to end of the building and a couple of sullen looking men in overalls were dealing out tin plates from piles they carried under their arms. There was a growl of conversation in the room in some language that was strange to me.

" What kind of language is that ? " I asked Dodds as he led me up a rough wooden stairway at the end of the room.

" Bohunk."

" What's that ? "

" Bohemia, Hungary and thereabouts. We call the people between Germany and Russia Bohunks. There are so many races around there we can't keep track of them. They've let so many riff-raff into this country from that part of Europe that a white American can hardly get a job any more."

" Are they as good as the American labour ? "

" They'll work longer hours for less pay and that's all most bosses care about."

The top floor also was one sole room except for the tiny partitioned-off cubby-hole where I was to sleep with Dodds. Only as high as my head the partitions reached . . . the rest open to the roof. The walls of the big room were lined with two tiers of bunks in which many men were lying, rolled in dingy looking blankets. The heat was less oppressive here, being supplied only by the stove-pipes from below on their way to the roof and the air which flowed up the stairway and through the cracks in the rough, boarded floor. But the foul reek was the same. It was as though the concentrated foulness of all the slums and other evil places of the earth wherein men lived in droves had settled in this place.

I walked to a window and noted that it was nailed shut. Rubbing some of the frosted filth off the glass I could see outside a jolly looking hemlock with powdered snow on its branches like the white powder on the branches of a toy Christmas tree. I took out my knife and began to work on the pane.

" What are you up to ? " asked Dodds.

" I'm going to get some air if I have to sleep here."

" The men will raise hell. Fresh air doesn't suit their kind."

" They can raise all the hell they like. I'm not going to sleep in this frowst."

The timekeeper looked up at me enviously from his five feet four inches. " I might have tried it myself if I'd been your size," he remarked, half defiantly. Then he slapped his thigh. " God Almighty ! I've had a hell of a time here by myself."

" What did you stay for ? " I asked as I got my knife under the edge of the window-pane and prised it loose from its flimsy putty fastening. A whiff of cold air swept inwards. It felt cool in my lungs like water on the tongue of a thirsty man.

" Jobs are scarce and I've got to eat," Dodds replied sadly.

A puff of wind outside shook the powdering from the hemlock branches and swept a cold draught in through the glassless square in the window. A chorus of growls and unintelligible curses arose throughout the length of the big room. A showdown was coming. That was evident.

" Shut goddam window ! " someone shouted in a guttural foreign voice.

" Come and shut it yourself ! " I shouted in reply. If I was going to live in this hoggery for a couple of months I might as well establish my status right at the beginning, I felt. So far in America I hadn't seen anything that looked half as tough as the material that used to drift into mining-camps in Africa. So I wasn't unduly worried.

We heard a ponderous tread come down the long room towards us and a big foreigner in dirty overalls stood at the door of our cubicle.

" This is ' Big Mike,' the foreman," volunteered Dodds.

I looked the man over carefully. He looked as big as a hippo and about as agile. His large square face showed about as much intelligence as a hippo too. But those long arms would crack a man's ribs if he were fool enough to get inside them. A long-range fight was the tactics, I decided . . . if it should come to a fight.

" Shut goddam window ! " he repeated frowning.

I still held the pane of glass in my hand. Now I pushed it diagonally through the opening so that it fell outside in the snow. Then I turned and looked at " Big Mike."

He scratched his head and his brow wrinkled. " Too much cold make man sick," he explained in a less truculent tone . . . no fight in him. That was evident.

" This is over my bunk and I'll take the whole window out if I want to." I took my knife from my pocket again and began to pry round the edges of another pane.

" No . . . no. Pleese Meester. Man too much sick for cold."

" All right then. One will do."

Still scratching his head he lumbered off and I heard him haranguing the men at the other end of the room. He was probably explaining away his loss of face. At any rate I had no more trouble from the Bohunk gang.

" Where do we wash ? " I asked Dodds as we came downstairs in the almost pitch blackness of six a.m. next morning.

He pointed to the tin wash-basin on a box near the door. There was some dark looking fluid in the basin which matched in colour the marks on the skimpy towel which hung on a nail above it.

" I think I'll rub my face in the snow outside," I remarked. I had already decided to grow a beard in that camp and not for anything would I have rubbed my face on that towel in the leavings of sixty men.

" Let's have a bath in the snow," cried Dodds beginning to tear off his sheepskin coat.

We stripped naked in the overheated room in front of the scandalised stares of the men who were sitting down to break-fast—it was not our nakedness that scandalised them but what they thought our loss of sanity. Dashing outside we dived into a snowdrift, rolled like puppies, rubbed each other vigorously with balls of snow and dashed back to dress by the stove. As I sat at the table with a glowing skin and blood pulsing through me I thought of the prophecies of old African friends when they heard I was going to winter in the States. That the malaria in my blood after years in the tropics would allow the cold to make a speedy end to me had been their prophecy. But Dodds and I repeated the snow bath every morning till spring without even catching cold.

There was only one other episode worthy of note in the two months I spent in the Osceola Mills camp. Towards the end of my sojourn there it was. The big shovel was already set up and I was waiting till the tests on it had been run. Spring was on its way. Patches of dun-coloured earth were already beginning to show through the snow. Little swellings on the bare twigs of the bushes showed promise of a leaf crop. God, how glad I would be when the country turned green as I had first known it on my arrival the summer before. The northern winter had seemed inexpressibly dismal to me after the green aliveness of the tropics. The bare dusty dun-coloured spaces of German South-West Africa had been unpleasant but they had seemed in keeping with nature, displaying their barrenness honestly. But the starkness of this country of leafless tree-growth seemed as though some disaster had overtaken nature. Deceitful were these northern climates. Seducing by their verdure in summer only to condemn the seduced to desert conditions for half the year. Some time later I was to meet an Australian woman on her first visit who had just travelled from west to east across the country in the depth of winter.

"How did you like the country?" I asked her.

"Looks like there'd been a hell of a bush-fire from one end of it to the other." My own reaction had been something like that.

"It's a good healthy country all the same."

She laughed. "Breeds healthy virile people, I expect. That's just what one ought to do with it. Use it to breed your ancestors in."

Now, borrowing a clean towel and a cake of soap from the cook I strolled down towards the little creek below. For a couple of days now it had burst its ice cover and its music of nights had floated in through my open window-pane and made me homesick. I stripped naked on its banks among some dry tufts of grass and prepared to step into the water.

A slight noise startled me. Something like a miniature baby's rattle. For a moment I did not connect it with anything. Then

I stiffened. It could only be a rattlesnake. There were plenty about in the summer in these mountains from stories Dodds had told me. Stepping gingerly back to my clothes I took my pocket-knife and cut myself a pliable sapling about six feet long. Then I hunted for the snake. The moment I moved forward he rattled again. So did others. In all directions I heard rattlings and dull brown shapes with black markings moved sluggishly among the grass-tufts. I smote lustily at anything that moved, acutely conscious of my bare feet and legs. When I could see or hear no more of them I dressed as quickly as possible. Then I went to count the bag. Over twenty I had killed and many more must have escaped. According to Dodds, rattlesnakes "hive up" in big balls in holes in the ground to keep warm in the winter. What I had walked into must have been the disintegration of a rattlesnake ball into its component parts with the warmth of spring.

Dodds looked pathetic when he shook my hand in farewell after he had driven me to Osceola Mills station.

"Don't forget me if you see any good jobs lying around loose," was his farewell as the train moved off.

"I won't," I shouted in reply. I meant it too. The cocky little sparrow of a man was too good for that kind of camp.

My next job was in a little coal-mining town called Wyano, not very far from Pittsburgh in Pennsylvania. My instructions were to wait at a hotel in Pittsburgh until the superintendent of the mine came to fetch me. I took to him at sight when he walked into my room and introduced himself as Bill Bitard. It is worth while describing the man in detail as he and I were destined to hunt in couple during most of my eight years' stay in the country. A slender man of middle height he was, about my own age of thirty years. Pale blue eyes, which he usually dimmed behind big tortoiseshell glasses—Heaven alone knows why, because his eyesight was excellent. He had the intellectual face of a college professor. An expression of disarming mildness belied, as I was to find out in more than one tight place later, a fiery temperament and a burning ambition. If you put the disposition of an Airedale into the ingratiating exterior of a setter you would get his prototype in the dog world.

In Wyano we were housed in a great stone farmhouse with

the date 1814 cut into the keystone of the arch of the door.
Walls three feet thick it had, and narrow windows which made
me believe that Indians had been not unknown in the district at
the time it was built.

CHAPTER III

A FIGHT FOR INDEPENDENCE

IT was just before my projected departure from Wyano that Bill Bitard came and sat beside me on an old log from where I was watching the big shovel rooting in the high cut of rock and earth like a monster boar into a river-bank in search of roots.

"What do you think of our proposition here?" he asked, taking off his glasses and polishing them with his handkerchief.

"First class." I had been thinking just that when he came up. A good thick seam of coal they had—eight feet thick and the best quality, while the overburden on top was not too thick to move cheaply. The price of coal was good and getting better, while the mine was situated advantageously to supply the great Pittsburgh steel industry with its coal. Cheap operating and a good market . . . the two prime conditions for the success of a mine. If the place was well managed it should make a pile.

"I've bought my partners out." His glasses still in his hand, he was looking at me keenly out of his faded blue eyes.

I stared. I knew he was a partner in the enterprise, of course. That was common talk in camp. But it was common knowledge also that Bill was a poor man. His family had been numbered among those of the coal barons once, but his father had come a cropper during the war and Bill had been left to start again.

"What did you use for money?" I asked.

Bill grinned. When he did that he made a man's heart squirm.

"Got no money. Bought on credit. Twelve monthly payments and the title stays with the sellers till the last one is made." He fished a folded document out of his pocket and slapped it with the back of his fingers.

I took the document from him and read it through. The conditions seemed fair enough. If he defaulted on any payment the property reverted to the original partnership. If he completed the payments the property was his.

"Where's the money coming from? It's a big figure." It was so big it took my breath.

"Right there," he cried, pointing to where the shovel was working. "If I can keep that baby moving she'll make the monthly payments easy."

"At the present price of coal she might. But suppose the price drops?"

"The price won't drop. There's a miners' strike brewing. That'll put the price higher yet."

That was likely enough. The United Mineworkers of America, under their leader, John L. Lewis, seemed out for another round with the Coal Operators.

"But suppose the price does drop and you can't meet the payments?"

He waved his hands in an airy gesture. "Then I revert to my original status of junior partner. All I'll have lost will be a lot of hard work and worry."

"How did you persuade your partners to sell?" I knew his partners were a couple of retired business men in Pittsburgh.

"They didn't need much persuading. They're afraid the coal strike will shut us down for months and break us."

"Won't it?"

"Not if I can find anyone with guts enough to hold this job down through some rough weather. I'll be busy myself with the selling end of the business."

That set me thinking. I was not much in love with my job as erecting engineer. I could see that it would be all right for a while, but there seemed little future in it. I would travel the U.S.A. for years, with an occasional trip abroad, building steam shovels and excavating machinery till I was sick of the sight of white plumes of smoke spurting out of prehistoric looking steel monsters. Sleeping in mining camps. Consorting with the same kind of people from one year to another. Then, the final reward. When my middle began to bulge and my hair to grey, a soft seat in a swivel chair in the Bucyrus administrative offices. Besides, I felt constrained. My first job, it was as a small cog in an immense machine. Fine people the Bucyrus Company were, and the officials kept a patriarchal status to their employees. Men stayed with that company. Some of those grizzled old chaps with whom I had worked in the shops had been with the company since they had left school. But such a future was not for me. God forbid. Suburbia. Already I felt like a springbok trapped in a fenced field. However good the grass may be inside, the buck will jump the fence. Besides, I saw opportunity in this stripping method of mining. New it was. Only a few enterprising men like Bill Bitard had got into it yet, although there were scores of coal areas where the method could be used to advantage. Unless I missed my guess every bit of coal suitable for stripping would be snapped up within a year or two. Cost of operation was the reason. Underground shafts were costly and the men who worked in them—the United Mineworkers' Union—more expensive still. Every few years the United Mineworkers, under that fighting bull of a leader, John L. Lewis, had gone to the mat with the Coal Operators and won each round, forcing their wage-scale up and with it the price of coal mined underground. But the stripping business was too small as yet to have made itself worth the domination of a powerful union among its workers. The men who worked in the stripping mines were mechanics, not miners. Unorganised. They owed no allegiance to the mineworkers. With a strong hand at the helm Bill's mine might well keep running through the strike. It would need a strong hand though. Striking miners had rough methods by all accounts and would stop at nothing to shut down any mine producing coal while they were on strike.

I had almost made up my mind to ask Bill for a job when he spoke again.

"How tight are you married to the Bucyrus people?"

"Not too tight. I'd have to give them proper notice, of course."

"How long?'

"A month."

Then he staggered me. "I need a partner to run this mine. Will you take it on?"

When two men want to travel the same road it is not hard to make a deal. A month later I was back in the Wyano camp as mine superintendent and partner.

There was a strike coming. No doubt of that now. The belligerence of the miners' rumblings was unmistakable. It behoved me to look to my defences. Only a mile away was the great underground coal-mine of Wyano, employing a thousand men. A thousand United Mineworkers and their families lived in that chessboard town of wooden houses which I could see in the valley from my window in the great stone boarding-house. Of a dozen foreign breeds they were, Russians predominating. Only a thin leavening of level-headed native American miners lived as though on sufferance among them. Ninety per cent. of the adults in that town could speak only the most broken English if they could speak it at all. Most of the daily papers they read were even printed in foreign languages. Once the strike started their inflammable foreign temperament would be kindled by agitators, set ablaze by the cheap bootleg liquor sold them openly, in defiance of the prohibition law, in the local " speak-easy " saloon which kept its doors wide open to the street, doors from which I had seen more than one drunken man fired like a projectile to lie in sodden stupor on the sidewalk. Whatever happened our mine must be kept working, in spite of that menace. To be shut down for a month would break us. Even a week's shut down might make the difference between failure and success. Every day we lost would be a nail in the coffin of our hopes.

Our only defence was bluff. The local police authorities would be hand and glove with the miners. We could expect no help from them. But, with a stout-hearted crew behind me, I was willing to bet that I could see it through. I began to run my mind over the roster of the fifty men we employed.

The timekeeper of a mine is the key-man who acts as the superintendent's assistant. Mine was a sappy youth with a leprous soul. Not much backing to be got out of that weak sister, I judged. I walked through the building to the room we used as an office. The youth was there. As I watched him, unperceived, I saw him take a photo from his pocket and gaze at it. Moving closer I saw that it was the picture of a popular ballet dancer, her dress fluffed out half-way up her shapely thighs. As I watched he tilted the picture and tried to peer up her skirt to get a more comprehensive view. It was not the boy's pornographic mind that decided me, but his lack of brain. I sent a telegram to Osceola Mills. Within a week Dodds was with me and the incompetent photo-tipper had gone. That little cocksparrow of a Dodds was so delighted to get into a decent camp that his loyalty was assured. Game he was too, I judged. He was to prove me right before our acquaintance ended.

Four men to the crew of the big shovel and two to the smaller coal-loading shovel. They would do, I decided. Native Americans all. Hard-bitten citizens who had spent most of their lives in camp wherever dirt was flying in railway construction. They could be trusted to hold their own if there was trouble. The two men who ran the "dinkey" locomotives were native Americans too. Solid old chaps who had once run locomotives on the big railway systems and been retired because of age.

There was Collins, the track foreman. Strangely enough he was a college graduate, a qualified civil engineer, condemned to earn his living with his hands by the shortage of white-collar jobs for the host of college graduates which the American educational system turned out in tens of thousands each year, regardless of the capacity of the industrial machine to absorb them. An athletic looking man of twenty-five was Collins. Sound enough although disappointment in his profession had given him somewhat of a complex and he used to boast a bit of his intellectual attainments. Collins ran a gang of twenty "gandy-dancers" who tamped ballast under the mine railway track, carried wooden ties, laid and spiked rails to the tune of Service's poems, chanted by Collins as he plied bar and hammer with them. Italians, the "gandy-dancers" were. They worked well and Collins had them well disciplined—at the least sign of insubordination his fists came into play.

Then there was Dan. "Dynamite Dan" he was called because his task was to set the charges of explosive that loosened the rock in front of the big stripping shovel. A little wizened old man was Dan. A first-class man at his work when he was sober, but he had a spark in his throat that drew him to the "speak-easy" every second Saturday as regularly as the moon changed. Dan would always be back by Monday morning, but his hand would be too shaky for his delicate and dangerous work till Tuesday.

The rest of the crew were foreigners of one kind or another. I weeded them out as fast as possible and replaced them by young farmers recruited from distance enough to assure that they would have no affiliations with the local miners.

My well-trained crew were working efficiently and coal was

pouring from the mine in a stream of a thousand tons a day. The more rumblings from the miners, the higher rose the price of coal in anticipation of a shortage, till there was a considerable monthly surplus of cash after we had paid our expenses and made the monthly payment. A few more months of this and we would be clear of debt. Safe. Our position assured.

At last came the strike. The great Wyano tipple over the railway track ceased crashing its stream of coal into the string of waiting railway cars below. The miniature electric trains no longer came shrieking from the black maw of the pitmouth to dump their loads into the tipple. A thousand unemployed miners hung around the town in groups or caroused in the "speak-easy" before they staggered home to their sad-eyed central European wives.

The day the strike began I announced that our crew would receive double pay for every day of the strike we kept our mine operating. The men sailed into their work with gusto and swore that no foreign gang was going to drive them from it.

It had always been Dodds' job to fetch the mail each morning from the post office in the town. Now I decided that his diminutive stature would be too much of a temptation to the local bullies, so I got into the habit of fetching the mail myself because there was no other unoccupied man on the mine to do it.

Groups of sullen men would eye me balefully as I walked through the town each day, but they confined their animosity to looks. There seemed to be no fight in them. Either they weren't hungry enough to be dangerous, I decided, or their hearts were not in the strike. The latter hypothesis was the correct one. The strike dragged on for a few months while mines began to drop back into production here and there throughout the country with increasing frequency. Then it collapsed. The miners accepted their old wage-scale—a generous scale it was too. Under that wage-scale the coal-miner in the U.S.A. was about the best paid workman on earth. But John L. Lewis had been too greedy, asking for more, and now he had sustained his first defeat at the hands of capital. Coal prices dropped vertically almost overnight, but we were in the clear. Our mine was paid for. Bill and I owned outright a coal-mine in full production. We could now number ourselves among the ranks of the Coal Barons, the proud hierarchy of the industrial middle-west.

We were as yet only little barons, it was true. We had only a single mine, while some of the vested aristocrats of the industry numbered their mines by the score. Still, one could almost hear the clanking of the armour as the august assemblage we had entered turned to scrutinise the two young parvenus. Most of the hierarchy were in their second generation, some in their third.

No strike could break us now. That danger was over. What now menaced us and must still menace us for long would be our competitors. The great Pittsburgh coal interests formed one of the most strongly entrenched capital groups of the country and they hunted in a pack. They regarded their industry as fully developed. They owned most of the big coal deposits, keeping as reserve such as they did not wish to work at once . . . almost a monopoly of coal they had established. There remained free only such small acreages as were not worth the high cost of an elaborate underground working. But here were a couple of youngsters mining coal by a new method . . . by means of surface machinery which could be readily dismantled and erected elsewhere . . . moved from place to place as small acreages were exhausted. A threat to the market. That's how the big barons regarded us. But they had troubles of their own at the moment although the miners' strike had collapsed. With a mental promise of some stern discipline in the future if we did not go broke in the meantime they left us alone for the time being.

CHAPTER IV

STRIKING MINERS, DEPUTY SHERIFFS AND
OTHER TROUBLES

BILL and I now owned our mine outright. Not a cent did we owe to anyone. But in spite of that our troubles were by no means over. For one thing we had no capital in reserve. The end of the strike and the consequent collapse of coal prices had almost exactly coincided with the time we had made that last payment on the property which had cleared us of debt. For another thing the year 1921 was on us. That grim year in which American industry paid the price of the post-war boom of 1920. Mines all round us began to shut down for lack of industry's normal demand for coal. We, ourselves, were working from hand to mouth. Tottering financially because coal was almost unsaleable.

But Bill was indefatigable. We had our teeth deep in the haunch of fortune and he would not be shaken off, let fortune career ever so wildly. His was the selling end of the business and sell coal he did in spite of lack of demand. Backwards and forwards he criss-crossed the State of Pennsylvania in his car. Hunting smoke-stacks. Wherever he saw a tall factory chimney whose plume of black smoke betokened a coal user still in business he went in and fought for sales. A fifty-ton lot here ; two hundred tons there. At any hour of the day or night the mine telephone was liable to ring with Bill's voice at the other end of it telephoning an order. More than once he crossed the border into New York State and sold our coal there. He even telephoned me from Canada once. Ten whole cars were in that order. Seven hundred tons. Enough to keep the mine running almost one whole day.

My part was a minor one. All I could do was to keep the mine force together with a minimum of working hours and cut expenses as much as possible. We kept going . . . somehow. Then came the winter with a slight increase of demand.

Houses must be heated when blizzards sweep down from the north. The price remained stationary, but coal was easier to sell.

Then prices began to rise. Ever so slightly. But rise they did. It looked as though we had weathered the storm.

By this time there were rumours of more trouble with the United Mineworkers. The Coal Operators were to be the aggressors this time it seemed. For the first time in his stormy career John L. Lewis was to be on the defensive. The Coal Operators declared they could not pay the present wage-scale and keep operating at the low prices still ruling—with justice, even with our lower cost of production we could hardly make both ends meet. They announced their intention of cutting wages. To the belligerent and so far almost invariably victorious miners this was like a bottle of petrol to a kitchen stove. They flared.

Back and forth the war-talk flew till it was evident that both sides were out for a battle to the death. Not much chance this time of the miners caving in as easily as before. Their heart had not been in the last strike. Their wage-scale had been generous enough to enable an illiterate miner to keep a better car than his boss. The most highly paid among them could earn about forty dollars in an eight-hour day, while even the boozy old foreigner who doddered round the mine, stabbing errant bits of paper with his pointed stick, received his seven dollars a day, the minimum wage under the scale, for work that any small boy could have done. The miners knew their scale was generous, but to cut that scale was another matter. Just as the miners had driven their scale up strike by strike, so could the Operators drive them down cut by cut once they were allowed to establish a precedent. There was a grim and bitter war ahead it seemed. The miners would fight to protect the fruits of twenty years of victory, the Operators for their very existence.

Bill came out to the mine a week or two before the date set for the strike to begin.

"It's going to be a scrap all right," he remarked with a grave face.

"We kept going without any trouble last strike."

"This is going to be a different kind of business. You haven't been in the country long enough to know the foreign element, but I was around during the steel-workers' strike in McKeesport. There were enough bullets flying to make a battle. This will be another hot and heavy one like that."

"We could shut down for a start and see how it goes," I suggested, "if you think it's going to be too hot."

"Trouble is if we shut down we'll never get going again. Only chance we've got is to keep going. Besides, a shut-down would break us. We've only just been holding our own. There's been no chance to accumulate a reserve of cash."

"Right-o. We'll run then."

Bill looked at me gratefully. "Can you keep going, do you think?"

"I expect so. It'll have to be pretty hot before we quit. It'll be costly running though."

"Damn the cost. Go the limit as long as you keep coal coming out. Prices are already beginning to jump and they'll go sky high before it's over. We'll both make our immortal pile if we can keep going." Then he slapped his thigh. "By God! I wish I had this end of it to run," he cried. "You'll have such a pile of fun." Bill meant it too. He was as belligerent as a bull terrier. One of the most courageous men I ever met was Bill, in spite of his "college professor" exterior. Our ideas of fun differed somewhat, though, I am willing to admit.

"What do you need to keep going?" he asked.

"I'll hire an extra crew so that we can keep the machines going day and night, double shift. I'll pick as many hard cases among them as I can . . . in case we have to fight. Then the day the strike starts I'll announce double pay for every day we keep running, same as we did before."

"What about weapons?"

"Send me out half a dozen Colt automatics so that we can arm the key men. We've got any quantity of dynamite here and I'll make some dynamite bombs to keep on the shovels and in the boarding-house in case of a rush."

"Do you know how to make a bomb?" asked Bill doubtfully.

"Fix a stick of dynamite in the middle of a pound of six-inch nails."

Bill doubled with laughter. "Christ, they'd be pulling nails out of themselves for a week if one went off near them."

About that time I noticed in the papers that a force of Pennsylvania State Police had been stationed in the district to keep order during the coming strike. This pleased me a lot. There was no protection to be had from the politically-elected local authorities. But the State Police were different. When I heard that a detachment of them had been stationed in the village of Yukon, only five miles away, I felt that luck was really with us. I drove over in my car and happened to catch them up riding along the road just before I came to the village. One look at their seat in the saddle and the kind of horse they rode was enough for me. The Royal " Mounties " of Canada couldn't have looked better. I pulled up ahead of them and held out my hand. In a second the beaming round face of the sergeant was bent down to the window beside me where I sat at the wheel.

" Any trouble, Partner ? " he asked wistfully. I could tell he was just spoiling for some excitement.

" Not yet." I laughed. " There's hopes though. That horse you're riding is the best thing I've seen in this country." It was a beauty. A great upstanding bay. I got out and looked it over. The throat latch of the bridle had twisted. I set the narrow strap straight.

" Know something about horses ? " he queried, pulling a cigarette case out of the pocket of his smartly-cut tunic and offering me one.

" A bit. I'm cavalry." I accepted the cigarette but could hardly keep my eye off the horse. So long it was since I'd seen that kind of a horse. In this country horses had almost disappeared, with the exception of the great cart-horses pulling ploughs or wagons . . . and it wouldn't be long before tractors had driven them off the roads and into the category of museum exhibits. Actually the sergeant and his men were the first I had seen riding horses in the U.S.A. To a man practically brought up in the saddle that meant something important missing out of life. So much of what is colourful in the history of mankind has been made from the saddle of a horse. It suddenly came to me how different was my present environment from the one in which my earlier life had been spent.

" There's a spot in the bottle in my room in the Yukon hotel," remarked the sergeant. " If you like to drive ahead I'll follow."

" How many mines are going to try and run in this district ? "
he asked as I rose to go an hour or two later.

" We're the only one. All the rest are tight union."

" If you have any trouble send word to us quick. We'll see
you through."

I had a sudden thought. " I'll give you good quarters if you
care to move into our camp."

He laughed and shook his head. " Nothing doing. We're
here to keep order only. If we took up our quarters with you
there'd be a howl from the miners. 'Discrimination' they'd
call it. 'Hired assassins of capital' or something like that. But
if you have trouble send for us quick. There'll always be a
couple of us at the hotel, even when the rest of us are on
patrol."

As I drove back to the mine I felt for the first time that the
forces of law and order might be behind us in our refusal to stop
using our own property at the word of a lot of foreign miners
with whom we had nothing to do.

It was on the very eve of April 1st, the date set for the strike,
that I met in the Wyano Post Office a native-born American
miner of my acquaintance called Jim Walters.

" I hear you're going to try to carry on when we shut down,"
he remarked.

" That's right."

" You'll have trouble."

" We're ready for it."

" This is a bad business." He shook his head.

" The miners are damned fools. They ought to know that
the Operators have got to cut wages or go broke."

" I know that. All us American miners know that."

" Why do you strike, then ? "

" It's the foreigners. Lewis can stir them up to anything he
wants."

" Did the Americans here vote against the strike ? "

He looked sheepish. " I wasn't at the meeting when the vote
was taken."

" So you let the foreigners run your union without even
bothering to vote ? "

He flushed. " If I'd attended the meeting I'd have voted
against the strike. Then there'd have been a bomb explode

inside my house or something like that. A man's got his wife and kids to think of. So I didn't attend."

"I'll give you a job with us if you like."

He looked startled. "Good God! no. That'd be 'scabbing.' I would be in trouble if I did that. But we'll do what we can to hold the foreigners peaceable. There won't be any violence if the American miners can help it."

The strike started on schedule. Once more the great Wyano tipple was silent and the busy electric trains ceased to dart in and out of its gaping pit-mouth in the hillside across the little valley. About a week after the strike started came my first opportunity to conduct an offensive against the enemy . . . the fellow who lands the first blow is often the winner of the battle. I was walking towards the boarding-house from the big shovel when I saw a man running to meet me. Fast he ran and some instinct set me running towards him. Dodds, panting and almost incoherent with excitement.

"Miners. At the boarding-house . . . trying to scare the men into quitting."

"How many?" I asked.

"An automobile full."

Dodds at my heels, I started to run in the direction of the big stone building which was only a quarter of a mile away, although out of sight from where we were. When I topped the rise I could see a car halted in the road outside the building. Then I remembered suddenly that the road beyond was blocked . . . being repaired. I slowed my pace to a walk. The car was in a trap. It must come towards me to get away. Across a field I cut, dropped down a bank into the road and began to walk along it towards the boarding-house.

When I was within a couple of hundred yards some men began to rush from the building and pile into the car, which started to move towards me. This gave me confidence. The miners had evidently seen me coming and were trying to get away.

I drew my Colt from my holster and stood in the middle of the road. I remember feeling foolish, almost as foolish as that only other time I had worn a pistol for use against my fellow men, that time Major Richards and I had raided the widow woman's still. But, foolish or not, I felt that this was the crucial moment. If I let these miners get away they would be back in force. Then, if our men resisted, there would be bullets flying and men killed. But, if I could hold them now on our property till I got the State Police here, at least I would have some kind of charge against them. At the very least it would give our men confidence to know that they had some kind of protection.

The car was a battered Ford without a top. As it came closer I saw that there were five men in it. I raised my pistol and pointed it at the driver, a little swarthy man. When the pistol muzzle came up I saw his face screw into a knot, but he still continued to force the car towards me, swaying and bumping over the rough country road. Then, a few yards from me, his nerve went. He braked so suddenly that the back wheels skidded to a stop.

I walked to the side of the car, my pistol threatening. Five pairs of hands shot up.

" Get out and line up against the bank," I ordered. " Keep your hands up."

They complied promptly. All but one. A big brute who looked like a Polak.

"Eenglish sunovabeetch," he lowered his hands to shake a fist at me. " Me got five keeds. You break strike. Sell coal. Same as steal food from my keeds."

When the pistol muzzle swung his way his nerve cracked, however. Hands in air he lumbered to where his companions were already lined up against the bank by the side of the road.

I lowered my pistol and began to slip it into its holster. My captives immediately lowered their hands. I still felt foolish, but elated too. I had these men where I wanted them. Had them cold.

A cry from Dodds startled me. " Christ ! hold the gun on them. They haven't come up here unarmed."

At once I raised the pistol muzzle and the five pairs of hands shot up as though geared to it.

" Go over them and see what they've got," I ordered Dodds.

Dodds was wrong. Although he searched them thoroughly they carried no weapon more deadly than a pocket-knife.

" Jump into their car, Dodds. Go like blazes to Yukon and bring the State Police back with you."

In a moment the car was careening and bucking down the road and I was left alone with my five prisoners. A good bag they were, now I had time to consider them. By a great stroke of luck I had captured all the officials of the local branch of the miners' union. Foreigners. Not a native-born American among them. Five blasted central-European peasants who had come up to intimidate my men, organise them and force them into their own cursed union where their right to work for their living when and where they liked would be taken from them. It made me boil. I walked up and down before them, pistol in hand. I matched the big man's scowl with a glare and swung the pistol towards him.

Then his nerve broke completely. " Pleese, Meester. Me got five keeds. Let me go before p'leece come." Hands still in air he lowered himself to his knees and wept loudly, tears running down his face.

The other four, small swarthy men, still stood in line, hands up, faces hang-dog, but hatred in their eyes.

By this time the news had got to the nearby boarding-house. Men came running. Soon every man not on duty was lined up on top of the bank against which the prisoners were backed. Silent. Non-committal, while I had expected their enthusiastic backing. If the prisoners had made a concerted attack on me, I am not sure to this day whether those American workmen would have raised a finger on my account, although my actions had been taken as much to protect their jobs as my own property. Their attitude chilled me. There were fighting men among them, I knew. But I suddenly realised that any fighting to be done to keep the mine running would have to be done by me unaided. Dodds, alone, could I count on, but Dodds was not of the fighting type.

It seemed ages, although Dodds swore afterwards that it was not more than half an hour, before I heard a car top the rise behind me from the direction in which Dodds had gone. My heart twisted at the sound. The news of my coup might easily have spread already to the town, in which case there might easily be a procession of cars on the way towards me, each one filled with belligerent coal-miners bent on rescuing their union officials. Out of the corner of my eye I could see the car that I had heard but it was as yet too far to be recognised. Then, to my relief, I saw two horsemen top the rise behind the car. Then two more. Two and two the horsemen sped behind the car, their horses stretched to the uttermost. The State Police sergeant and three troopers slithered their horses to a stop as the old car jerked to a standstill beside me with a protesting squeal of brakes.

The sergeant slipped from the saddle and strode to where I stood. With a suppressed grin he surveyed my bag.

" What's the trouble ? " he asked quietly, but his eyes gleamed with the joy of excitement as he spoke.

" These men were in my boarding-house trying to incite my men to strike."

The sergeant turned his back on the prisoners and frowned at me. I took it for a signal that I had said the wrong thing.

" Trespass," he remarked judicially. " That's a serious offence now with a strike going on. Do you accuse these men ? "

" Yes."

" I'll take them in charge, then. You'll have to attend before the Justice of the Peace to-morrow in Yukon to give evidence."

" All right."

" Come early. I want to talk to you first." This was said in a low voice.

I nodded.

He turned to his men. " Put the bracelets on them and bring them along."

The prisoners were handcuffed and marched off. Two of the troopers rode ahead, the sergeant and the other trooper behind. When one of the prisoners tried to hang back and argue the sergeant rode his horse at him and knocked him down. They disappeared over the rise.

" That's first round to us," I remarked to Dodds.

The little man's face was glowing with excitement. " That's fixed the sons of bitches," he cried. " They won't be back here in a hurry."

I wasn't so sure, but anyway we had won the first round.

My workmen on the bank drifted back to the boarding-house without a word.

Next day I was in the police sergeant's room in Yukon an hour before the time set for the hearing. He grinned widely when I entered.

" We did all we could for you," he remarked. " When we passed through the town of Wyano we marched your prisoners up and down every street so that all their friends could have a good look at them. The result was that the local union called a meeting then and there and threw every one of them out."

"But they were all high officials of the local union."

"That's right. But they're not even members of it now. Their fellow-members didn't approve of their having been held up by one man—I took care to spread that story. John L. Lewis hasn't any use for failures in his organisation. The other miners didn't like to see their leaders marched round by the police either. Ridicule. Anyway, they threw them out and elected new officials. The new men are all native-born Americans. That means the miners round here will be easier to control from now on. So you've done a good turn for law and order and in return I'm going to see you through your troubles."

"I thought the prisoners were the ones in trouble."

The sergeant grinned again. "That's all you know. What have you got to charge them with?"

"You mentioned trespass yesterday."

"I did that to help you out. They were on your property, but that doesn't constitute trespass unless they've been previously warned. For all you know they may have been only paying a friendly visit to your men."

I had no answer to this. The workmen in the camp had been very reticent about the visitors when I had questioned them. Dodds had heard them threatening someone, but he was a bit vague about whom they had threatened and what they had threatened him with.

The sergeant stuck his hands in the pockets of his riding breeches and looked at me with a frown, rocking slightly on his heels as he did so.

"What right had you to hold those men up with a pistol on the public highway?"

"My God, man! I've got to keep that mine running. If I hadn't held them up they'd have scared my men into leaving. You know that."

"Whether I know it or not, that doesn't constitute any legal reason. Those men have got a penal case against you if they like to press it."

"What am I going to do about it?" I hadn't thought of the legal aspect of the case before.

The sergeant laughed. A jolly sort of laugh he had. His round, good-natured face puckered up like a child's and the twinkle in his eyes was almost hidden behind the wrinkles.

"I said I'd see you through," he cried. "Sign that." He pushed a legal looking document in front of me. "Damn it. I'd have done the same in your place—that is if I wasn't a policeman."

I examined the formidable looking document. It was evidently a list of the charges I was preferring against the five miners' officials—ex-officials now—I had captured. Couched in such legal jargon that I couldn't make head nor tail of it.

"What the devil does it mean?"

"Look," he explained. "If we can keep those Wops and Bohunks scared enough they won't think of charging you. They're good and scared already. My boys have seen to that. At this moment they're not sure whether they're to be sent up for life or shot at daybreak. They've been trying to hire a lawyer but none of the local sharks want to play with them because their union has thrown them out . . . disgraced. When you've signed the charges we'll go down to the J.P. and have them brought in."

I signed the awe-inspiring thing and handed it to him.

"Now tell me what I've signed," I asked as he folded it and put it in his pocket.

"You've charged them with about every offence I could think up which they could possibly have committed in your boarding-house if they'd thought of it. They won't understand any more of it than you did and that will scare them worse than ever. Then the J.P. will bind them over to keep the peace and let them go. They'll be so relieved that they'll never think of charging you with anything."

The sergeant was right. The five were so glad to get clear that they left the court-room almost on the run as soon as they had been bound over to keep the peace by the J.P. Further-more, their fellow-miners made their lives so unhappy with jokes about their recent experience that they left the district shortly afterwards.

On my return to the mine I found Bill there. He was delighted that we had scored the first trick against the miners, but the occurrence had frightened him into insuring against a shut-down.

He showed me the insurance policy. I liked the first part of it all right. The insurance company was to pay us the sum of one thousand dollars for every day the mine was shut down during the strike by violence, intimidations or any other subversive action on the part of the miners, but when I came to the conditions I didn't like it so much.

"God, Bill. You've committed us to employing six deputy sheriffs," I cried.

"Don't you want them? Supposing the miners come again. You mightn't be so lucky next time."

"I'll take my chance with the miners. I can handle them, but I don't guarantee to handle a lot of deputy sheriffs. They'll be more bother than they're worth and they won't be any help if there is any trouble." Before coming to the States my opinion of deputy sheriffs had been culled from literature of the wild west variety—keen-eyed, two-gunned sons of the south-west, who shot from the hip with both guns together, lightning-quick on the draw. Since arrival in the States, however, I had heard a different tale about them—boozy good-for-nothings, who would sooner loaf around with a big gun strapped to their hips than do an honest day's work. I had never actually met a deputy sheriff—the one full-blown sheriff I had met hadn't impressed me—and I didn't want to. Still less did I want six of them parading round the mine. They'd be a nuisance when things were quiet and conspicuous by their absence if trouble did come. My doubts were intensified when I drove to Greensberg, the county seat, next day and collected my six protectors from the sheriff's office. Six poor-looking specimens they seemed to me, with the bloated pallor which comes from hard drinking and soft living. But their weapons startled me. A heavy revolver caressed each well-rounded hip and in each pair of flabby-looking hands was the rear half of a twelve-bore shot-gun, the barrel sawn off some four inches from the breach. Ghastly-looking weapons. I could imagine the mess they would make of a man's stomach at a few yards' range. They'd blow a hole big enough to put your head through.

My doubts changed to certainties before the deputies had been long in camp.

"This food ain't what we're used to," complained their spokesman the day after their arrival.

"I don't doubt that," was my rejoinder. The food was first-class. Our cook, Oley, was one of the best I have ever eaten after.

The man pondered my reply for a moment before catching its implication. Then he changed ground.

"There ain't no liquor, neither. Most jobs stand a man a shot of liquor once in a while."

"This job doesn't. There's no liquor allowed in camp." With a number of thirsty souls like Dynamite Dan about the place it would have been a pothouse if I hadn't enforced that rule.

The deputy went off grumbling. A few days later came the sequel. The mine telephone rang and an American voice at the other end enquired for me.

"What is it?"

"We'd like to talk to you."

"Who's 'we'?"

"The committee of the Wyano branch of the miners' union."

"What about?"

"We'll tell you when you get here. We'll be in the post office."

I considered a moment. The committee was no longer made up of foreigners and I believed they were now making an effort to conduct the strike peaceably. The closer touch I kept with them the better.

"I'll be right down," I replied.

Five men were waiting for me in the big building which combined the functions of post office and supply store for the miners' town . . . empty at this time of day. One or two of them I knew slightly. Decent citizens all they seemed. Of British descent. By their names they were descendants of Welsh "Taffies" who had come to the States a generation or two before when the coal-mining industry was young.

"We want to tell you that you'd better shut that mine down," began the spokesman, a dark-haired man with a square bull-dog face and the short stocky frame of one who has grown up in low coal galleries underground.

"I can't do that. It's my job to keep it running."

The man bent over to squirt a stream of tobacco juice into a spittoon.

" I know all about that," he replied when he straightened up. " You and young Bill Bitard are having a cut at making your fortune. We don't think any the worse of you for that. But there'd be less chance of trouble if you shut down."

" We won't shut down."

He expectorated again. Scoring a dead centre at two yards' range.

" Well, the bit of coal you mine don't make much difference. Another thing, too. That hold-up of foreigners didn't do us Americans in this town any harm. If you didn't have those damned deputies, things might be different."

" What have the deputies done ? "

" One son-of-a-bitch went down to the ' speak-easy ' and tried to hold the place up at the point of a gun for a bottle of liquor."

" What happened ? "

" He got beat up bad." He flexed one hand reflectively and rubbed skinned knuckles.

" Did you kill him ? " I asked hopefully.

All five laughed.

" We took the artillery off him and then I cleaned him up. He's not hurt bad. If you clear the deputies out we may be able to hold the foreigners in."

I explained why I couldn't get rid of the deputies.

The spokesman shrugged his shoulders. " There'll be trouble and it won't be our fault. Those damned skunks come strutting through the streets hung all over with hardware. It's just asking for trouble."

" I can hardly stop them going to the town," I stated. " But supposing we disarmed them before they got there ? "

" That might work. But they'd get beat up some. The men don't like them."

" Beat them up all you want to. I don't like them either." I thought for a moment. " I'll make you a proposition," I continued. " I'll build a shanty alongside the road where it crosses the boundary of your mine and ours. If the miners' union will keep two men on duty in that shanty I'll undertake that every man of mine hands them his weapons before he crosses the boundary. In return you fellows keep the miners off our mine."

" We can't guarantee your men won't get beat up by some of the hotheads here."

" That's their look-out. I can't keep them out of town if they want to come when they're off duty—I'm not running a girls' boarding-school up there. But there's no man on our mine has any business in this town except me when I come down for the mail every morning."

" That's fair enough."

" But I don't want to be beaten up."

They laughed again. The atmosphere had cleared completely. " That's your look-out," remarked one. " But we'll see the foreigners don't gang you."

" I'll take my chance."

" We'll have to call a meeting and put it to the union," explained the leader. " But I guess it's a go."

Within a few days a wooden shanty stood where the road crossed our frontier . . . like a customs station it was. I stopped at the door as I went for the mail at seven next morning, slipped my pistol off my belt and handed it to the two American miners who were sitting on a bench near the door, ruminating peacefully.

The scheme worked well and for many weeks there was no more trouble with the miners. Now that the excitement of recent events was over I began to reflect on something that had been puzzling me—the behaviour of our own men—their air of strict neutrality—when I had held up the five foreigners near the boarding-house. Their attitude had been a shock to me at the time. They had always seemed to like to work for me . . . in times of peace there was always a long waiting list of men who wished to be employed on our mine. Their jobs were good ones at all times and during the strike they were doubling their regular high rate of pay. And yet they had made no move to help me in a crisis, that is with the exception of Dodds. In other countries men thought a boss worth working for was worth fighting for too.

I put the question to Collins one day by the mine railway tracks as we sat on a pile of wooden ties and watched his " gandy-dancers " shovelling ballast. He lit a cigarette reflectively when I had asked him but he remained silent.

" Why did they act like that ? " I queried. " They're not afraid. I know that. There was some other reason."

" They're Americans."

" What's that got to do with it ? "

" The other fellows were foreigners."

" Well. How does that explain it ? "

" You see you're a foreigner too. If it had been a white American holding up those five, our boys would have been all over them . . . eaten them alive. But as you're a foreigner too, they waited to see what would happen. We Americans don't mix much in affairs between foreigners."

I felt a cold spot inside me.

" Do you mean to say I'm classed with that riff-raff ? "

" A foreigner's a foreigner to them."

This was a new viewpoint to me. Hitherto I had looked on Americans much as I did Australians, New Zealanders, Canadians or my own South African fellow-countrymen. Men of my own kind who liked the things I liked, had the same ideals and the same ancestry. True, the Americans had a flag of their own, but so did all the British dominions. The Americans had a different political system and had elected to remain outside the federation of nations which composed the British Empire—that was all the difference I could see. I had known Americans in Africa. They had been simply other white men to me and I had never stopped to consider whether they were foreigners or no. Now I felt just like as a man would feel who had dropped in for a meal with a friend and equal and been served in the kitchen with the servants while his host dined in state. My mind raced back over the years since I had landed in the country. A lot of things that had puzzled me explained themselves in that instant. I had missed the casual hospitality of my own country . . . and that in a country that prided itself on its hospitality. Hospitable the Americans undoubtedly were—to those who came over as guests. But the Americans keep a barrier between themselves and the hordes of European peasants with which they had flooded their country to get cheap labour for the development of their vast territory. That I understood—it was the protective instinct of the minority on which the very existence of that minority depended. But that there should be no discrimination ! That, because I came to work, I should be classed with every Central-European peasant and criminal who had boarded an emigrant ship one jump ahead of the police of his own country ! I felt that the United States could never be a real home to me after that, even though I should live there the rest of my life. And in my innocence it had taken me nearly three years to find that out.

CHAPTER V

A STRIKE WITH VIOLENCE

WITH every day of the strike the price of coal crept up. Day after day the shovels spurted their white plumes of steam—triumphant, the diminutive "dinky" locomotives shuttled back and forth, pulling their trains of dump cars to the loading plant, whence the big Pennsylvania Railway "Road-Hog" locomotive each evening pulled away to market a long string of the big fifty-ton hoppers of our coal. I saw little of Bill these days. In the two little rooms of our Pittsburgh office suite he was conducting by telephone what amounted almost to an auction sale of our daily drag of over a thousand tons of coal. A few months back he had been driven to go, almost hat in hand, to a coal buyer who was having a thousand tons offered him for every one he could use. Now the position was reversed. The buyers came to us. Our 'phone was ringing from every nearby state and even from far-off Canada. Coal at almost any price. Any kind of coal that would burn. We were one of the small handful of mines in the country which had managed to keep going and we were reaping the harvest of our determination.

Then came the Herrin massacre . . . screaming across the headlines of the country's press. Two states from us in Illinois the miners were on strike as they were throughout almost every coal-mining district in the country. In Illinois there was a man named Lester, who owned and operated a coal-stripping property of the same type as ours, near to a little town called Herrin. Like us, when the strike began, he resolved to keep working and to that end fortified his mine against the miners, hiring deputy sheriffs and mounting a machine-gun for the mine's defence. The deputy sheriffs proved a continual source of irritation to the striking miners just as ours had done, till, in the third month of the strike the growing tension flashed into action. The striking miners besieged the mine. Lester's men defended it and killed several of the attackers. Enraged by their losses the overwhelming numbers of the miners swarmed over the defences and took prisoner the garrison. Then they led their prisoners to a nearby open field and told them to run. When they obeyed the machine-gun was turned on them and something like a score were killed. Like the news of a declaration of war it was. The half-million members of the United Mineworkers of America roared with the noise of a hiving swarm over the half-dozen dead they had lost in the attack. The press of the country screamed vigorously for restoration of order. Political recrimination shot back and forth across Congress like snowballs in a wintry school yard. Most of the few mines which had still managed to continue working shut down hurriedly before they met a like fate to Lester's men. The Government began to move soldiers into the mining districts. The national situation became tense and riots, amounting almost to civil war, seemed imminent.

I knew nothing of this when I strolled next morning to the post office for the mail. God, if I had known the situation I was walking into, the mail would have stayed in the post office. I did notice, idly, that the two miners on guard at the frontier looked queerly at me when I handed them my holstered pistol. The big room of the store and post office was filled with miners, nearly a hundred there must have been, talking and arguing excitedly. The moment I entered every voice was hushed. There was dead silence as I walked to the wicket to get my mail. Not a soul returned the greeting I threw to the men present whom I knew.

At the window I opened my morning paper while the postmistress sorted the mail for the mine. There it was— H E R R I N M A S S A C R E—splashed right across the front page. I had hardly got the gist of what had happened when a big Bohunk standing near me grabbed the paper from my hand and threw it on the floor. " Scab sonovabeetch," he cried as he did so. " Pret' soon we keel you too."

My reaction was purely automatic. I lashed out at his jaw and knocked him clean off his feet. A moment he lay still, before sitting up and blinking stupidly.

I was afraid then ; sick afraid. Not of the man I had knocked over. He was bigger than I, but built like the coal-heaver he was; clumsy as a cart-horse. I knew I could settle his business in a couple of minutes. It was the mob that scared me. That gang of foreigners would stand on no rules if they attacked me. No case of forming a ring and fighting it out like white men do. I had a horrible vision of the mob swarming over me, while those heavy hobnailed miners' boots came into play as soon as I went down. There was a queer empty feeling where my stomach should have been. My dry tongue stuck to the roof of my mouth.

The man continued to sit on the floor and blink at me, rubbing tenderly the angle of his jaw. In dead silence the mob stood. Motionless they were, but I could see their eyes focused on the sitting man as he blinked and rubbed his jaw with a confused look on his stupid features.

Something pushed me in the back. I turned my head to glance at the wicket. With wide-open eyes the postmistress pushed a bundle of letters into my hand. Pasty white her face was. Mine was just as white, I imagine.

" Get out quick," she whispered.

Trying not to show my fear I walked slowly at the crowd between me and the door. In dead silence they parted to give me way. I heard the spring mechanism of the door close behind me. To the middle of the street I walked. It took every ounce of determination I could muster to keep my head from turning to look back. My ears tuned themselves to the sound of that door. I could have heard a fly walking over it almost as I walked away. If it opened again it would mean a mob at my heels. The door remained silent, but I heard a buzz of excited talk break out in the building as soon as I left it.

Once in the street I turned right towards our mine. Something gave a twist inside my chest when I saw four horsemen drawn up in line at the next cross-roads. The state police sergeant and three troopers. The sergeant spurred his horse towards me.

" You crazy son-of-a-bitch," he cried. " What in the name of God possessed you to go into that wasps' nest this morning ? "

I had just knocked a man down for an identical epithet, but from the sergeant's lips it sounded like the benediction of a friend.

" I didn't know about Herrin when I went in."

"We came over just in case you were fool enough to go. Knew you went for the mail every morning. Reckoned there'd be trouble if you went in to-day."

I rested one hand on the withers of his horse. My knees were weak.

"You all right?" he asked anxiously, looking into my face.

"I'm all right. I could do with a drink though."

"What happened?"

I told him briefly.

"Lucky you plastered that Hunky right off. If you'd hesitated they'd likely have mobbed you."

"Think there'll be more trouble?"

"Not now." He laughed. "Look at that." He pointed back towards the post office.

Men were coming out of the building in little groups, laughing and talking naturally as they scattered to their homes for breakfast.

"They've let off steam now. Mobs are funny things," he explained. "There's usually a psychological moment when something will take the steam out of them . . . open a safety-valve. You seem to have hit that moment." Then he slapped me on the back. "You're the luckiest guy I ever did see. Always walking head on into trouble, but your luck always pulls you out. If you fell into a cesspool you'd come out with a diamond necklace you'd picked up off the bottom of it."

When I got back to the mine I found a stormy meeting of my own men in progress. Bill had called up from Pittsburgh, it seemed, just after my departure for the mail, in order to give me the news of the Herrin massacre and to warn me against going into Wyano. Dodds had taken the message in my absence and had immediately spread the news. My American workmen had raved . . . it seems that the attackers of Herrin had been foreigners while the massacred garrison had been American born. They were busy organising a party to rescue me from the strikers when I walked into the meeting. Just on the point of sallying out towards the town in a body with what weapons they could raise. The welcome they gave me was a warm one. Uproarious it became when they heard what had happened. I could see that they would back me to the limit now—even though I was a foreigner.

But the excitements of that day were by no means over. On that day of all days, Dynamite Dan must succumb to the chronic thirst which for ever tortured him. I suppose the excitement of the morning had fanned the spark in his throat to flame. Some time during the day he left his work and wandered across fields in a roundabout way to town to quench his thirst at the " speakeasy." As soon as he entered he was greeted by cries of " scab." The feeble old man was badly battered before being thrown out into the street.

As poor old Dan dragged his aching bones back to camp along the road he met a young Texan in our employment who was walking towards the town—I have a shrewd suspicion that he was bent on the same errand which had taken Dan there.

"What have they done to you, Dan?" demanded the Texan at the sight of Dan's battered face.

Dan told his story.

"I'll fix those Bohunks," grinned the Texan, lifting his coat to show a revolver tucked into the waistband of his trousers.

Evading the border station the Texan marched into town by a side street. When he reached the door of the " speak-easy " he kicked it open unceremoniously and lounged in the doorway with his hands tucked negligently inside his belt.

"Who beat up Dan?" he drawled, his smooth southern accent seeming to pierce easily the roar of drunken argument inside.

"I did," cried a big foreigner at the bar. "I'll beat . . ."

But the Texan never did know whom the foreigner was going to beat up. Before the man could finish his sentence a bullet from the Texan's pistol barely missed his ear and broke a bottle on the shelf. There was a stampede for the windows and in a moment the crowd had gone and taken the window-frames with them in their rush. In the words of one of the occupants of the " speak-easy " when he described it to me afterwards, " One second there was seventeen men and four windows in that place. Next second there was only one man and no windows."

The Texan was left alone in the " speak-easy " with an array of bottles before him and a burning thirst in his throat.

It was dusk of that evening before I heard anything of this beyond the ill-treating of Dan. My first news came from a telephone call. I recognised at the other end of the wire the agitated voice of Davis, superintendent of the Wyano mine.

"Your men are shooting up my town." The voice was almost anguished.

"WHAT?" If it were true Herrin was being avenged.

"Your men are shooting up the town."

"Can't be my men." I could hear the preparatory buzz about the boarding-house, which hungry men make before they are fed. Further down the road both shovels were snorting like a pair of fighting boars and I could hear a dipperful of great rocks crash on the spoil pile as I held the telephone. Most of my men were on the job at least.

"It is your men. First they shot up the "speak-easy" and now they're cleaning up the town. I'll hold you responsible for any of my men who are hurt. It's up to you to do something about it and do it quick."

I walked down to the mess-hall and found the men just sitting down to supper.

"Anyone missing?" I asked.

"Only Tex."

The Texan alone couldn't hold up a thousand miners, even if it were he. Puzzled, I got into my car and drove to the town a mile away. As I approached the place I could see that something unusual was going on. The usually brightly lit up place was in darkness. I inferred that the superintendent had turned off the current in the mine power-house. There was no sound of shooting. Dead silence.

Then a match flared behind a window-pane as someone inside the house lit a cigarette. A second later came coincidently the crash of breaking glass and the deep bark of a heavy pistol from somewhere on the dark road ahead of me. From behind the shattered window came frantic cursing in some foreign tongue.

Quickly I cut off my headlights. Then at a foot pace drove forward, the engine softly purring. At the next intersection I could see a dim form standing. Almost silently the car pulled up alongside. There was Tex. Swaying on his feet as he revolved slowly like a gun-turret looking for another mark, in his hand his pistol. Crouched behind him, almost in the crook of Tex's knees, was another form which turned as he turned, keeping almost under the coat-tails of the marksman, or where his coat-tails would have been had he worn a coat. Slowly the Texan revolved. Before his revolution brought me into the line of fire I spoke, ready to drop out of sight into the bottom of the car if he did not recognise my voice.

" Give me that gun, boy," I ordered sharply.

His gun hand dropped. I reached out and took the gun from it. No sooner had I done so than his satellite shot out from behind him and scuttled out of sight, a diminutive miner running for cover as some little night animal flees in the darkness. Without a word Tex climbed in beside me and I drove him back to camp hoping he would sober up enough to work next day.

Month by month the strike went on. The miners were adamant, but so were the Operators, and the Operators had the longer purse. When the fifth month of the strike dragged itself upon us it was obvious that the Operators would win. Families of miners began to drift away from those districts which still held out to others which were capitulating. The miners were hungry. Their funds were giving out.

All through those months my deputy sheriffs had been a source of continuous annoyance, sometimes a real potential danger. For a long time they had been afraid to go into town for fear of the miners, but they always somehow succeeded in obtaining liquor and they were drunken and quarrelsome. My men hated them as much as I did, but that cursed insurance policy of Bill's compelled me to retain them. It was only a few days before the final capitulation of the miners when I was congratulating myself that I would soon be rid of the deputies, that they stirred up their last piece of trouble and one of them, at least, got his deserts.

Oley, the cook, was the camp autocrat, as all self-respecting mine cooks are bound to be. A good fellow was Oley and a damned good cook . . . there's many a well-known eating-place that has no better. Good-natured. There was always a wedge of cake or pie for any friend in camp who dropped in to watch him rule in his spotless domain with his two white-aproned flunkeys to help him. The long kitchen range gave off delicious odours of giant roasts and bakes—Oley cooked for sixty hungry men—as he would stand reflectively poking the glowing heart of the firebox with a length of half-inch round iron from the blacksmith's shop, which served him for poker, meanwhile his helpers peeled potatoes or washed dishes at the great sink.

On Oley's cheery round face the smile of a dictator whose power is undisputed. But Oley did not like deputy sheriffs. "Them bozos think they're tough because they've got a lot of hardware hanging on them, but I never knew one yet that wasn't chicken-livered. I don't like them worth a damn and they gets no hand-outs from my hash factory."

Oley was busy one day taking pies from the oven. The magnetic odour of fresh baked pastry floated out of the kitchen door, up the stairs and into the room where the deputies slept when they were off duty, which was practically all the time. Presently one of them stepped into the kitchen.

"Gimme one of them pies, Cookey," he demanded.

Without any apparent notice of his visitor Oley continued the stirring of the fire with his iron bar.

"Gimme one of them pies."

"Get out of here. Them pies are for dinner and I'm busy."

The deputy stepped forward, flushed with rage at Oley's resistance to his demands, his hand fumbling with the pistol in his holster. But before the weapon was half drawn Oley slashed him savagely across the face with the hot iron rod from the fire. Down went the deputy, a hideous red welt across his face. As he struggled to his feet Oley was on him like a tiger, slashing him again and again till he lay quiet.

By the time I arrived on the scene some of our men had dragged the deputy into the adjoining dining-hall where the two non-chalant flunkeys were already beginning to lay the table, regardless of what looked like a battered corpse on the floor. The remaining deputies were standing, backed into a corner by a group of men who were enraged by the attack on the popular Oley.

The damaged deputy's face was a mess. Great blistered welts criss-crossed it. Nose and lower jaw broken. I reached for a dish of butter and plastered it on his face as first aid for the burns. The sting of salt in the butter must have stirred him for he began to move. Then he sat up groaning.

"What happened?" I asked.

The two flunkeys told the story between them, both willing to swear that the deputy's pistol was half drawn when Oley struck him.

When I called Oley he came from the kitchen, the iron bar

still held in his hand. Rage contorted his usually good-natured face. His eyes glared and he gripped his bar tighter when he saw his victim sitting up. If I hadn't been there I believe Oley would have had another go at him and I haven't a doubt that in his berserk Scandinavian fury Oley had meant to kill his man.

"There ain't no son-of-a-bitch can pull a gun in my kitchen and get away with it," he cried, transferring the battery of his glare to the remaining deputies, who had clustered round their mate on being released by the men who had been guarding them to prevent them storming the kitchen and shooting Oley out of hand.

"You'll go to the pen for this, you lousy bastard," cried one of them, shaking his fist at Oley.

Oley made a threatening gesture with his still-smoking iron bar and the deputies backed up hurriedly.

I thought it was about time to intervene before a free fight started. Feeling among my men was running high. Oley was the most popular man in camp while the deputies had succeeded in making themselves about as popular as Jews in Germany.

"Get your mate outside and into my car," I directed the deputies. "I'll send Dodds into Greensburg hospital with him."

"That sucker of a hash-spoiler's coming too," cried one of the deputies. "I'll arrest him right now." He took a pair of handcuffs out of his pocket.

"You can't arrest him without a warrant, you fool." I knew Oley would be badly beaten before he ever got to jail if they were allowed to take him.

"We'll damn soon get a warrant and come back then."

"As you like. But if you do take Oley I'll see that your mate goes to jail too. He pulled a gun on Oley before witnesses. Oley only knocked him about in self-defence."

"We'll see about that." They helped the battered man to his feet and out to the waiting car. I didn't think they would come back, but I wasn't sure.

"You'd better skedaddle, Oley. Those fellows might get a warrant for you. If they ever got you in jail they'd rough-house you half to death."

"Goddamit. The son-of-a-bitch pulled a gun on me before I hit him."

"You might be able to prove that in court, but it wouldn't

prevent you getting your face smashed to pulp while they held you in jail pending trial."

Oley's face puckered and he scratched his head. Then he heaved his poker back through the open door into the kitchen where it fell with a clatter on to the floor.

"I go," he decided dolefully. "Plenty jobs in other camps . . . farther west maybe." Suddenly his face cleared and wreathed itself in smiles. "Goddam," he cried, smiting his fist into his palm. "By God, always I remember that bastard. Like bacon in the pan his face fried."

I was sorry to lose Oley. But it was almost worth losing him to have got rid of the deputies. For the rest of the strike we would take our chance on our own . . . insurance policy or no.

A week or two later the long-drawn-out battle between the miners and the Operators terminated. The miners capitulated and accepted a scale a little lower than previously—the first time in a generation that their wages had been reduced. During all the five months that the strike had lasted we had not missed a day's work and I believe that we were the only mine in the country to hold that record.

CHAPTER VI

OBSTETRICS BY TELEPHONE

I HAD married again not long after Bill and I had gone into partnership—just after the end of the first strike it was, when our business seemed to have been surely enough established to justify the appeasement of a widower's loneliness. Her name was Margaret. The widow of a small farmer who ran her own farm near the mine, she was making a gallant attempt to educate two children . . . Minnie aged sixteen and Walter, two years younger. Pennsylvania "Dutch" they all were. In the district were a host of their relations who had come over from Germany only a generation before. Along with a wife and two step-children I acquired a model mother-in-law, a gentle old lady with a mutch cap and a perpetual smile. Not a word of English could she speak, while my German was limited to a few curses I had learned in German South-West Africa. Not one word did we exchange during the six years that she lived with us except a " good morning " on my part and a " *gut morgen* " on hers. We got along splendidly.

There were Fritz and Hans, Margaret's neighbours. Both Pennsylvania "Dutch." Two old bachelors of sixty, twins, who ran their own market garden, shaved on Sundays, and cooked their own meals—on the several occasions on which I imperilled my digestion with them the fare was always the same, a sound stew of pork spare ribs with whatever vegetables were in season. A more dissimilar pair I never encountered. Fritz was as close as the bark on a tree, while Hans' generous heart wanted to cherish the whole world in need. Fritz had an imaginary ailment in his back which precluded his doing any but the lighter and more pleasant tasks about the farm. Hans ploughed, hoed and weeded from daylight to dark. Among the tasks which Fritz condescended to undertake was the weekly trip to the nearest town peddling vegetables in the farm wagon. He said he did it always—in spite of the pain in his back—because Hans gave too much away on the rare occasions when he was allowed to undertake the jaunt. His real reason was, undoubtedly, that when he sold the vegetables himself he received the money and could hold a stronger position with his brother in the weekly argument about the proportion of the takings to be paid into the bank. If Fritz had had altogether his own way the brothers would have clothed themselves in old fertiliser sacks and lived on potatoes. For forty years had the two brothers pigged it in the old stone house on the farm. A few years later they received a good offer for the place—a workable coal-seam had been discovered deep under it—and, much to the surprise of all who knew them, accepted the offer and moved into the nearest town. Fritz, the miser, married a lively young woman in her thirties, wilted and died within the year. Hans bought a cheap car and almost any day would find him hanging over the fence and gazing wistfully at the fields he had spent a lifetime tilling. Within the year Hans too was dead—pure homesickness.

There was a distant relative of Margaret's called Aggie, who had a penchant for being infected with every new craze that came along. I believe that had an epidemic of nudism occurred she would have taken it in spite of the fact that she was metaphorically knock-kneed from virtue, presumably so, because she persisted in wearing her skirts to the ankle during those days in which the rest of the feminine world wore them about as long as a highlander's kilt. At the time I married Margaret Aggie was suffering from a bad attack of Christian Science and was about to have a baby, while her husband was on a prolonged journey to the other side of the country—he travelled, I seem to recollect, for some firm of agricultural machinery manufacturers while she ran their little farm. Aggie's first baby it was and she conceived the idea of giving it a Christian Science birth. Her husband had not returned when the time approached—possibly he had suspicions about Christian Science obstetrics. Both Margaret and I thought it strange that he should be absent from his wife at such a time, but before I was through with the affair my opinion of his intelligence had increased mightily.

I was inveigled into the business by stealth, so to speak. Aggie asked me to drive her into Steelport to interview a Christian Science " practitioner " of great local repute who lived there.

After considerable knocking at a dingy door in a dingy street a shambling-looking old man came out. His jaws worked continually like those of a masticating monkey. There was a little dribble of yellow juice at each corner of his mouth and two long yellow stains down his white beard gave testimony to the path of other dribbles. When I told him he had a client he came to the car and interviewed Aggie through the window.

"I'm going to have a baby and I'll need your help," she informed him.

The ancient shifted his cud from port to starboard, glanced with a goaty expression at her middle and expectorated. Then he turned to me.

"When is your wife due?" he asked.

"She's not my wife. You'd better ask her."

The "practitioner" looked scandalised.

"My husband's away." Aggie blushed. She mentioned a date.

The "practitioner" consulted a tattered little note-book.

"I can make it." He masticated with the contentment of an old ram chewing the cud.

"Shall we send the car in for you when the time comes?" Aggie still looked embarrassed. The old man obviously scented an affair. I suppose it is rather unusual for anyone but a woman's husband to arrange this kind of business.

My heart sank. A longish drive in the car with that ancient did not appeal to me. I should be elected, I was sure, along with my car. Aggie's husband had been astute enough to take his car with him on the trip.

The "practitioner" shook his head till his beard wagged.

"Heck, no. I do my stuff over the telephone. I ain't gadding round at night tending strange women. Not at my time of life."

For the first time since she had decided on Christian Science delivery, Aggie looked doubtful. For my part I began to get interested in the procedure for the first time. Up till now I had imagined that the "practitioner" attended the bedside and soothed the pains away by some sort of hypnotic process. But to have obstetrics conducted over the long-distance telephone! That was something new in my experience.

"My fee is a hundred dollars," continued the "practitioner."

Aggie looked startled. " But they told me you only charged twenty-five."

The ancient leered. " I said a hundred."

" That's what Aggie gets for running round with other people's husbands," I reflected.

Aggie looked pained and blushed once more.

" I'll take twenty-five for a retainer," the old man added. " You can pay the rest of it as soon as it's over."

Aggie fumbled in her pocket-book and handed over the money. I caught her side glance at me and hoped the twinkle in my eye was not too obvious.

" It is painless, isn't it ? " she asked pathetically.

" Sure is . . . if you got faith enough." The white beard wagged emphatically.

" Doggoned old robber," ejaculated Aggie as soon as we were under way. " I've a good mind not to pay him the rest."

" He'll talk if you don't," I warned her. She subsided with a flustered expression.

In silence we drove back through the steep cobbled streets with grim, ugly houses staring at us from either side, while overhead hung the black pall of sulphurous smoke, belched from the batteries of steel mills which lined the maybe once beautiful Monongahela River nearby. It must have been beautiful once, that river and that countryside. As recently as when British Braddock, with George Washington as aide, marched against French Fort Pitt and Fenimore's Chingadgcook trod the forest. But the white man had spoiled it. Ruined it utterly. The forest was gone. Vanished for ever. The one-time sparkling streams ran sluggishly now, stained with iron and sulphur from coal-mine drainage till the water looked like oily blood and the farmers' cattle turned their noses up at it. The once blue Monongahela River ran dark and sinister, its greasy surface blotted with patches of filth and garbage. The Indians were gone, a century since. The descendants of the *Mayflower* settlers had been too strong for them. But even that white American stock were becoming extinct, swamped by the horde of Central-European peasant immigrants. The Anglo-Saxon tradition of ethics was being replaced by the devious methods inherited from a score of centuries of oppression by European dictators.

Wealthy the region was, I knew. One of the wealthiest in the world. But at what a price!

The time of Aggie's confinement arrived without any sign from her husband other than a letter from that astute gentleman, regretting his inability to attend. I was for it. I had a premonition.

Margaret took the precaution of engaging the local midwife and expressed her intention of being present and lending moral support. I myself was to stand at the telephone and deal with the "practitioner" at the other end of the wire.

To my surprise Aggie raised no objection to the employment of the midwife. She even seemed slightly relieved, a fact which augured badly, I thought, for the painlessness of a performance in which faith was to be the only anæsthetic.

It was March. About the equinox. Aggie telephoned our house about dark and asked us to come over . . . scared her voice sounded over the telephone and it would have sounded more scared still if she had known that Margaret had just gone to bed with a bad influenza cold. She gave a gasp when I told her that she must get some other woman because Margaret could not come.

Hurriedly I finished dinner and got out the car, cursing the perversity of women for there was a man-size blizzard blowing. White clouds of snow were sweeping horizontally across the headlights and I had to get out every few minutes to clear the snow off the glass of the windshield so that I could see at all. I got to the village all right and roused the midwife. A wrinkled, toothless old beldame, but she had the rudiments of sense. She set a bottle and a glass on the table while she wrapped a shawl around her head. I took one and she took one. We needed them for what we had ahead. The blizzard was increasing all the time. The wild north wind howled among the leafless boughs. At times the force of the wind caused the car to sway as we ground slowly in second gear through foot-deep snow. When at last we turned into the lonely lane which led to Aggie's farmhouse the going was worse yet. The snow was drifted in places. Here and there boughs had fallen across the road and had to be dragged clear before we could pass. Finally we stuck fast in a snow-drift. I could neither back the car out nor move it forward and the snow was drifting deeper every minute. That

car wouldn't move again till it was dug out, that was plain.
Fortunately we were only a couple of hundred yards from Aggie's
place. The old beldame was game enough, but she was old and
as bundled in clothes as a Quaker virgin. Somehow I pushed,
rolled, dragged and almost carried her to Aggie's door. When
I hammered on it Aggie appeared. Her eyes looked wild but
relief flashed into them when she recognised my companion.

" I couldn't get the neighbour woman on the 'phone. Her
line must be down."

" What about the ' practitioner ' ? " I asked.

" God help me if we can't get him," she wailed. " He should
be praying for me now." She clutched her middle.

I called the telephone number. The " practitioner's " voice
answered.

" Better stand by," I warned him.

" Tell him to pray," screamed Aggie as the midwife led her
into the bedroom.

" She says to start praying."

" All right." His voice sounded sleepy. " I'm beginning
now. Be sure and call me when it's over."

That house was arctic. Aggie had let the furnace in the cellar
die down and one of the hot-water pipes had frozen and burst,
as I found out when I tried to get a fire going in the furnace to
raise the temperature to a liveable level. After about half an
hour of fruitless tinkering below I emerged into the living-room
as black as a sweep and just in time to hear Aggie's voice calling
me, anguished.

" Tell him to pray. For God's sake. This is killing me."

Again I got the practitioner.

" Pray. Damn it, pray. She says you're not praying hard
enough."

" Jehoshaphat, I'm praying. Ain't she near through yet ? "
His teeth were chattering audibly.

" She's just starting."

" Jesus. I'm frozen."

" So am I and I'm not getting paid for it."

He hung up.

Aggie's groans were audible through the door of the bedroom.
I don't remember ever feeling more uncomfortable in my life.
Cold. Freezing right through. I felt foolish, too. Further-

more, while the situation had seemed laughable in anticipation, the poor woman's suffering killed the element of farce and made it tragedy—hardly tragedy, because the midwife was competent and Aggie was a healthy wench, but somehow the fun was taken out of it. Every moment my anger was rising against the old impostor who took the money of credulous women on the pretence of saving them pain. Freely I admit that there's a lot to be said for Christian Science, but the amount of relief that old billy-goat could bring anyone was the measure of his deserts in Paradise.

With numb blue hands I fumbled at the kitchen stove and tried to kindle a blaze.

Groans and cries called me back to the living-room.

"Tell him to pray . . . o-o-o-o-oh . . . pray. Make sure he's praying. Make him do it at the telephone and tell me what he says."

Again I got the practitioner.

"Pray, damn you. Pray or I'll hang you with your own beard."

"I'm p-p-p-praying." His teeth rattled like castanets.

"Pray into the telephone so I can hear."

He began to mumble something that sounded like *Our Father*.

"Time's up," reminded the McKeesport operator.

"Keep me plugged in. For God's sake don't cut me off." I was repeating to Aggie the practitioner's mumble, improvising where necessary. The effort she made to repeat after me took her mind off her troubles somewhat.

"What's going on there?" asked the telephone operator suspiciously.

I explained the circumstances.

"Poor soul," she remarked, and kept the plug in till we had finished.

Somewhere in the small hours a baby was ushered into a very cold world.

The midwife and I were warming ourselves over the kitchen stove after it was over.

"We beeg dam fools," she remarked apropos of nothing.

"Why?"

"We leave the bottle at home."

I agreed with her heartily.

About a year after Aggie's our first child was born—in March of 1922, just a few days before the beginning of the great coal strike. A fair-haired mite she was. We called her Margaret after her mother.

CHAPTER VII

SOUTH TO THE FOUNTAIN OF YOUTH

A YEAR it was since Bill and I had won our battle in the strike of 1922. Two small rooms in the Fulton Building in Pittsburgh had been our office then. Now the whole of the seventeenth floor was ours to house the platoon of clerks and accountants who handled the business from our six producing mines. Six there were now. We had expanded fast. Five thousand tons of coal a day rolled from our mines along the railway network of the neighbouring states, a hundred great steel railway hoppersful. More than a million tons of coal a year from our mines to contribute to the dun pall of smoke which hangs for ever over the manufacturing districts of the middle west.

In front of me stretched a vast expanse of shiny glass-covered desk top. Clean of papers. I had finished for the day. The swivel chair squeaked as I swung it around, rose and stood before the window. Right below me oozed the sluggish yellow current of the Alleghany River. Across the river a monster building flaunted the sign of HEINZ, who manufactured some fifty-seven varieties of pickled, bottled and cachupped food. A hundred yards down the stream the Monongahela joined its sister Alleghany to form the great Ohio River. On the little point of land between the two I could see the restored log fort, the old French stronghold—Fort Pitt, from which the grimy steel manufacturing city of Pittsburgh took its name. The square log building of the fort looked puny and incongruous beside the towering sky-scrapers of " The Golden Triangle " which overshadowed it from our side of the river.

The darkey elevator man gave me a cheery " Good naat, Boss," as I stepped out on the ground floor. His grinning black face made me homesick for the land of his ancestors. The sun. God ! how I wanted the sun.

My car crept slowly through the streets with my headlights

barely piercing the pea-soupy fog which was as thick as much maligned London's best efforts. Going through Schenley Park it cleared a bit and flakes of snow began to fall ; black, from the soot which had stuck to them on their way down.

I put my car in the garage of the big house in which I lived in the fashionable suburb of Squirrel Hill. Good country it must have been when there were woods with squirrels in them on this bluff above the scene of General Braddock's defeat by the Monongahela River. I seated myself on a chair which allowed my bottom to sink in a full half-foot in the process of arresting the pull of gravity with the least shock to the human system. It was covered with a dust cover of some white cloth. All the furniture in that living-room was of that ultra-luxurious variety and all the upholstery was covered with the same white cloth. I never did see the real tapestry covering from the day that Margaret and I had selected it at the down-town department store until the day, years later, when it was exposed for sale. Luxury. All luxury and damned little comfort. That's what this life was. There's more comfort in a rough wooden chair with a rawhide seat than in any of your over-stuffed contraptions . . . that is if you've made the wooden chair with your own hands, there is. Winter coming again. Months of dreary fog, snow and thaw with rarely a glimpse of the sun. When you did see the sun it was like seeing the ghost of a friend . . . pallid, cold and ethereal. My fourth winter in the North and, God ! how I longed for the sun. But the sun had gone South. Southward stretched this great country, almost to the tropics, the delectable lands, where most of my life had been spent.

After a few minutes' thought I went to the telephone.

" Bill, I'm taking a vacation," I announced when I heard his voice on the wire.

" Pete, you can't do that." Neither of us had had a single day's holiday since we had joined forces more than two years before.

" I'm going, anyway. I'll bust if I don't."

" When ? "

I thought for a moment. I was going to camp all the way, none of the gilt and plush discomfort of big hotels for me. I'd need a day to assemble camping-kit.

" Day after to-morrow."

" Who's going to run your job ? "

" You are. When I come back I'll run yours for a month while you go away. What's the good of making money if we don't enjoy it ? "

I had hardly hung up when Margaret came in from the kitchen.

" We're going to Florida for a trip," I announced.

" Florida ! "

" Want to go ? "

" Do I ! "

" We're going to camp."

" But we've got no tent."

" I'll get camping-kit to-morrow while you're parking the baby. We start next day."

" But we can't start so soon."

" I've only got a month's vacation. Takes a week to drive to Florida and a week back. Every day we delay is a day off the two weeks there."

It was black early daylight when Margaret give her final instructions about feeding the baby to sister Kate who had come in to run the place during our absence. We climbed clear of the fog as we roared up Turtle Creek Hill on the Lincoln highway. Half-way up Turtle Creek Hill there was a man walking ahead of us carrying a suitcase whose weight seemed to drag his body sideways. When he heard our car coming up behind him he moved to one side of the road, set his suitcase on the ground and mopped his forehead, gazing pleadingly at us.

" We'll give you a lift if you can manage to climb in on top of our camping-gear in the back," I volunteered.

" Where are you going ? " I asked after the hill was climbed.

" New York."

" That's a long way."

" It's a bet. A friend in Pittsburgh bet me I couldn't hitch-hike to New York and back in a week."

" What's the idea of hefting a heavy suitcase on a jaunt like that ? One would think you'd travel as light as you could."

He laughed. " Would you have picked me up without the suitcase ? "

" Probably not. But why such a big heavy one ? "

Grinning he opened the suitcase. There was a toothbrush and

a spare shirt in it. "It's easy enough to make it look heavy. When I do have to walk a mile or two between lifts it's not hard to carry empty."

Up Chestnut Ridge we swept through woods aflame with autumn red—like the red spring foliage of the *umsasa* trees in Rhodesia it was. As we topped the Alleghany range the dark pall of the American "Black Country" hung in the sky behind us as though it had just lifted from my soul. On top we turned off the Lincoln highway and dropped our passenger—fifty miles of his bet he had made in our company—to wait for the next east-bound car. South we were heading now. Ahead of us, far, far ahead, lay the equator with its friendly encircling tropic bands. Beyond the equator lay the Antipodes, the land of "down-under," where I was born and bred. Vast was this land of the United States. One thousand miles and more it stretched ahead of us as I held the car's nose to a southerly course. But even when we should have attained the most southerly tip of its southward pointing arm of Florida we should have hardly reached the northernmost fringe of the genial tropics and the delectable lands beyond.

That night we camped in an oak thicket somewhere near the Virginia line. Scarlet leaves fluttered to the ground round our tent as the autumn wind moaned in the tree-tops. In front of our tent a tiny stream chortled. Clean water it was. Uncontaminated. I lay on my belly with my face to it and drank and drank and drank. For the first time in three years I drank as man was meant to drink.

Richmond. Capital of the old Confederate South. Wide leisurely streets with gracious white-porticoed houses standing sedately back in the streets of the suburbs like bustled ladies in an old-time southern ballroom. That night we pitched our tent in North Carolina. Here the leaves of the oaks were only beginning to turn their autumn tints and the air was warmer. Ahead, to the southward, summer lingered and we were catching it up.

Next night we camped among the Caribbean pines in South Carolina. Funereal trees with long drooping needles. In interminable array they stood around us, scattered like the timber on the South African *bushveld*. Evergreen too, as our trees at home are green. We baled our water from the well of a nearby squalid nigger shanty.

Next morning the asphalt surface on which we had driven from Pittsburgh ended and a wide clay road began. A dry clay road with a newly scraped surface. Mercury's wings had smoothed it. Swiftly the car ran, held to a gliding motion by the weight of our baggage in the back. Fifty miles an hour with little traffic to dispute our speed. Ahead was a country wagon loaded high with bales of cotton on which perched four cheery niggers, laughing and joking. The mule between the shafts jogged methodically towards us with its ears flopping. One nigger's body swayed rhythmically as his hands pushed and pulled at a concertina. Rapidly our speed cut down the distance. Suddenly with a noise like a gun-shot our left front tyre burst. Unruly as a charging rhinoceros the big car jerked her head free and charged the approaching cart. The steering-wheel fought my hands like the wheel of a sailing-ship in a gale. The piled-up wagon seemed rushing at me through the windshield, four pairs of starting-white eye-balls and four wide-open mouths in four black faces showed the agony of death. One nigger jumped with arms flung wide, half the concertina in each clutching hand. At the last moment I regained control and brought the car to a halt after missing the wagon by inches. The niggers piled off in a body to help me change the tyre.

" My Gawd, Boss ! You done saved us from one awful mess," remarked one reflectively.

Two days of clay roads through Georgia with the sun standing daily higher at the zenith and full-leaved peach trees lining the road with the last of the peach crop still unpicked. We were back in late summer already, beating the sun in his slow wheel towards the southern hemisphere.

On the fifth day out of Pittsburgh we crossed the Suwanee River, that of the old darkey song, a stolid stream on which great beds of hyacinth floated indolently. We were in Florida now. From clay surface the road changed to a rough sandy track. Flat the country was. All around us ranged the scattered boles of the long-leafed Caribbean pine. A dim shape in the distance, moving from shadow to shadow through the sunlight, was a darkey collecting the rosin which had bled from the tree-boles and which would be distilled into turpentine, the chief product of the region. On the scattered bunch grass between the trees some skinny cattle fed. For mile after mile there was no sign of human habitation. The solitude was heavenly peace after the warring hive of the North in which my last years had been spent.

Hour by hour the scene became more tropical. At Indian River we ate oranges fresh from the trees and Margaret exclaimed at her first sight of a banana growing on its stem.

" Look. They're growing upside down ! " she cried.

That night darkness almost overtook us before we chose a camping place, so eager were we to press on. As we drove southward through the dusk the beam of a lighthouse flashed out to our left. A dim sandy track led seawards. As we pitched our tent on the edge of the lonely beach a full moon rose like Neptune from the Atlantic ocean. We flung our clothing from us and rolled naked in the gentle surf, warmed by the Gulf Stream.

Palm Beach next day. The huge wooden mass of the Breakers Hotel. The playground of American society, a more hide-bound aristocracy than England had known since Queen Victoria died. Our travel-stained car and our rough dirty clothes, spattered with bacon grease from cooking over camp-fires, had no place here.

At Fort Lauderdale we saw a darkey fishing off a long wooden bridge. We bought some fish from him which we stopped and cooked as soon as we had reached the other end of the bridge. We bought a parcel of shrimps too, because he said they were good for bait and because we had fishing lines among our gear. We forgot all about the shrimps. Even when a tropical, corpse-like odour began to permeate the car a day or two later we did not connect it with the shrimps. Day after day the odour grew . . . almost viscous it became . . . until we turned out everything piled in the back of the car searching for a possible dead cat. The shrimps had slipped behind the cushion at the back. Their whereabouts was easy enough to trace.

Miami. A quiet fishing village with a few modern buildings along Flagler Street. A few tourists. Mostly shabby-looking people like ourselves who camped, cooked their own bacon and smoked their own toast over camp-fires. Companionable. We liked the atmosphere of Miami and swore we would come back some day. We saw no signs that within a few years Miami was to be the Mecca of every footloose person in the United

71

States, would grow in a single year from a fishing town of about fifteen thousand people to a metropolis of twenty times that figure. There were as yet no visible signs of the great Florida land boom of which Miami was to be the storm centre, still less was there any indication that I was to play a fairly prominent part in Miami's share of it.

We could drive no farther south than Miami. We were at the end of the southward reaching arm of the country. But the pointing finger of that arm still lay ahead—the long line of Keys which leads to Key West, the most southerly town in the country. Flagler's genius had bridged the gaps between the Keys and built a railway during the Cuban war of the nineties. From the train windows we gazed down through transparent blue water to the coral bottom above which great fish played . . . shark, barracouta and the great sting-ray, the latter flat as a table-top and about as big. Sometimes the train was out of sight of land, so long the bridges were. Before us and behind the long row of concrete arches diminished into invisibility. That night I gazed from my hotel window in Key West over the dark expanse of the Florida Straits to the southward. Beyond lay Cuba. Beyond that the Caribbean and its islands, the most fascinating expanse of water in the world. As I watched I saw faintly a constellation whose base almost touched the dark edge of the sea which cut short the star-illuminated sky. Almost down over the rim of the world it was, that star group which for most of my life had wheeled overhead, queen of the sky. The Southern Cross. The lodestone which draws back from northern lands the men from " down under " when they have wandered too long. Very dim and seemingly very far. But I could see it. That was something.

As we had come south down the east coast of Florida we decided to take the west coast route for the return. But southern Florida was as yet largely undeveloped. West of Miami were the Everglades, pioneer country still. A few years later plenty of hardship was in store for me in that waving sea of saw-grass, rooted in slime. As yet unconceived was the Tamiami Trail which was to bridge the Everglades with a sixty-mile-long ribbon of asphalt on which cars could travel at sixty miles an hour. As yet the only passage of the Everglades was in a narrow dug-out canoe propelled by some stolid Seminole Indian who had his home in the swamps. So back up the east coast we must drive to Melbourne, two hundred miles. At Melbourne we loaded our automobile on a railway flatcar and, sitting in it, were pulled across the Kissimmee Swamp by a diminutive wood-burning locomotive with a smoke stack the shape of an inverted crinoline skirt. Tampa that night. In a hotel. The first we had slept in since leaving home. An industrial port which smacked of the North. We cleared out early and set our course for Silver Springs.

The sun was low in the sky when we reached the springs, a limpid pool of water a hundred yards across; ringed by forest as silent as when the Seminoles had hunted in it; clear; so clear that the water was invisible when you looked directly into it. We hired a glass-bottomed boat from the concessionaire. Out in the middle we stopped. A small silver coin was clearly visible all the way as it sank to the white sandy bottom thirty feet below. There the sand was boiling as Nature's hydraulics somewhere in the mountains of Georgia, hundreds of miles to the northward, forced the water through mysterious underground channels to find its level. Fish swam below us in the invisible medium and rose to take breadcrumbs from our hands. This spring was the magnet which had first drawn the Spaniard to Florida—the Fountain of Youth, which had been Spanish Ponce de Leon's goal. After dinner that night we stripped and swam naked in the starlight. The concessionaire had gone for the night to some nearby town where he lived. That glorious crystal depth was ours.

Some years later I came back to enjoy the springs. A row of gimcrack wooden villas ringed it, built where the forest had been cut down. Divers from half a dozen springboards raped the once placid surface of the water. Refuse from picnic-parties littered its shores, while in the centre a gramophone blared from a garish barge. Without even getting out of my car I turned and drove away.

Four days after leaving the springs on our way home we topped the Chestnut Ridge once more. Late it was; hours after dark. The smoke pall which hung over the " black country " ahead was invisible. A howling blizzard blew from the north and clouds of snow whipped past us.

CHAPTER VIII

MINES, RAILWAYS AND AEROPLANES

IT was that Moshannon coalfield which really got us into trouble, although our troubles did not begin till long after we had opened it. Five thousand acres of the best quality coal in the Pennsylvania coalfields. Fifty million tons of coal which was easy to mine albeit somewhat hard to put on the railway systems of the country. The great Charles Schwab had it under option when we first heard of it. He wanted it for his steel company, the great Bethlehem Steel octopus. For months his engineers ran levels, made maps, estimated tonnage and finally sent him an adverse report on it. "No roof" was their verdict. The coal lay in scattered islands near the surface and therefore underground mining costs would be high because the natural rocky layer above the coal—the "roof" in mining parlance—was rotted by the weather and would not hang in place when the coal was removed, but would display a tendency to fall on miners' heads with consequent costly stoppages of production and still more costly payments to extinct or partially deceased miners. "No roof!" Schwab's engineers had failed to take into consideration the new stripping method by which we and others like us were profitably mining just such "roofless" seams of coal. "No roof" to us meant low cost of production. Just what we were looking for.

The Moshannon seam of coal it was, with its high fuel value, that first brought the steel industry to Pittsburgh and was consequently the first of Pittsburgh's several coal seams to be worked out. When Nature laid out the Pittsburgh region she had been prolific of her coal. A million years or so before the *Mayflower* sailed westward she had built the region up neatly with layers of coal and rock, laid level as the layers of a cake. But Nature was then younger and more frisky than she is to-day. In the course of her cataclysmic gambollings she cracked her layer cake badly and tilted up pieces of it so that rivers began to run in the depressions with their feeder streams. Rock exposed to weather becomes soil. Soil washes away. Deep valleys form where rivers run. Some of Nature's neatly stored coal was eroded away—the top layers naturally eroded and disappeared first. The Moshannon seam was the best, the sweetest. So, like the icing of the cake it lay on top and like the icing it melted first. By the time man appeared on the scene and appraised the five-foot layer of black potential heat in the Moshannon seam, only a small percentage of the original area of Moshannon had survived. In addition, by the time we entered the arena, for fifty years the Pittsburgh steel mills had burned Moshannon coal to melt the iron ore which the great ore-boats carried down the chain of great lakes all the summer. By the time Bill and I had won our spurs in the coal business the mills were perforce using other and inferior grades of coal. The Moshannon seam was gone, all but the five-thousand-acre patch which Charlie Schwab's engineers had turned down.

"I'd like to have a go at that chunk of Moshannon coal," remarked Bill, wistfully looking at a map of the coalfield which lay on his desk.

"Why not?" I had visions of developing a good-sized stripping operation instead of the short-lived patches which our various shovels round Pittsburgh were operating. "The reason Schwab turned it down makes it ideal for us. Our big 'muckers' will make hay of that rotten roof." I pored over the map. It intrigued me. The coalfield was right on top of the Alleghany Mountains, forty miles from the nearest town of Clearfield. Real country that must be up there. Unspoiled. Deer and bear up there, they said. I'd have to superintend the development and that would get me clear of the office for a while.

"It would take some getting down from the mountain-top to the railway." Bill was watching me, almost furtively.

"We'll get it down by rail."

"A railway will be costly. Forty miles of it would be needed according to Schwab's plan."

"We'll cut that down." I had been talking to one of Schwab's engineers. "Schwab's men made their survey on the basis of using ordinary railway haulage which means a maximum two per cent. grade. We'll run our grade on a basis of eight per cent. That'll cut our mileage down to less than half."

" You're crazy, man. No locomotive will face an eight per cent. grade."

" We'll use one of those new-fangled geared locomotives. They'll operate on anything up to ten per cent.

Bill whistled. " That's an idea." Then he gazed at me seriously. " This'll be big stuff. So far the big-shot Coal Barons have let us alone because we're only operating short-lived properties that will be worked out in a year or two. But there's fifty years' work in this Moshannon job. Fifty years monopoly of the best coal in the Pittsburgh sales area. I have a fancy one or two of the big fellows are already after it now that Schwab has let his option lapse. If we take it on we'll have a fight on our hands for sure."

" That'll be your trouble. My job is to get the coal out."

Bill grinned. To get into a knock-down, drag-out fight with big interests had long been Bill's ambition, I knew. Like some young swordsman, sure of his skill, who longed for a D'Artagnan to give him gauge of battle. For my part I wanted to see ourselves operating a really big property. Tangible, my ambitions were. I wasn't so keen on a fight with intangible values as Bill. Even he was to get his bellyful of that kind of fight by the time we had finished.

" But you'll have to move quick to get an option now the field is open," I added.

Bill's teeth flashed again. That grin of his always did twist something inside my chest. He pulled open a drawer of his desk and flipped a paper at me. It was an option on the five thousand acre field in question. Eagerly I scanned it. No cash required. Only a ridiculously small royalty on each ton of coal as we dug it out. There was a time clause, of course. A gift it was, except for that time clause, and even that was within our powers to meet provided we had an even break of luck. We must be actually operating within six months or the deal was off.

" How the hell . . . ? " I began.

" The owner got disheartened when Schwab turned it down. Walked right in here this morning and fairly pushed it at me. Said he was tired of dealing with the big fellows and that we ought to be able to do the job if anyone could. Seems as though we're beginning to acquire a reputation."

The sun was almost setting next afternoon when I stopped my

car on a ridge. Two hundred miles had I driven since leaving Pittsburgh that morning, the last thirty on a rough winding mountain track. Before me lay a rolling plateau. Bright green were the leaves of the second growth timber, the green of middle spring. Here and there in the light green sea were sombre dark green islands where the clumps of hemlock stood. Lighter patches, like shoal water in the darker depths of the ocean, were little clearings of the mountain folk. They were scarce though. Little columns of smoke rose from their chimneys, miles apart. Room to breathe here. The tang of the hemlock burned my lungs as I distended them to the bursting-point. To my right the plateau fell away sharp for a thousand feet to the yellow streak of the west fork of the Susquehanna River—our railway must climb that sharply tilted slope. On the near side of the river ran a railway track, a branch of the New York Central system with which our railway must connect to get our coal to market. Beyond the river was pine. Rank upon serried rank the white pine marshalled on the mountain-side as far as my eye could reach. Of the once vast pine forests of Pennsylvania this was the last remaining stand, they had told me. Even as I looked the screech of a circular saw from somewhere behind a mountain spur reminded me that even this last stronghold of the pine would soon be gone. That river there below me had not so many generations since carried its great rafts of pine logs to market, on each raft a fort to protect the "river hogs" who manned it from the arrows of the red men on the bank. Now the Indians had gone. The "river hogs" were as extinct as the Indians and the pine would soon be the same. But the open country still remained, thank God. Strange it was that I, who so loved the open, should be always destined to break ground for the industrialisation of such peaceful scenes.

We got our job through well within our six months' limit. Our railway was fifteen miles long when it was finished. Like a letter Z it zig-zagged up the mountain slope from the siding by the river until it reached the level plateau where a great steam shovel snorted not far from the long wooden building which we had built to house our men. For the convenience of the mountain folk of the region we bought a passenger car which we hooked on to the back of our coal train to connect with the single passenger train on the New York Central line below.

More as a joke than anything else I had some complimentary free passes printed . . .

THE BITARD MOSHANNON RAILWAY EXTENDS FREE THE FACILITIES OF TRAVEL ON ITS LINES TO   FOR THE SPACE OF ONE YEAR.

Signed (P. W. RAINIER),
Vice-President.

I filled in names and sent them to the presidents of several of the great American railway systems. They were good sports. In return I got complimentary passes on enough railway mileage in the United States to give me free travel all over the country. It was a pity I had not the time to use them.

The new property looked from the start like being a success. Incidentally this development was to bring me a compliment. Years after it was. Ten years about. I came back from Colombia, South America, to New York with an emerald mining proposition which I needed to finance. I was advised to put it up to Charles Schwab. He was as hard to meet as the president of the United States, but eventually I was ushered into his office. A grand looking old man with a head like a Roman Emperor on a coin. He was sitting at his desk without a paper on it wrinkling his brows at my card which he held between his fingers.

" Sit down," he boomed. " Don't speak. I'll place you in a moment." Then his face cleared. " I've got you now. YOU'RE THE YOUNG SQUIRT WHO DEVELOPED THAT MOSHANNON COAL-FIELD WHEN MY ENGINEERS SAID IT COULDN'T BE DONE."

That was the greatest compliment I have ever been paid. To have one of my achievements remembered after all those years by a really great man. He didn't take my emerald proposition. Too old he said he was to be getting into new things. Getting out of business instead of getting in. Retiring. But he sent me to Chester Beatty, the copper king of Rhodesian " Roan Antelope " fame. Chester Beatty's secretary made an appointment which he cancelled a few days later because the copper magnate had the 'flu. As soon as he recovered I got another appointment. But the day before it I received a telegram from my step-daughter Minnie, who had long since married a man named

Bob Spencer and was living in the little town of Irwin, near Pittsburgh :

BOB'S DEAD BEING BURIED TO-MORROW.

I was horror struck.   I called up Beatty's secretary and postponed the appointment, wiring Minnie :

SHOCKED ARRIVING SIX TRAIN TO-MORROW

I was astounded to see both Minnie and her presumably dead husband on the platform to meet me.   The telegraph company had made a mistake.   " BOB'S DAD BEING BURIED TO-MORROW," the message should have read.   Never having met the old gentleman I dashed back to New York to get another appointment.   I did eventually meet Beatty, but only when he was hurriedly cleaning up loose ends to catch a boat for England—something had gone wrong with copper shares and he had to go back and plug the leak.   He turned the emerald proposition down flat, but I had the impression that it might have interested him in a different mood ; also it might not.   But that's how these financial adventures go.   All this is parenthetical, however.

Hardly was our Moshannon property working smoothly when Bill sprung another one on me.   Being partners with Bill was about as peaceful as hanging on to the tail of a comet.   The man couldn't have slept more than half the normal human ration and his waking hours were as active as if he had had a galvanic battery hooked to his tail.   River transportation this time.   One of the great electric power companies was going to build a generating station at Philo on the Muskingum River in Ohio, some miles downstream from Zanesville.   Ten thousand tons of coal a month they would use.   Somehow Bill got wind of it and immediately secured an option on the nearest coal-field upstream—a few miles above Zanesville.   This meant river transportation . . . a fleet of boats and barges to be built and operated. It would be my job to supervise, of course, in addition to the various properties I was already finding difficulty in visiting once a week, so scattered they were.   Two hundred miles east of Pittsburgh lay our Moshannon mine.   This new Ohio coal-field lay about the same distance west of that city.   In between were scattered the half-dozen lesser operations for whose smooth operating I was responsible. I felt that one visit a week was the minimum I could honestly give each of them, but already this was entailing two whole nights a week driving in my car. Air travel was the only answer to my problem that I could think of. I chartered a plane and had provisional landing-fields cleared and rented in the vicinity of each mine. The landing-fields were hayfields or cow pastures. The plane was an old Standard two-seater in which the passenger sat in front with the wind blowing his head off and the pilot just behind. It had been a good plane once. It was still a good plane except that one wing seemed to develop a wobble at too high a rate of speed. But the pilot-owner swore by it and he ought to have known. A Captain Robinson he was, late of the Royal Air Force, with half a dozen Germans to his credit in the war.

Robbie always insisted on having several stiff drinks before he would fly. He said he couldn't fly sober. He said that in the war they had always filled them up before the dawn patrol, that the results had been successful and that he intended to keep the practice up. I can't say whether Robbie could fly sober or not because I never saw him try. But he could certainly fly when he was tight. Still, flying with him in his old Standard plane was not without its tense moments, although I must admit that none of them were ever due to any fault of the pilot. There was the Zanesville landing-field, for instance, frequented by inquisitive cows which had the habit of suddenly appearing from behind a tree just as the plane was taking off. To the south of this field there was a high-tension cable. When the field was hard and the engine behaving nicely we cleared the wires easily. When the field was soggy with rain or the engine had indigestion it was problematical. Robbie would hold the old plane's nose at the level of the wires, striving for height. If he could get height enough we cleared with a foot or two to spare under the landing wheels. If not, when a crash with a hundred thousand voltage looked imminent he would dive under the wires, brush the tops of the bushes underneath, skim the placid surface of the Muskingum River and zoom upwards before the other bank was reached.

Then there was an unforgettable occasion on one of our weekly visits to the Moshannon. Fog shrouded the Alleghany Mountains, like a great white tablecloth beneath us. For what seemed an age we circled the vicinity of where we thought the mine ought to be, trying to pierce with our gaze the fog below to recognise some familiar landmark. We might as well have tried to gaze down through the ocean to recognise some spot in the depths. Not even the island of a mountain peak stuck up to guide us. After a long time which seemed even longer than it really was I felt a tap on the shoulder. Robbie, pointing upward to the petrol gauge above my head. To my horror I saw the needle flickering about the zero point. Below was fog, transparent as a white wool blanket. Beneath the fog we knew were the rounded heights, wooded slopes and narrow valleys of the Alleghany Mountains. I realised then why the minor range of the Alleghanies was more dreaded than the great Rocky Mountain chain by the trans-continental mail-plane pilots.

The engine stuttered once. Robbie cut it off and turned the plane's nose downward, holding one thumb aloft in the gesture of the old Roman arena. With no sound but the whistling of the wind in the struts we glided downwards and the cotton wool rushed up to meet us while the sun shone brilliantly from the clear blue sky. Once in the fog we were blind, like wearing frosted glasses. Smothered. I screeched something incoherent as a dim black shape ahead rushed at us, but the engine caught and roared for a second—Robbie had saved the last carburettorful of petrol for just such an emergency. The plane took the leap like a startled springbok and black glistening tree-tops sped backwards beneath our feet. The engine stopped again and we continued our glide to the unknown, wisps of vapour flying past us. I leaned back and braced my feet for a crash. Then we were suddenly out of the fog and gliding beneath it down the valley of the Susquehanna River with a level seeming cornfield just ahead of us. In the cornfield we landed.

"We've got the luck of a pox-doctor," remarked Robbie calmly as he began to climb out of his seat. "About the only place in miles we could have landed."

"Did you have any petrol for another burst if you had needed it?" I asked.

"Not a drop." He grinned as he vaulted to the ground.

When I reached the ground my knees felt weak and I sat down. Sitting down I vomited. When Robbie saw me vomit he followed suit.

The farmer came running up. In his Ford we sent him to
the nearest mountain village for petrol and took off again within
a couple of hours into a clear sky.

The neatest thing I ever saw Robbie do was to put his plane
down in an emergency landing near Johnstown when the engine
suddenly conked out. He landed in a farmer's yard—pancaked
—between the manure pile and the threshing machine. To get
the plane out we had to take the wings off her and tow her
down the lane with the farmer's tractor till we came to a field.
We had her together and reached home safely that same day.

But Robbie came to a sad end. When he left me he took a
contract sky-writing, a form of advertising which was then just
coming into vogue. Using a sea-plane with floats he spent
several months writing LUCKY STRIKE across the sky above
Philadelphia until one day—he must have either mixed his drinks
or taken one too many, or else, just once he might have broken
his rule and gone up sober—he forgot he had a sea-plane under
him and tried to land it in the municipal airport . . . on land.
Exit Robbie and the plane. Both complete " write-offs." But
poor old Robbie had taught me something. Since those days
I have flown a lot. Been in a plane buffeted by up-and-down
currents among snow-capped Andean mountain peaks. Ridden
battered by a blinding sand-storm in the Libyan desert. I've
even been passenger in a bomber while a bored pilot practised
dive bombing as he travelled his route or hedge-hopped rocky
desert ridges, reaching downward at Bedouin tents with his
landing wheels while panic-stricken Bedouins vied with their
camels and donkeys in reaching a distance in one mad rout.
But I have never got squeamish since Robbie's day. He and
his old Standard had inured me to thrills.

We got a good deal of publicity in the Pittsburgh papers from
using a plane for routine mine inspection work. It was due to
this publicity that enough local interest was aroused to form the
Pittsburgh Aero Club, of which both Bill and I became foundation members. There was plenty of money in the club to cover
almost any expenditure, but there was a great scarcity of sites
for a landing-field in the hilly country round Pittsburgh. Finally,
we got an option on the only suitable site which had the advantage of being close to the business section of the city, near the
County Workhouse. The price was prohibitive, but we sub-

scribed sufficient money among the members—the downtown business district of Pittsburgh was not named "The Golden Triangle" for nothing. With sufficient funds in hand to buy and level our optioned site we approached the city authorities. We proposed to donate free the landing-field to the city in return for permission to use and keep our private planes on it. Surely a generous offer on our part, but, to our surprise, some hitch developed. The city of Pittsburgh did not seem at all keen on acquiring a landing-field, not even a free-gratis one. The club appointed a committee to wait on the mayor.

A red-faced beefy individual, he looked like a retired brick-layer. A white goatee beard waggled as he greeted us when we filed into his office.

Our spokesman put our case. He put it well, too. Surely in the development of aviation no city ever had a better proposal from the public spirited among its sons!

The mayor shook his head after some consideration. " Naw." His beard waggled. " I guess not."

" But why not, Mr. Mayor? Here's a city of a million people. The nearest landing-field is an hour's drive away from the city limits. It takes as long to get to it as it does to fly to Chicago, almost. We're offering the city a landing-field right downtown free of cost."

" Because of the County Workhouse. That's why."

" But what has the County Workhouse to do with it?"

" Think we want you young squirts flying about over it and dropping files and saws and things to the prisoners?"

We pleaded, but the mayor was adamant. His reason was ridiculous, of course. The real reason was that the owner of the far distant landing-field had enough political influence to block us. We got up a press campaign, but the party political machine was strong enough and the next election far enough away for the mayor to thumb his nose at our efforts. Finally our option on the land expired and it was snapped up as a site for tenement buildings. For almost a decade—the decade which covered the great commercial development of the aeroplane—Pittsburgh was without a landing-field adjacent enough to the city to make flying anywhere from Pittsburgh worth while. Finally, Pittsburgh did acquire a nearer field but at an astronomical cost.

About this time our second daughter was born. A jolly little red-haired thing with what promised to be a sunny disposition. We called her Dorothy after a favourite South African sister-in-law of mine.

CHAPTER IX

RIVER NAVIGATION

THE town of Marietta on the Ohio River had been a famous river port in the old "flat-boat" days when Pittsburgh was the jumping-off place for western settlement, and the easiest road to western pioneering was down the river. At Marietta also, the Muskingum River joined the parent stream and at Marietta two river steamers and a string of coal barges were being constructed for our Zanesville mine. For a hundred miles above Marietta the Muskingum meandered between the fat rolling farmlands of Ohio State; broad, placid and yellow. The haunt of bass and muskelonge. Peaceful. Then came Philo, once a tiny village but now bristling with weird-looking excavating machinery noisily digging the foundations for the great electric power plant which the Ohio Edison company were constructing. Soon great dynamos would be whirring in the huge, gaunt building, whose steel framework already lay scattered over the lush river meadows where cows had so recently chewed the cud. Stolid fat-looking boilers would generate the steam to keep the dynamos driving electric power into the network of high-tension wires which criss-crossed the continent. The boilers would burn coal; our coal. Bill had spent a month in New York City, dealing with the New York Edison directors, and had returned to Pittsburgh with a contract in his pocket. And such a contract. On to each point of a deal Bill would hang like a bulldog on to the nose of a bull, shaken and battered by superior weight till by sheer hanging on he wore the opponent down and gained his point. A ten-year contract at a fancy price. We got the price because we had optioned up—thanks to Bill's foresight—the only tract of coal capable of being transported by water to the Philo plant. Our competitors had perforce bid on a basis of railway transportation. Costly. Our coal would travel in our own barges. Cheap. Years later, in the grim days of the coal business, when overproduction had killed the market till mines were lucky to work two days a week, there were two mines which ran steadily, making a profit when most of the others were running at a loss. Those two were the Moshannon, with its lack of competition for its own particular grade of coal, and Zanesville, with its lack of competition for cheap river freight. True, we had long since lost our connection with them, but the mines lived on as our monument, as proof that the structure we built was not based on sand. It is years since I had word from that part of the world, but to the best of my knowledge the Moshannon and Zanesville mines are working still—sixteen years later.

Ten miles above Philo was the industrial city of Zanesville—named after one Zane who had been prominent in fighting Indians thereabouts. At Zanesville three drawbridges crossed the river—two of them for two of the great trans-continental railway systems and the other for a great trans-continental highway, one of the great traffic arteries from east to west. At Zanesville the naturally navigable portion of the Muskingum River ceased as, above the city, the current swiftened and the upper river lost its depth.

But the upper Muskingum River was navigable. It had been made so by building locks—at the cost of a good many million dollars of the tax-payers' money. There had been up till now no justification for the expense. Locks were not needed for the occasional picnic launch or fisherman's skiff which had been till now the only traffic on the upper river. But Congressmen seeking re-election are apt to hunt for concrete achievements to flaunt before their electors on election day. The upper Muskingum navigation scheme had been subjected to what, I believe, is technically known as a "log-rolling" process. This operation is conducted somewhat as follows. Congressman Blather has on hand his upper Muskingum navigation scheme for which he requires to obtain from Congress the necessary appropriations to dangle before his constituents as the red-skin warrior of a generation or two before dangled the scalps at his belt when seeking command of a war-party. Congressman Dither from the far west has, let us say, a highway project in his state while Congressman Puff might have an irrigation dam. Blather approaches Dither in the lobby of the house or in some nearby pub where Congressmen congregate.

" I'll swing my gang's vote for your highway if your gang will vote for my navigation scheme."

Dither having agreed, both Dither and Blather approach Puff with a similar proposition for mutual aid. So the log rolls on till sufficient votes have been accumulated to ensure all the appropriations required for all the schemes of all concerned.

But the fact that the upper river had been made navigable had not increased the traffic for the simple reason that there never had been any industry on the upper river to cause any traffic. During the decade which had passed since the millions had been spent no boat large enough to force the drawbridges to raise had passed upstream beyond the city of Zanesville. For ten years the lock-keepers upstream had lounged in the sunshine and fished for bass or cultivated their firesides during the winters with only the excitement of an occasional summer picnic launch to break the monotony of waiting till they had accumulated sufficient years of service to draw a pension.

Now, a dozen miles above Zanesville our barge-loading plant was being rapidly constructed on the river-bank, while a mile or two of railway connected it to the edge of the coal-field where a giant steam-shovel was already taking shape under the efforts of another gang. Down-river, at Marietta, our fleet of boats and barges were building.

Finally, our fleet was ready. Bill and I drove down to Philo and caught it on the way upstream. Two stern wheel paddle-boats of the conventional river type, each dragging behind it half a dozen great open barges to carry the coal. On the bridge of the front boat we took our stand beside a red-faced be-whiskered captain who looked as though he might have stepped off the page of one of Mark Twain's books. And were we proud ! Our own fleet and standing on our own bridge ! No new-fledged member of the board of the Cunard ever felt prouder than we did that day, as the big stern paddle churned the tow upstream.

Below the first Zanesville drawbridge we blew the specified number of blasts, a peremptory signal for the drawbridge to be raised.

" The St. Louis express flyer is about due now," remarked Bill. " Wouldn't it be a joke if she had to wait till we had passed." She would have to wait if she came along just then. Navigable waters take precedence of all other means of transportation under United States law.

But the bridge did not open. After waiting a few minutes the captain sounded the siren again till its echoes rang from the barn-like factory buildings of the nearby town. The bellow of that siren would have awakened Rip Van Winkle out of his nap.

Nothing happened.

" Did you notify the railway that we were going to pass ? " I asked Bill.

He laughed. " What for ? There's going to be a tow pass here every day. You don't have to notify anyone when you use Uncle Sam's water. Drawbridges are supposed to open on demand. That's why they are drawbridges."

At the third try a man in overalls slouched out of the small watchman's hut on the bridge. Annoyed he looked, as though our noise had disturbed his nap. Idly he gazed downstream till a blast of profanity from the captain seared his ears. Then he suddenly galvanised and his eyes popped wide as he realised that there was a real live steamer blowing its head off and an inflamed skipper blasting him from the bridge with a flow of riverman's profanity. The watchman dashed back into the shanty. Evidently he telephoned someone because, a few minutes later, we saw a gang of labourers frantically pushing a work car on to the bridge. Then there was the blue flame of an oxy-acetylene jet and the sparks of molten metal dropping into the water with a hiss. Only then did we realise why the bridge had not opened as required. A decade had passed since the opening of the upper river to navigation had compelled the railway company to install a drawbridge in place of a solid steel span. During that decade the railway had probably replaced rails all along their high-speed line, among them the original rails cut to allow the bridge to open in the centre. As the bridge had never been required to open and there was no indication that it ever would be required to open they had omitted to cut the new rails when they laid them. The railway track lay solid across the river. Now they were cutting the rails. Cutting them in a hurry . . . under fire of a fine profusion of curses and ribald remarks from the skippers and crews of two steamers, a series of tunes from two steamer sirens and profound and wrathful bellows from the locomotive of the St. Louis express whose sacrosanct time-table was being seriously disorganised by the delay.

At last the bridge opened and we splashed majestically through between crowds of hilarious spectators on either bank.

Round the bend was the trans-continental highway bridge. No rails to cut here. With a screeching of long-disused machinery the two halves of the bridge raised before us as we came into sight. We passed between them as they pointed skyward like the rifles of sentries at the "present." After we passed they continued to point skyward. The rusty machinery had stuck. Some hours it was before they got that drawbridge down and road traffic restored. Meantime, they told us afterwards, the busy highway was packed for twenty miles in either direction with parked cars and buses.

The third bridge gave no trouble and we steamed into the virgin upper river, startling fishing lock-keepers pop-eyed when we whistled for passage.

That night we anchored our own fleet at our own wharf beside our own loading plant and next morning watched the black stream of our own coal falling into the barges from the long conveyor belt which projected beyond the wharf edge. We were beginning deliveries on our ten-year contract with the Ohio Edison plant downstream.

"That's that," remarked Bill. "We've put the first commercial navigation on the upper Muskingum River and every soul in Zanesville knew it when we passed."

89   D

CHAPTER X

MOUNTAINEERS, HOLY ROLLERS AND A MINING PROMOTER

BILL and I were coal barons now. Full-fledged. Two big long-lived properties were ours as well as smaller ones. When the small properties were worked out we could move their equipment on to the big Moshannon or Zanesville mines. There was enough coal in those two to last for longer than we should want to stay in the coal business, even working them intensively with all the steam-shovels we owned. To Bill's shrewd brain we owed our success. I had been merely the hand to execute the Machiavellian schemes which conceived themselves, were born and sprang full-fledged from behind his disarming smile and artless expression. A financier was Bill and a damned good one, too. A little over four years before we had hesitatingly tip-toed into the Pittsburgh coal business. Once established, we had flung ourselves like a comet into the sooty Pittsburgh firmament. So sudden had been our advent that the stately planets which there revolved had not as yet moved from their orbits to intercept our passage. The long established community of coal magnates had not as yet given any sign of hostility, but we knew that they were watching us closely and might be sure they would not withhold a stroke should any weakness in our defences be exposed. Our debt was our weak spot. Our various mining companies owed a large sum of money when their debts were combined, and yet not unduly large when the solidity of their assets was calculated. Still, the debt was our Achilles' heel. But it did not worry us unduly although everything we had was in our mines. Neither of us had ever drawn on any profits beyond the bare necessities of living. All our accrued profits had been reinvested in the business. But it was a sound business. Although the price of coal was on the downward swing and although many of the more expensive operations were finding a difficulty in making a profit, our own operating expenses were low and our mines were making money. One more year at the present rate would see us completely out of debt and in an impregnable position.

Dull months those were. The year in which we had organised our two big mines had been too full of work to be boring. But now my old longing for the South returned. Not the southern states of the country in which I lived, but the southern half of the African continent . . . I wished to carry on where I had begun and where my life had been interrupted by war and tragedy. In any case this damned industrialised northern land was no place for a man of my upbringing. When first I arrived in the north I had trod the path of my profession diffidently, overawed by the greater erudition of college-trained men. But I had found that I could hold my own with the northern men, could hold my own with most in the profession of mining—the sweetness of the running of our mines was the proof of that. What I lacked in technical training was more than compensated by the resource engendered by my apprenticeship in the wilds where a minimum of equipment had to be balanced by a maximum of ingenuity. Many a man who was reckoned an expert, let us say in Milwaukee, would have been at a loss in Mozambique or Nigeria where my first mining experience had been gained. Successful in the north I had been, but I felt stifled. To me the northern winters and summers were alike uncomfortable. The difference between them seemed to be that in the winter one stifled in an overheated house or froze outside, while in the summer one stifled equally indoors or out. I longed for the perfect climate of the equator—four thousand feet elevation and zero latitude give the nearest to the perfect climate in my estimation . . . cool, equable, sunshiny, with enough rain to avoid monotony. Less luxury and more comfort was what I wanted. Nostalgia beset me for the old days when I could stroll out with a rifle on my shoulder and take my choice of game for the pot. I longed to be gone.

I would go before long, I was resolved. Once the mines were out of debt I should be able to realise on my holdings in the coal business. The battle would have been fought and won then and there would be no question of deserting Bill. He and I had entered the arena together and I would stand by him till our position were secure. Then back to Africa again. With capital too. There was a railway already built through my old land concession of which the war had deprived me in Mozambique —the railway I had prophesied when I first took up the land. God ! what that land must be worth by now and it would have cost me next to nothing if I could have kept up the payments on my concession . . . but the war had already knocked that scheme on the head . . . no use to think of it even. Still, there was plenty of good cheap land left in Africa, although the frontier would have moved northward in the years I had been gone. Land was the thing. War, pestilence, depressions and all the other ailments to which our modern state is prone will be survived by land.

One break in the monotony I had when I went to Washington as one of the delegates of the coal-stripping Operators, when the next wage-scale agreement with the United Mineworkers came up for renewal. For days I sat across the table from that wily bull buffalo of a man, John L. Lewis. The Operators demanded a cut in the miners' wages. Lewis threatened another strike and only climbed down when his followers showed signs of wavering—that hard-fought battle of 1922 was still too close in retrospect for them to chance another. The miners finally accepted a slight reduction in wages which still left them very highly paid men and the Operators breathed once more. The price of coal was slowly sliding downwards and another two years' agreement at the present wage-scale would have ruined many of them.

I dined one night in Washington with a young American official of my acquaintance and his fiancée, a beautiful girl of a prominent Washington family. After dinner we all repaired to his apartment. When he produced a couple of bottles of home-distilled gin I left them . . . I had inured myself to " bootleg." whisky, but my experience of home-distilled gin had proved disastrous. It was usually warm from the still, had a tinny taste and a delayed-fuse action which was treacherous.

When I met him casually next day he appeared worried.

" How's the poor head ? " I jeered.

" It's worse than that."

" What is ? "

" I'm in a hell of a fix."

" How ? "

" When you left us last night we took a drink or two. Then Betty got ambitious and bet me she could get to the bottom of a gin bottle before I did."

" Did she ? "

" She passed out in the second half. Couldn't get her round so that she could get home in good shape so I took her into the bathroom, stripped her and dunked her into an ice-cold tub of water . . . used up all the ice in the ice-box to make it cold. That seemed to fetch her to a bit. I dressed her in a hurry because it was getting late, got her into the car and drove her home."

" As long as she doesn't talk you're all right."

He shook his head. " She got wobbly again in the car but I found her latch-key in her pocket-book, opened her door quietly, steered her to the stairs and hoped to God she'd last out till she got to her bedroom on the next floor. Then I went home after leaving the latch-key inside and shutting the door."

" So far you're all right."

" Like hell I am. It seems she flopped on the landing. Made enough noise to wake her mother, who came out, undressed her and put her to bed."

" That's nothing to worry about."

He looked at me mournfully. " Her mother has just called up and asked me to explain how Betty's underwear came to be put on upside down."

Bill and I had sworn to expand no further but to concentrate on the properties we had already acquired. We kept our resolution too, except for one extraordinary mining venture which was almost forced on us and on which we spent no money. We were sitting in Bill's office one morning when a man named Ferguson came in to see us. It appeared that some friends of his had a fluorspar mine in Kentucky which was not paying under its present management. Our mines paid, it seemed. Therefore theirs might pay if we assumed the management.

" What the hell is fluorspar ? " asked Bill.

I explained that fluorspar was one of the ingredients of steel besides being used for a number of other things.

Bill raised his eyebrows at me.

I shook my head. We had plenty on our hands without taking on more responsibilities.

Ferguson pressed.

"Who are these friends of yours?" asked Bill.

Ferguson named some names that caused us to raise our eyebrows. He had named several of the leading bankers in the important manufacturing town of Youngstown.

"Sorry," explained Bill. "They'll have to hoe their own row. We've got ours to hoe and it doesn't look too straight either."

But Ferguson wouldn't take no for an answer and we finally agreed to meet the mineowners in Youngstown and at least hear their proposition.

The accumulation of wealth owned by the gathering must have been enough to buy up one of the smaller European countries. Smug ultra-respectability was the atmosphere of that meeting. The atmosphere of a churchwarden taking round the plate. Anything those chaps wanted to let go of wouldn't be worth having, I felt.

The mine, it seemed, was situated in Western Kentucky near Irwin Cobb's native city of Paducah. It bore the significant title of the Bonanza mine. Only, unlike its famous prototype, it had never paid. There's a good deal more to making a mine pay than naming it after a paying property. A man named Caruthers had first promoted it a decade before in New Orleans. A hundred thousand dollars he had raised, all spent, it seemed, in sinking the shaft and tapping the vein of fluorspar two hundred feet below the surface. The mining company had then gone into bankruptcy. Caruthers had bought it in again at the bankrupt sale for a mere thousand dollars or so. Again Caruthers had promoted it, formed a new company and raised another hundred thousand dollars. This time the money merely sufficed to buy a mill to treat the ore. As there was no working capital this company also went bankrupt. Again the mine was auctioned and again Caruthers bought it in for a song. Now a third time Caruthers had formed a company and it had been financed by the august assembly whose swan-song we were hearing.

I made a rough mental calculation.

"I can't see why Caruthers wanted your money," I remarked. "That is if the mine is any good. The shaft and the mill together couldn't have cost a quarter of the money he raised in his first two promotions. If the mine were any good he would have kept it himself. He ought to have had plenty of working capital because it looks as though most of the money he raised has stuck to his pockets."

The bankers looked at one another with a pained expression. It occurred to me that they had only recently reached the same conclusion.

"Who is actually managing the mine?" I asked.

Again the exchange of pained glances.

"Caruthers," replied one of them.

Bill and I exchanged glances and I am afraid we smiled.

"Will you gentlemen undertake the management?" The president of the board leaned forward eagerly, one hand fiddling with the end of a white moustache.

"We don't want it," replied Bill.

But they would not take no for an answer. I have never seen bankers so persuasive. My experience of them is that the other fellow is persuasive while the banker is as unresponsive as a pillar of stone.

"Will you let us talk it over together outside?" asked Bill finally.

"Bill, we don't want that mine. It's a dud," I exclaimed as soon as we were outside in the corridor. "How the devil did that crowd of bankers ever get stuck with a deal like that?"

Bill laughed. "Caruthers must be some story-teller."

"But we don't want it."

"I'm with you there, but on the other hand we can't afford to offend those bankers. Always make friends with a banker if you can. He's like a six-gun in Texas. You don't need him very often but when you do need him you need him bad."

We finally agreed that we would offer to undertake the management but would make the terms impossibly stiff. We would make it a condition that we be given fifty-one per cent. of the stock of the company . . . control of the voting power . . . that meant virtual ownership under the hard-boiled code of the mining game in the States. That would get us clear, we calculated. However bad a mine was no one ever gave it away, especially when there was a lot of expensive machinery included.

But my heart sank when we presented our ultimatum. I saw a look spread over the faces of the bankers, the same look one sees on the face of a pack-mule when the heavy pack is removed after a long and tiring day. Those damned bankers positively beamed as they jumped at our offer. They had been afraid that the mine would go bankrupt once more, this time with their august names tied to it.

That night I left on the train for Kentucky . . . and a whole series of unusual events which I did not anticipate. If the mine was really as worthless as I expected, at least I would waste no time in pulling out the pumps that were keeping the water-level down, shutting her down completely and getting the best price I could for the machinery.

My preconceived opinion of the property wavered slightly as I stood beside the hoisting gear at the top of the shaft. On the surface it looked like a good mine to me. A nice wide vein of good quality fluorspar ran along the surface of the property, showing against the grey country rock like the white line down the centre of a clay tennis court. Six feet thick that vein was. Payable if there was any depth to it. But my original opinion was seemingly confirmed when I got to the bottom of the two hundred foot shaft—a nigger youth in greasy tattered overalls let me down casually in a cage which looked as though it would fall apart at every jerk his inexperienced handling gave to the hoisting cable. All I could see of the vein down there was a narrow streak the width of my hand running through the rock. "Pinched out" in mining parlance. And yet on the surface that vein had not looked like one that would "pinch." In a nearby little village I borrowed a theodolyte from the village engineer and did a bit of surveying on my own with the nigger youth to help. One day's work did it. Then I felt pretty sure of the answer. The cross-cut from the bottom of the shaft was too short to reach the real vein. If there had ever been any experienced miners down that shaft before me they must have been drunk or blindfolded not to spot the trouble. For the benefit of those who have never made their living—gnomelike —hundreds of feet below the earth's surface I give the following explanation. Stand a bottle upright on the table and lean a piece of cardboard against it. The bottle is your shaft. The cardboard is your vein, dipping away from the shaft at an angle. It is obvious that the deeper the shaft the farther the bottom of it will be from the vein. Therefore a tunnel is driven from the shaft to give access to the vein from which the ore must be mined. That tunnel is called the "cross-cut."

There seemed to be no miners about the place, no one but the darkey boy and his brother who relieved him for the night-shift to keep the pumps going and the water-level down. Caruthers came once a week, they told me. Saturdays, their pay-day. But I didn't want to see Caruthers till I had the mine properly sized up. It was miners I wanted. In the village I got a couple. Six feet more of cross-cut did it. Two days' work. At the second round of shots the grey worthless rock turned to milky-white. Fluorspar. Eight feet wide the vein was and first-class ore. If the bankers had hired a good mining engineer instead of panicking they wouldn't have given away a first-class mine. If Caruthers had suspected its value the bankers would never have got a smell at it even.

Hardly had I made my discovery when a smartly uniformed darkey handed me a note from Caruthers himself, who had apparently just discovered that I was in the neighbour-hood.

"Mr. Caruthers would be delighted to entertain the new mine-owner for the night if he would come in the launch the servant was bringing." Not half a mile from the mine was the beautiful Cumberland River. As the launch sped upstream the mysterious wooded shapes of the Kentucky mountains passed behind in stately procession—feuds, moonshine, Daniel Boone, bears and wild turkeys—I vowed to penetrate their mysteries before I returned to the smoky hell of Pittsburgh even if Bill should burst a gut-string at my absence.

Caruthers, I found, ran a miniature palace on a wooded island in mid-stream. Oily, that's how he struck me. A small dark man with a smooth face, well-slicked hair and a voice as unctuous as a high priest seducing a virgin. His *ménage* was made up of a houseful of well-trained darkey servants and a highly polished, peroxided blonde lady whom he introduced as his secretary. After he had dined me with six perfectly served courses and wined me—in prohibition time at that—with the appropriate wines we sat down to business. Glad I was that the meal was over. That oily rascal's food choked me, good as it was. Most of the wealth which he expended so smoothly was filched from the pockets of small investors by crooked promotion . . . I was convinced of that. The money of widows and orphans stuck in my throat.

"Well, Mr. Rainier," he cocked one plump leg over the other and pressed his well-manicured finger-tips together. "What part have you and Mr. Bitard assigned me in the new scheme of things?"

"No part at all," I replied bluntly.

His finger-tips pressed till they turned white. "You mean that you don't intend to employ me?"

"Exactly."

"But I can help you."

"How?"

"You will need capital."

"Not yours, we won't."

He paced the floor rapidly for a moment. Then he advanced one plea after another for the management of the property to be left in his hands. Almost hysterical he became at the thought of losing his connection with the mine down-river. He didn't even know the mine was a good one but regarded it as something convenient to wrap a swindle round. I boiled as I watched him. Too many honest mines of my acquaintance had been ruined by men like him and left to languish without the capital that is a mine's life-blood because a crooked promoter had used them to line his own pockets. A mine's reputation is as hard to keep unsmirched as that of a maiden who keeps fast company. I wouldn't have had him round any property of mine at any price. A forty-foot pole with tar on the end was too short to touch him with in my estimation.

Finally he stopped in front of the chair in which I sat smoking. "Dear Mr. Rainier, pray with me to the Almighty God for guidance."

"I've nothing to pray about at the moment."

He knelt down before me and lifted up his face to Heaven, hands clasped in supplication. "Lord God, forgive this man for his trespass against me for he knows not what he does."

I left him praying. Later that night I went to his bedroom to ask that his launch might take me back to the mine early in the morning. A darkey showed me the room and knocked on the door. As it opened for Caruthers to emerge I glimpsed a luxurious double bed in which lay the peroxided secretary, a low-cut night-gown of some bright colour seeming to clash loudly with her hair. Her eyes raised and she caught sight of me. One eye-lid dropped in an unmistakable wink. Caruthers harboured his own Nemesis, I decided. Like many another man before him he kept the future cause of his own ruin in his bed, In any final redistribution of his ill-gained wealth, I surmised, that gold-digger lady would have her full share. I hoped she would fleece him soon. At least she was not oily in her methods.

Bill and I had a fluorspar mine now ; what looked like a good one. The mine owed some debts in Paducah, so Caruthers had told me . . . about ten thousand dollars. We'd need about the same sum in addition for working capital. Ten thousand dollars isn't much in the mining game, but even that comparatively small sum could not be squeezed out of our coal business. I knew that Bill would throw a conniption at the bare suggestion. Yet without it we could not get the mine going.

In Paducah I called a meeting of the creditors. I was quite frank with them and gave them the full history of the mine.

Beaming they congratulated me. " We'll be getting our accounts paid now," they gloated.

" I guarantee to pay them out of the first profits," I promised.

Their faces fell a little. They had expected me to immediately take a cheque-book out of my pocket.

" But we first need ten thousand dollars working capital," I continued.

" You'll raise that in Pittsburgh easy enough."

" I'm going to raise it here."

" Not much loose money in this town."

" I'll be frank with you. All this mine has cost us up till now is my railway fare from Pittsburgh. If you creditors will put up the ten thousand dollars as a loan for working capital we'll go ahead with the mine operation. Your loan plus your over-due accounts will probably be paid off in a few months. If you won't put up the money I'll leave for Pittsburgh to-night and wash my hands of the business. We'll be out of pocket my railway fare and you'll be out the money that's owed you."

After a bit more pressure they capitulated and I passed round the hat.

I wired Bill :

MINE WAS DUD BUT HAVE DEVELOPED PAYABLE ORE COMMA RAISED WORKING CAPITAL AND AM BEGINNING MINE OPERATION STOP WILL BE SHIPPING THREE THOUSAND TONS FLUORSPAR MONTHLY STOP UP TO YOU TO SELL.

Bill wired back :

NOT BAD FOR FIRST WEEK STAY THERE AND PULL MORE RABBITS OUT OF HATS.

A week or two later Caruthers made the first move in the attack which I expected. He tried to throw the mine into receivership as a prelude to still another bankruptcy. However, the Kentucky lawyer whom I hired was too smart for him and the judge refused his petition. The mine was working gaily by this time and shipments of fluorspar already on the way to market.

There was a " Holy Roller " church in Klondike. I saw a crowd round the building one Sunday afternoon and elbowed my way to a window of the simple little barn-like building. The church was full. Every bench was jammed with people whose eyes and open mouths were fixed on the old white-bearded preacher who ranted and raved on the raised platform at the far end. Before him, on a sort of mourners' bench sat a row of people, wrapt, entranced. As I watched, one of them sprang to his feet and leaped about the platform, uttering wild unintelligible cries.

A moan came up from the congregation. " The Holy Ghost ! The Holy Ghost ! " they breathed.

Another from the bench—a woman, matronly—howled like a wolf and rolled on the floor with utter abandon, arms and legs jerking, frothing at the mouth. From her lips poured sounds. A maniacal jabber like that of a demented ape.

" She speaks with tongues ! She speaks with tongues ! " moaned the body of the church.

So it continued till a dozen or more had fallen into the hypnotic state and recovered to reseat themselves on the bench, white and trembling with exhaustion. When no more souls seemed to fall to his exhortations the preacher led the way outside to baptise his harvest.

A cold drizzling afternoon. A foretaste of winter. Through dank meadows we spectators splashed after them to the village duck-pond. Wide, shallow and muddy ; duck feathers and filth floating on the surface.

With a shudder of anticipation the preacher waded bravely into the centre of it and stood waiting. One could almost hear his teeth chattering from where we stood on the edge. Around the border, ankle deep, stood the converted, reluctant, the icy, dirty water completing the reaction after the religious fervour which had been burning them.

At last one woman picked up her courage and her thin cotton dress in both hands and waded out, her skirt billowing round her in the cold breeze. Swirls of mud came to the surface as her feet sank in the oozy bottom. Slimy-looking weeds caught her legs and trailed behind her as she waded. Duck-feathers floated proudly round her, rising and dipping in the heavy sea of her ripples. At last she stood before the preacher. For a moment they shivered at one another. Then, with violence, he grabbed her by the hair, pulled her to him and thrust her under the surface, cutting short her cry of protest. She rose spluttering, half drowned. Weeds, duck-feathers and muddy water spurted from her mouth. " God ! " she ejaculated as she dolefully began to plough her way ashore, meeting in her passage the head of the procession which were now wading out to have the hot metal of their fanaticism tempered by the icy waters of the village duck-pond.

It must have been shortly after the baptismal episode that I found a man waiting for me at the shaft-head when I arrived at the mine one morning. A tall bearded mountaineer in faded blue overalls. When he saw me coming he leaned a business-like rifle against the mine headgear and advanced to meet me, his brown beard undulating as his jaws masticated the inevitable quid of tobacco.

" You the boss man of this outfit ? " he queried, with a straight glance from a pair of piercing black eyes.

" Yes."

" Huntin' fluorspar, ain't you ? "

" We're mining it here as you can see."

" I got a dandy fluorspar vein on my place up in the hills. Wider vein than this one." His glance travelled along the six feet wide streak of fluorspar outcropping which ran through the grey rock on which we stood.

" We've got about all the fluorspar we can handle here."
My own gaze lifted longingly to the blue line of the Kentucky
hills across the Cumberland River.

" Come and look at mine, anyway. The missus and me'd be
proud to board you. It'd be kind of rough like, but you look
like you wouldn't mind that."

" It wouldn't be fair on you. We couldn't buy your mine
now, however good it looked."

" But you'd know about it. Then some day you might want
a mine, or some of your city friends might."

I looked doubtful. I was dying to get clear of the so-called
luxury of civilisation and into the real comfort of primitive sur-
roundings, but it was up to me to get back to Pittsburgh as soon
as possible. I owed that to Bill. I resolved to refuse, but
wavered as my eye caught the well-oiled barrel of the rifle
where it leaned against the base of the towering headframe.

" There's a sight of things to be shot up there and Cappy
Jake is the man to find them for you." His eyes twinkled.
" There's b'ar once in a while and there's always lashins of deer
and turkey."

I fell.

Cappy Jake and I left next morning. We travelled up-river
for an hour or two and left the river steamer at some little landing whose name I forget if I ever knew it. Two buildings it
had. A tiny combined store and post office and a still tinier
building where the combined storekeeper and postmaster lived.
Jake strode off across the flat river meadows with his rifle over
his shoulder. I followed. Soon the ground swelled beneath
our feet and the driving thrust of leg-muscles came into play
to push us up the slope. The conscious effort of each stride
combined with the smell of the wild to stimulate my body. I
drove upward fast upon Jake's heels and he quickened his pace
as he felt me pressing. Up and up we went along little twisty
paths through scattered pine and funereal hemlock, breasting the
ridges and braking on our heels on the down slopes. The smell
of the pines burned my lungs as I breathed the deep breaths of
the mountaineer.

About noon we stopped at a tiny cabin—built of logs and it
might have belonged to Daniel Boone himself by the look
of it.

"Reckon you was born in the hills, mister," remarked Jake. "Figgered to stop here for the night seeing as how I had a furriner along, but you travel most as well as I do myself and we'll make my place come sundown easy enough."

A bearded mountaineer, almost a replica of my companion, brought out a stone jug of about a gallon capacity. My companions beamed approval when I hooked my left thumb through the handle, raised the body of the jug on the crook of my left arm and drank the hot moonshine whisky—made of the mountaineer's own corn—in as audible series of gulps as I could compass. While they followed suit I congratulated myself on having acquired the Kentucky technique during my stay at the mine.

"That's a fine corn patch," I congratulated my host as I gazed at the hard-won acre or two growing corn below the cabin.

"Might be worse," was the reply. "Reckon she'll give twenty gallons to the acre.

Mrs. Cappy Jake was a motherly woman of indeterminate middle age, clad in a striped calico garment which was slung from the shoulder line and hung straight down to her ankles. In the log cabin were two ground-floor rooms and an attic which was reached by a " chicken ladder "—simply a notched pine sapling inclining up to the trap-door. One climbed up it by placing one's toes in the notches. Up there was a bed made of deer-hide thongs stretched on a wooden frame. The sheets were white as snow.

Cappy Jake and I shot more than one deer together although it was out of season. Game laws had small effect on a people who had prided themselves for generations on distilling their own whisky in direct contravention of the laws and in spite of anything that Uncle Sam could do about it.

One day at midday dinner we heard the drone of an aeroplane far overhead. Cappy grabbed his rifle and dashed out. I followed just in time to see him aim and fire at the big United States mail-plane which looked like a monster buzzard wheeling at about five thousand feet, carrying the westbound mail.

"God, Cappy!" I cried. "You can't shoot at Uncle Sam's mail."

"Can't I?" He fired again.

"But what for?"

" To keep them bastards high. Don't want them flying low and snooping round over my still." He lowered his rifle and scowled at the fast disappearing plane.

Mrs. Cappy once asked me to go down to the community still to replenish the big stone whisky jug which she handed me together with a dollar bill.

" Where is it ? " I asked, nothing loth. I had always wanted to see one of the famous Kentucky mountain stills, but Cappy hadn't given me much encouragement on the several occasions on which I had dropped a hint.

" You goes down the trail to the big pine-stump by the creek," she directed. " Then you puts the dollar bill on the stump and the empty jug on it. Then you comes back up the trail a piece without snooping in the bushes—snooping ain't healthy round there. After a bit you goes back and finds the dollar bill gone and the jug full of corn licker. That's all there is to it."

I followed her directions implicitly and found she was right.

As regards the business part of my visit I made a compromise with my conscience by making a sketch-map and writing a geological report on Cappy's fluorspar vein. It looked pretty worthless, but I felt that I had to do something to pay for the good time I was having. I would have liked to stay for months, but after a couple of weeks my conscience became troublesome and I announced my departure for the following Monday. Cappy and I were promptly " shooed " out into the woods to shoot " a mess of wild turkey " for Sunday's dinner.

Mrs. Cappy put on a noble spread that Sunday. Three great turkey gobblers graced the centre of the plain board table, garnished with carrots, turnips and anything else the little settlement of log cabins could provide. The local preacher was the other guest of honour, a lean skeleton of a man in faded overalls, the skin of his face drawn tight over his cheek-bones like waxed parchment. There must have been a dozen of us at the table altogether.

I can taste that wild turkey yet. I gorged. As I leaned back in my chair, replete, I was startled by a horrible sound which issued from the preacher's mouth. Like the belching of a miniature volcano it was. As though the inner pressure of his internal arrangements had forced a blast of invisible gas from him. Self-consciously I looked away. To my embarrassment one after another of the guests belched. Erupted. Shame-facedly I caught Mrs. Cappy's eye. She was beaming at me expectantly. Then her face sobered.

"Mister, you ain't enjoyed your dinner," she stated reproach-fully.

"Indeed I have," I assured her with utter truth. "I never ate a better."

"Well, you ain't belched once," she argued.

Then it dawned on me that the belching was intentional, the local method of expressing appreciation of good food. Almost a grace after meat.

CHAPTER XI

A KNOCK-OUT

THIS is to be a very short chapter but a very pregnant one. It is painful to me to write about it . . . even fifteen years later.

By about the middle of December, 1925, Bill and I considered our position among the coal operators of Pittsburgh was approaching the impregnable. Our load of debt was decreasing monthly. In spite of an adverse coal market our mines were still working at a profit. Within the year at the present rate we should be free of debt. Solid. In Bill's fertile brain I knew there were already schemes hatching. Vast projects which would be financed by the revenue from our mines till he could step from the minor barony of coal in Pittsburgh to the greater hierarchy of Wall Street.

But my ambitions did not run in harness with Bill's. Africa was calling me back. With the solid capital that I should possess within the year my future there should be assured. Land. I would own land. Somewhere in the Rhodesias it would be, I thought. Somewhere where the shooting was not too bad. In the dewy Rhodesian mornings I would mount my horse and ride about my land. Down in the *vleis* the mealies would be ripening in mile-long golden rows while the fat backs of grazing cattle, rounded with contentment, would be visible among the ridges. Give me ten thousand acres of good farming country in Rhodesia and I could defy the world. There my children would grow with the appreciation of the simple things which the industrialised northern people have forgotten. The heart-leap which the sun gives a man as he poises for a moment on the horizon, clad in his pink night robes of splendour, which he throws from him for them to linger in the sky while he himself leaps with renewed vigour to his daily task. The reverent worship of beauty. The glittering jewellery of the Rhodesian veld at sunrise. A million tiny spiders have worked all night at the weaving of a million tiny webs and the night angel has bedecked each one with dew diamonds so that the first gaze of the sun is reflected in a million glittering jewels, finer than any that Sheba got from Solomon. The joy of creation, of producing food for men from land on which nothing grew before except the grass on which the game herds subsisted. My children would grow up sanely, close to the simple things, close to nature and so, in the pattern of their future lives, all things would fall into their right proportion. Whereas if they grew up here in the north the yardstick by which they measured values would be radios, automobiles and "keeping up with the Joneses." Two girls as yet I had. But they could learn to shoot and ride once I got them in the southlands. And there yet might be a boy. Margaret was fruitful. My heart leaped at the thought of walking with my son on the Rhodesian veld and showing him how to keep his sights on running game while he squeezed the trigger.

And then we crashed. All of our companies owed some money . . . money that was being rapidly repaid. Our competitors—there was more than one of them in the conspiracy— bought up a few small debts in each company of ours. Then they struck. There was a law in the United States whereby any three creditors can go before a judge and demand a receivership. That is what our competitors did to eliminate our competition and eventually to get our mines into their possession. They did it to each of our coal companies. On December 15th we were solvent. Within a week all of our coal companies had gone into receivership and were being operated by the courts to whom we had been compelled to hand over the keys of our office suite. Chucked out on our ears. Only the fluorspar company remained. It was paying by now with all its debts settled. We thanked God that we had it. It was all we had left from the wreckage of our four years work because we had always put back our profits into the business to facilitate the quicker paying off of our debts.

For about two days we thanked God for leaving us the fluorspar mine. But those smug bankers in Youngstown had regretted handing us the mine ever since we had made it payable. They hired a smart lawyer to find a flaw in the transfer of rights which they themselves had drawn up in our favour on the day on which they had almost forced the mine down our throats to clear their names from the impending bankruptcy which they thought was in store for it. The fluorspar mine was also thrown into litigation and we had no money to fight a case. So we lost that too, although it was several months before the case was actually decided against us in the courts.

"What are you going to do?" I asked Bill when we had finally closed the door of the office which for years now had been our daytime home.

"I'm going to stick around a bit and try to pick up the pieces."

"What chance is there?"

Bill frowned. "Damned little chance. If this were an ordinary receivership, asked for by legitimate creditors because they stood no chance of getting their money under our management, it would be different. In that case the mines would be returned to us as soon as the receiver had paid off the debts from mine profits under his management. But this . . . this is a blasted steal. Those debts will never be paid off under the receivership and the mines will be forced into bankruptcy. Then our nice friends who are behind it will buy them in for a song. Whatever money they pay for the mines at bankrupt sale—it will be precious little—will go to the creditors . . . so many cents in the dollar. We're out of it . . . you and I. Once we had the house nicely built they threw us out . . . God damn them."

Bill took the soft felt hat off his head, twisted it into a ball, made as though to throw it into the gutter, then thought better of it and replaced it on his head, all crumpled though it was.

"What are you going to do, Pete?" he asked after a minute.

"I'd like to get out of the country but I'm too broke. I'll go West, I think. Try to make enough money there to get back home."

Bill laughed. "There's damned little money in the West. The money's here in the East. Better stay here and we may play another hand together."

I shook my head. Money or no money I was sick of eastern industrialism and I wouldn't have stayed in the eastern states for another set of mines such as we had just lost. The eastern states must have been good country once. But they were no longer. Ravaged. Raped by the ogre of industrialism. Their beauty gone . . . prostituted.

Bill put his arm over my shoulder. "You've been a stout partner, Pete," his voice was a bit husky.

"So have you, Bill." There was a constriction of my throat and I could not talk much.

He straightened up suddenly and smote me between the shoulder-blades so that my back smarted.

"My God boy, they knocked us out but they knew we'd been in the ring. Believe me they knew it, even the biggest of them."

"So long, Bill."

"So long. We'll play another hand together yet. Something tells me."

I had that sort of feeling myself, but I should have been astonished if I had known how soon Bill and I would play another hand together and what a crazy hand it would be.

PART II

THE GOLDEN WEST

CHAPTER I

WESTWARD HO!

CHRISTMAS Eve. Dodds and I were going West. To-morrow would be Christmas day and I was headed away from home with only fifty dollars in my pocket. It was Dodds' car we drove . . . mine had been sold to provide Margaret with the wherewithal to live for a few months. The situation she had accepted nobly. I never met a stouter hearted woman than Margaret. When I had told her I was going to leave her and seek better fortune in the West she had raised no argument. Her only criticism had been that I had given her the lion's share of what little money we could raise from the wreckage of our coal business. Dodds too had been faithful. When he heard I was going West he said he was going too. Never seen the West and always wanted to, he said, but I knew that he was sticking to the man who had pulled him out of that awful mining camp at Osceola Mills five years before. A good lad, Dodds. Yes, it was his car we drove along the ice-bound roads. Turn and turn about. One driving while the other slept, wrapped in blankets on the back seat. Turn and turn we would drive, we swore, non-stop, till we reached the Chino copper mine in New Mexico State, the best part of three thousand miles away.

Across the bleak winter landscape of the middle west we drove. Snow was falling thick as our chain-clad wheels rattled through Colombus, Ohio. At Indianapolis I stopped the car at a drug-store to get some glycerine to smear on the windshield. So intense was the cold that my breath had been freezing on the glass as I drove and coated the inside of it with hoar frost. The thermometer outside the drug-store was registering six degrees Fahrenheit below zero . . . thirty-eight degrees of frost. All that night the car roared westward along the great trans-continental highway—the same highway that Bill and I had blocked hundreds of miles farther eastward when we had brought our tow of barges through the drawbridge at Zanesville. St.

Louis was our next objective. We had listed mentally the main points in our three-thousand-mile drive. As we passed each one we ticked it off in our minds. So much energy expended and one less obstacle to pass. Like hurdles in a steeplechase those cities were to us. As we cleared one we keyed up our flagging energies to lift us through the next. Tired when we started, we became more so as the asphalted miles sped back behind us. But that was what I needed . . . bodily fatigue to dull the flaming riot in my overtaxed brain. St. Louis . . . I would drive as far as St. Louis before I handed over to Dodds and buried myself under the blankets, pretending to sleep.

Sometime after midnight it must have been when the thought came to me, with St. Louis still twenty miles ahead. God! how cold it was and how I hated the cheerless bleak winters of the north. Vandalia swept along the headlight beams towards me, a tiny town with a sign-post pointing south. CAIRO was written on the sign-post. Cairo, the river town where the Ohio and Mississippi rivers join. Cairo, almost across the river from Paducah, where I had interviewed the creditors of the fluorspar company and talked them into putting up the money to run the mine so that their debts would be paid . . . and paid they had been. It would be warmer in Cairo, down there hundreds of miles to the southward.

The chains screeched and the back wheels skidded on the icy surface as I swung the wheel violently round and we turned southward at left angles to our former course. God! how my head ached with the strain of the last few years. All the cumulative nervous tension of the past years of overwork seemed to have descended on me at once. Chino copper mine Dodds had picked as our destination because he had read a wild west thriller once in which the cowboy hero rescued from bandits the daughter of the mine foreman of the Chino copper mine. That's what Dodds had said, but I knew that he had thrown the name at random at me to try and distract my attention from sitting rigid in my chair and holding my once steady hand out in front of me at intervals to see whether by will-power I could check its palsied tremblings. His random shot had hit the mark and awakened my interest. Chino . . . in New Mexico, where it would be warm and not over-populated. I must go somewhere to steady up and as well Chino as elsewhere. It was a monster mine, I knew, and there I could surely get a job of working with my hands which trade unionism in the eastern states denied to me unless I joined a union. Hard work with my hands. That was what I needed. Hard physical effort like those early years of mine in Mozambique had given me. Six months of that and I could face the world again and hack another road to fortune.

The car sped south. Dawn broke, pallid winter dawn. The sickly winter sun shone in through the left-hand windows of the car . . . I had driven all night. In the rear vision mirror I could see the shapeless lump stir under the blankets of the back seat. Dodds' head appeared and he blinked stupidly at the sun-rays.

" This western country's a damned queer place," he remarked, scratching the back of his tousled head reflectively.

" Why ? "

" Where I come from when you're headed west the rising sun shines in through the back windows instead of the side."

" We're going south to Cairo. Cross the Mississippi there and travel south-west through Texas. It's warmer down there. We'd freeze to death along the northern road."

" Suits me." He yawned. Then he sat up suddenly. " Christ ! You've been driving all night. Why didn't you wake me ? "

" I wasn't sleepy." We stopped and I turned the wheel over to him. Once under the blankets I fell asleep at once, the first real sleep I had had for a week.

Cairo was distinctly warmer, but Cairo, Illinois, is a dismal place at the best. A roaring town it must have been in the old river-boating days when hordes of rivermen thronged the streets nightly, making the round of the drinking dens and fighting with all who were not of their own persuasion. But the river men were gone and they had taken every vestige of a colourful life with them. Only the drab stage remained where they had been used to act their part. Haphazard streets lined by haphazard decrepit houses. That was Cairo as we saw it. To make it worse, a cold drizzle was falling. After breakfast at a cheap riverside eating-house we drove the car on to the ferry.

Not for a couple of hours did the ferry start. The mile-wide, muddy river was running bank high. Ice-blocks as big as small houses were riding the flood, dashing downstream on the flood-waves, curtseying and bobbing in the eddies. Sinister. Dirty grey monsters of every conceivable shape.

When the ferry did finally get out towards midstream those ice-blocks bore down on us as though alive, vicious monsters from a frozen world, charging at the big wooden ferry-boat which dodged and turned to escape them. An hour it took us to cross instead of the usual ten minutes, and the ferryman tied his boat up on the western bank and swore that was his last crossing till the ice had ceased to run.

But we were across. The great American south-west lay ahead of us. That day we crossed the state of Arkansas and night caught us in Fort Smith. By now the asphalt road had turned to dirt and the icy surface to slippery mud. Next day Oklahoma and the famous Cherokee strip, scene of a race for land as exciting as any of South Africa's diamond rushes. Tulsa. A modern city built from oil. There was money in Tulsa and where money was there should be work. We broke our vow to go straight through to Chino and stayed a day or two in Tulsa.

It was in and around Tulsa that I first met the American Indian. The state of Oklahoma is the only one in the United States where he survives in any numbers, excepting always the handful of Seminole Indians who still live in their natural state among the fastnesses of the Florida Everglades—I was to have a good deal to do with the wild Seminoles later . . . the remnant of the Seminole nation which had remained in their native Florida swamps—unsubdued—when the majority of their race had surrendered to United States authority after the Seminole War and been transported to what was then thought worthless land in Oklahoma, to become rich in oil a generation later. As the eastern states became populated by white settlement their original Indian inhabitants were removed to the then considered worthless Oklahoma territory and given reservations on which to live. Poor land it was. Barren, as compared with the fertile hunting grounds from which they had been displaced. Then oil was struck in Oklahoma and the hitherto worthless Indian reservations happened to embrace the richest oil formations. The tribes became rich on their oil royalties. Some of them fabulously rich. Tall, stolid looking braves with lank black hair stalked the streets of Tulsa. Clad in blue overalls they were mostly, but in the pockets of their overalls was liable to repose a roll of high denomination currency thick enough to choke a boa-constrictor. Queer tastes they developed, these descendants of warrior tribes, once their pockets became well enough lined to make them free of the resources of civilisation. Hearses were the fashion among them when I was in Tulsa. Instead of coffined dead the glass case would hold a fat squaw and a quiver full of stolid looking papooses, very much alive although contentedly squatting on their heels along the sides. In the driving seat would sit the brave, tooling his sombre conveyance through the city traffic, pride radiating from his wooden exterior.

There proved to be no work for us in Tulsa. Trade unionism seemed as tight there as in the East. It did occur to me that there was money to be made in thinking up new stunts to attract the fat bank rolls of the Indians, but that was a bit out of my line.

South we headed now and crossed the Texas line. Fat rolling grasslands with the roads made of gumbo clay which clogged the wheels of the car in great sticky masses, sloshing continuously against the fenders. Houston and Fort Worth. Both thriving modern cities of the pattern which seems almost universal in the United States. Westward now we chased the setting sun and before it balanced on the horizon ahead of us the country changed. Vast flat spaces with freakish mountain shapes humping themselves against the sky. Cattle ranged freely among the scattered sage-bushes which looked not unlike the uninviting *karoo* bush of southern Africa. A weight began to lift from inside the back of my head. This was what I was looking for. Clear air. Fresh and invigorating, distilled by the sun from clean uncontaminated leagues. Warmth radiated from the sun-baked flats. Space. Plenty of room for a man to breathe. Separated by miles were the wide flung ranch buildings.

"Christ, this is it!" I cried, pushing the accelerator to the floor and charging the car along the not too smooth surface of the sandy road. "Dodds, we've arrived. Here's your West. Cowboys and all." Against the sunset was silhouetted the figure of a man who rode in a peaked saddle with the long stirrup and slouching seat of a Boer *Takhaar* from the western plains of South Africa.

Dodds shivered, although the air was warm. Hunched in the

seat beside me his small frame seemed to shrink even smaller. His face was worried.

"Great Guns, it's empty," he piped. "We haven't passed a town for hours."

All night I drove while Dodds slept. The moon rose. The magic of empty spaces clasped me like a passionate woman. The road became rougher. Deteriorated into an ill-defined trail along which the car crept slowly, the low humming of its engine seeming one of the noises of the night. Over a ridge I crept, cut the engine out and glided slowly by gravity down the further slope. Like a great noiseless beast the car inched forward round a bend in the road, its eyes glaring through the semi-darkness like the eyes of some great cat animal.

There was a sight. A forest of ears pointing skyward. The little hollow into which the road dipped held hundreds of jack-rabbits. Monster hares, many times the size of a prize Belgian but built for speed like greyhounds. Ears like jackasses. Caught in the headlights they sat hypnotised. Erect. Noses working. I cut the lights out for a second and they were gone. Dim shapes in the moonlight which scattered, making for the horizon with smooth swift bounds. It has always puzzled me to account for that concourse. Like a convention of elderly gentlemen they had no doubt met to discuss some juicy scandal of the jack-rabbit world.

Two days of driving through the monster state of Texas and we were in El Paso on the River Rio Grande. *El Paso del Norte* of the Mexicans. The "northern pass" across the river to the lands of the western states which had once been theirs. A quiet city, El Paso, whose air of dignity verged on the Spanish. The quiet of a city with a history, whose turbulent youth is past. One is apt to forget that the Spanish settlement of the Americas antedated by a century and a half the sailing of the Pilgrim Fathers in the *Mayflower*. Men in wide-brimmed hats sat around the central square and chatted sedately with dignity and poise. I liked El Paso. Of the many cities which I have known in the United States only five seem to me to have individuality. Boston is a sedate old maid very jealous of her virtue. New York is a raucous street woman with so little virtue that she is careless of what little she has left. Washington is a charming southern lady whose ethics are possibly not quite as rigid as she would have the world believe. Miami, Florida, is frankly a gold-digger; while El Paso is the dignified Spanish *Senora*. Of the other United States cities that I know—and they are numbered in hundreds—so many are built on a pattern that were one jettisoned, blindfold, in a parachute into the main street it might be the main street of Peoria, Indianapolis, Colombus, Zanesville or Pumpkin Centre for all the difference one could note.

West of El Paso we crossed the Rio Grande where it swung north away from Mexico, to where the great Elephant Butte dam held its waters in pawn for the irrigation of its banks.

West to Deming. A tiny wooden town sitting for no apparent reason among drifting sand-dunes. At Deming they told us of a short-cut across the *mesa* to the Chino copper mine. All the afternoon we followed a rough track through the sage-brush in air as clear as that of Table Mountain. The sky was blue, the soft pale blue that one sees back of the sunset glow. A cool air blew across the plain, on it the fragrance distilled by hot sunshine from square leagues of sage. Strong air. It rasped my throat, burned my lungs, steadied my shaken nerves like alcohol. Such air I had not breathed for years. Towards sundown the great imperceptible swell of land over which we had been travelling reached its crest and began to slope away from us almost as imperceptibly towards the setting sun. The Continental Divide. Not spectacular just here, although I was to suffer considerably before long in recrossing it at a more mountainous part. On the divide was a town. They had told us about it. One of the " ghost towns " of the West. Born of mining camps the " ghost towns " died when the mines petered out. " Big Lake " this one was called, I believe, after the once famous but now defunct silver mine of that name. God knows why it bore such a name, because there was neither lake nor water for miles except the flask we carried in the car and the one-gallon tin for refreshing the radiator.

We drove into the dusty main street between wooden houses whose doors swung creakingly on half-rusted hinges and whose clapboard walls were patched leprously here and there with the peeling remnants of their initial coat of paint. Ahead of us swung a sign whose legend was illegible from age. The saloon evidently. The door swung open as though to welcome us.

When we had entered it creaked lugubriously ajar behind us, leaving the great bar-room in a half light.

" Man, this is spooky," cried Dodds, giving the heavy door a violent push open. The strain was too much for hinges rusted by a generation of weather. The heavy wooden door crashed outward on to the street, raising a cloud of dust which moved ghostlike between the rows of sightless houses. Dead. That's what this place was. Not only abandoned but it had died when the breath of human life had removed itself from it. Daylight now streamed into the great room in which we stood. Along the whole length of it ran a wide bar. Mahogany showed, fine grained, when I rubbed the half-inch layer of dust off it with my finger. Behind the bar what had once been a mirror stretched from end to end also. Dull too. Dead. Splintered here and there with bullets from what had probably been the last wild jamboree to drink the balance of the liquor up before the town was abandoned.

" Big Lake " had a history. The silver mine had been started in the early seventies by New York capital, at a time when the dreaded Sioux Indians still roamed the adjacent plains. The New York capitalists sent a manager out. A good man he must have been. He had faith in the mine in spite of initial poor success. Time after time when the New York owners wanted to close it down he persuaded them to put up still more capital to keep the shaft going deeper. The mine was good . . . he was sure of that. There must be payable silver ore. All indications showed it. Sooner or later a rich pocket would be found that would recoup all their losses. Then one day he went hunting antelope on the plains. While he was away his prophecy came true. The mine workings burst into a pocket of almost pure silver. Rich. Fabulous. The " Bridal Chamber " they called it because the walls of the cavity were hung with silver. A name that lives in mining history till to-day because from the " Bridal Chamber " the world's record silver nugget was extracted. They sent a messenger galloping to the manager in his camp out on the plains to tell him the news—that his faith had been justified . . . that the mine would be famous and he with it. The messenger found him—dead, with a Sioux war arrow sticking out a foot between his shoulder-blades. The mine's prosperity waxed till the " Bridal Chamber " was exhausted. Then it waned. An Indian arrow had removed the driving force. When poor ore was once more encountered the owners closed down the mine rather than search deeper for another rich spot. Then the mine died and with it the town. As Dodds had said, it was spooky. The sun blazed up in the west, touching the peaks of the Caballo Range across the Rio Grande with pink. The wind dropped. But in the still air doors still gently creaked. Queer little shuffling noises became audible—they were pack-rats, scurrying about the dead houses to collect any bits of hardware that fell from rust to take them to their nests, as pack-rats do. In those houses across the street men had lusted. In the bar where we stood they had caroused and fought and died. Now the place was dead and their ghosts had come back. Ghosts of hard-fisted miners. Cowboys with wide-brimmed hats and pistols in their hands. Ghosts of painted women with long skirts and ruffles. The ghost of a man with a fighting face and an Indian arrow in his back. Without another word we got into the car and drove rapidly away. Far out on the *mesa* we slept on the cushions.

It was the next evening before we arrived at Chino. First we came to mammoth smelters alongside a railway track. From their tall chimney evil fumes floated. Fumes which had blasted every bit of vegetation within leagues. Ten miles ahead the mine lay, they told us. Years before they had removed the smelters from the vicinity of the mine because their fumes caused sickness.

Over barren flats we drove into the setting sun . . . three thousand miles we had followed the sunset from the industrial East only to find ourselves once more in a similar setting. But Chino was only a small sore on the face of Nature, while in the industrial East Nature's face had gone. Far to our right rose a peak shaped in the likeness of a praying nun. Kneeling with her hands clasped in prayer. Human sculptors could have made no better image. Green copper stain had oozed from the rocks about her head till she seemed to be coifed in green.

Then the mine. A sizeable town running up a gentle slope. At the foot of the slope was the copper-pit. Vast. Several hundreds of feet deep and maybe half a mile across. On spiral railways ascending its steep sides locomotives belched black smoke as train after train of copper ore was dragged labouring up to the rim whence it sped along rails to the smelter we had just passed. Black smoke swirled about the bottom of the man-made crater. Plumes of white steam like shrapnel puffs burst through the black smoke pall as a score of great steam shovels rooted and grunted down there, digging the copper ore and loading it on to waiting trains. Here was an isolated fortress of industrialism transplanted into the wilds. Dodds' face was beaming, but I drove the car to the mine office in the town with a sinking heart.

Dodds got a job at once. Timekeepers were scarce out here and there was no such thing as a timekeepers' union to keep a man who wanted to work from doing so—free. Me they agreed to put on the waiting list provided I joined the local mine union, a slave to any politically minded union official who wanted to exploit me. My heart lightened as I refused. If I could have worked here a free man I would have done so because we had come so far with this mine as our goal and because I needed the money. But I was almost glad of the excuse to refuse. Work in this great organisation was not what I needed. As well work in the industrial East. True I had only ten dollars left, but that did not worry me. This western country was my kind of country. I could make a living in it unless I were mis-taken, so like the South African *veld* it was. Almost was I back in my native environment. At least in this western country I would be dealing with men of my own kind. Close to Nature. As quick with a helping hand as with a blow and guileless of intrigue.

CHAPTER II

THE LOST LEAD OF GUTNER'S GULCH

IT was at a filling station in Chino town that I first met Shorty. The day after I had arrived in Chino I had read in an El Paso paper, abandoned by someone in my cheap lodging house, that there had been a sensational strike of alluvial gold in Hillsborough County, a couple of hundred miles north-east of Chino, across the continental divide. I discounted about ninety per cent. of the newspaper splurge . . . give a newspaper something like gold to write about—something that catches the popular fancy—and he will make a sensational strike out of the few minute grains of gold that a miner shakes out of his bag when he is going to fill it again from a new clean-up. But I still thought there might be some nucleus of truth behind the newspaper's rhetoric. The problem was to get to Hillsborough County. Ten dollars wouldn't go far in buying transportation. Therefore I hung around the filling station in hopes of getting a lift in some car going in the right direction.

A dilapidated Ford roadster pulled up near the filling station but did not attempt to drive into the region of the petrol-pump. On it was the dust of many western miles. Tires worn smooth. Top full of holes. Just tired. I could almost imagine its battered radiator sniffing hopefully in the direction of the petrol pump—like a thirsty horse tied up out of reach of the water-trough. That its tank was empty I would have bet all of my ten dollars.

At the wheel sat slumped the driver—a short dumpy youth with a weak round face. Good-natured. Broke, too, from the hopeless look upon his face. A drifter, caught short before he could land a job. The look of a lost puppy about him. I walked across and leaned my elbows on the side of the car.

"Which way are you heading?" I asked him.

He turned his head slowly to look at me. His eyes were wolfish. The boy was hungry.

"I'm buffaloed. Came here job-hunting but they've got no jobs."

"Moving on?"

"Broke and the tank's empty. I'll have to sell the Lizzie, I suppose, and buy railroad transportation, only I don't know where to buy it to. Jobs are scarce everywhere."

"Does this appeal to you?" I took the cutting from the newspaper out of my pocket and handed it to him. He took it and read it slowly aloud:

SENSATIONAL PLACER GOLD STRIKE NEAR ANIMAS PEAK.

"Old timers in Hillsborough County, New Mexico, will remember the rich Gutner's Gulch diggings from which at least one lucky claim-owner took out in a few months the value of fifty thousand dollars in gold dust and nuggets. For a time Gutner's Gulch flourished, but the rich lead seemed lost when it reached the cañon through which the gulch ran to reach the flats below. Then the diggings petered out. All this happened in the 'seventies, nearly sixty years ago. Since then many western prospectors have tried to find the extension of the fabulously rich lead . . . but all have failed hitherto—all but one. Pete Hanson has found it. Better known in western mining circles as 'Gold Dust' Pete. Keeping his find to himself, for months he has worked assessing his claims, which he now owns outright. Pete has ground to lease on shares and he has even expressed willingness to sell part of his extensive holdings. 'This is going to be no Big Company job,' Pete told our reporter. 'It's the working man I'll sell to. Any man who is willing to work his own claim with his own hands can buy a claim from me or lease it from me on shares.'"

There were several more columns in the same strain ending up with a regular panegyric on the opportunity given to the working man to become independent by buying a claim from Pete.

Shorty's face glowed. "God! A man could make a stake there. Get rich maybe." Then his face fell. "But I haven't a cent to buy gas," he wailed. His face puckered like a child's about to cry.

"Don't worry about getting rich. Not many men get rich on even a rich gold strike and this one sounds a bit fishy to me. But there ought to be a job or two going."

"But how to get there? It's miles from any railroad, even if I could sell the car for enough to buy a ticket."

"I've got ten bucks. That ought to get us there in the car and buy a feed or two along the way."

Shorty's face lit up like a child's when it sees a sugar stick. He patted his tummy about which his belt hung loosely. "Could we start off with a feed? I haven't had my nose in a plate since day before yesterday."

After he had breakfasted we left.

That evening we ate *tamales* and *chile con carne* in a little Mexican eating-house halfway up the continental divide . . . very different to cross here from the long easy slope up and down which Dodds and I had driven a few days before. With only an hour of daylight left we drove the lurching little car up the long steep grade and round hairpin bends. Rocks rattled down steep slopes when our wheels displaced them. Over the top and down the farther side lay our destination, in one of the dry gulches radiating from the eastern slope of the very range we were climbing. But darkness caught us before we reached the top. Shorty's car did not run to lights and the road was too dangerous to attempt in the dark. There was nothing for it but to stop where we were.

Cold. Six thousand feet above sea-level and midwinter. True, we were well south, but even so the thermometer must have been below freezing-point because the water in our radiator froze that night. No blankets. The blankets in Dodds' car belonged to Dodds, and I had not even told him that we were going. A note I had left in his room when he was at work . . . to say good-bye. If Dodds had known that I was leaving him he would have insisted on throwing up his new-found job to come with me or else on sharing his salary with me till I found work. I had no intention of being a charge on Dodds nor did I want Dodds for ever hanging on my heels. Town-hungry Dodds was no fit mate for me. I liked the lad and he had been a true friend in adversity. But now he was well fixed up with a job which he liked and a good salary.

God! how cold we were on that high mountain-slope. A bitter wind from the north began to blow. In the lee of a boulder we huddled, Shorty snuggled into the curve of my body, shivering like a pup who has been thrown into cold water and sits miserable on the bank.

At last dawn came. In a few minutes we had topped the divide and could see a cluster of tents on the plain far below— they must be our destination.

The sun was just rising when I stopped the tired car before a big marquee tent from which delicious breakfast scents were pouring.

"Christ, I'm hungry," cried Shorty. "How much money have we got?"

I took out of my pocket the few cents which remained. Barely enough to buy a cup of coffee.

Shorty's face fell like a child's.

A Chinaman came out of the big tent and struck an iron triangle. Men began to swarm from the other tents. As they filed into the big mess-tent I noticed that the Chinaman collected from each one a blue ticket which they tore from small books. The ticket system was evidently in operation in this camp. By this system the boss issues a book of eating-tickets to each workman. The man pays for his meals at the camp caterers with the tickets, the price of which is deducted from his pay. The caterer collects from the boss according to the number of tickets which he presents.

"Come on, Shorty. Let's eat," I cried and led the way to the tent.

"But we can't pay for it," he wailed, following behind me nevertheless.

"They can't take it away from us once we've eaten it."

The Chinaman at the door glanced at me inquiringly as I approached. He held out his hand.

"Got no ticket yet, Wan Ling. Boss just took us on. We'll give you two tickets each for lunch."

"All lightee," was his calm response. His face split in a grin.

We found places at the long table inside. And we ate. How we did eat! Great stacks of corn cakes with maple syrup. Ham and eggs. Coffee almost by the gallon . . . strong and sweet.

After breakfast I left Shorty dozing in the wintry sunshine while I sought the acquaintance of "Gold Dust" Pete. A clever-looking man of thirtyish I found him. Although dressed in the conventional blue overalls of the working man they were too neat for the part. Even pressed. He gave me the impression of a man who had lived more in cities than in the open . . . that in spite of the newspaper account of his many years experience of prospecting.

"My name's Rainier," I introduced myself. "Just blew in with a partner. We took the liberty of inviting ourselves to breakfast."

He laughed pleasantly. We shook hands. Then I knew him for a city man. Soft his hands were. Mine were soft too after years of Pittsburgh, but under the softness were hard places where the callouses had been. His hands were soft all through. Like a girl's. The bars of El Paso had been the scene of most of this chap's prospecting, unless I missed my guess. I had suspected something fishy about this show from the newspaper spread. Real gold strikes don't get advertised in the newspapers until after the rush has taken place. The man that makes the strike is the last man to grant an interview to a newspaper reporter . . . he wants to keep it quiet till he's got all his friends in on the rich ground. Any worth-while gold strike gets advertising enough anyway by word of mouth. The very birds carry news of a real gold discovery. Yes. There was something wrong with the business and yet I did not dislike the man himself. He impressed me as well-meaning, albeit inefficient.

"Come to try your luck?" he asked.

"Come to look it over," I replied non-committally.

"Help yourself." He laughed with a wave of his hand towards the landscape. "You'll find me around when you've picked your claim. You're first on the ground."

Once clear of the camp I stood and looked around. Half a mile west—the direction from which Shorty and I had travelled —the gaunt shoulders of the continental divide stood up against the sky. Steep rocky slopes, seamed with age, wrinkled like the face of an ancient prostitute, painted with vermilion on the red ledges and dotted here and there with black tufts of mesquite that looked like tufts of hair on an ancient beldame's face. Opposite me the face of the hills was slit—the cañon of Gutner's Gulch, I judged. Beyond that cañon there had been a real gold strike once. Men had made fortunes there in a few weeks. That was an authentic fact, I knew. Something solid on which to base my deductions. Gold above the cañon. None apparently in the cañon itself—in the cañon the rich lead had been lost. Here below the cañon where I stood there was some gold probably . . . the light dust which had washed through in the rains . . . there must have been rain at times even in this dry country—without rain no gulches would have formed. The ground where Gold Dust Pete had staked his claims might even be payable—even though the heaviest gold would have remained above the cañon—if there were water to work it. But where was the water? The hills were dry. Bone dry. Gutner's Gulch looked as though no water had run down it since Noah's time. East of me the vast dry plain dipped almost imperceptibly to a narrow strip of green thirty miles or so away. The Rio Grande that must be . . . its banks irrigated and made green by water from the Elephant Butte dam. Here and there on the plain skeleton cattle grazed. Cattle implied some water in the neighbourhood. But there was no water here and to mine gold normally one needed water on the spot—a stream of it.

At the jingle of a curb-chain behind me I turned. A cowboy was riding towards me. A lean sun-burned man of middle age in a wide-brimmed hat and leather chaps from thigh to ankle. Sitting long-stirrupped in the saddle. Easy. Swaying with the horse. Like our own South African plainsmen he rode, part of the beast under him.

Beside me he reined in and pulled tobacco and cigarette papers from his pocket. Rolled and lit in silence. As silently I pulled out my pipe, filled and smoked.

" You from there? " he queried after a minute, jerking his head sideways towards the camp.

I shook my head. " Just blew in this morning. Sizing it up."

" How big does it size? "

" About knee-high to a duck."

He laughed. " Sounds like you know something about mining? "

I nodded. " I've mined a bit."

" You'll be pulling out soon then."

I shook my head. " Too broke to travel. I've got to get a stake out of this somehow."

His face flushed. " Broke! Who isn't broke here? It never rains these last years. When I came here twenty years ago there was grass knee-high all over these flats. Finest bit of country I'd seen this side of Texas, so I located here. Then I brought in two thousand head of cattle—good cattle. My share of my old man's estate in Texas. In five years I'd doubled their number and had money in the bank. In ten years I was rich. Then the droughts came. Year after year. The grass died and left the soil bare. The soil blew away and left only rock and sand but I figured it must rain again sometime. Spent my money bit by bit in shipping food in for my cattle by the railway that runs down there by the Rio Grande. If only I'd known enough to pull out then and let my cattle die . . . but it's hard to let them die when you've reared them from calves. The last of my money gave out a month or two ago. Then I sold my mineral rights to that bar-fly Pete. Calls himself 'Gold Dust Pete' nowadays ! " The cowboy laughed scornfully and flicked away the smoking butt of his cigarette. " Anyway, I got enough cash from him to carry on for a month or two more. Maybe it'll rain by then. There's still a thousand or so critters dragging themselves about and eating mesquite for a living. Enough to make another start with if I could save them." His eye travelled along the steel blue sky above the far Caballo Range, looking for a cloud that would betoken rain.

" There should be some light gold in these little *arroyos* below the mouth of Gutner's Gulch," I remarked. " If there was only water to wash it."

He grunted. " You do know something about it," he admitted. " There is gold. You can get a fair pan in any *arroyo* below the mouth of the gulch. But the only water this side of the Rio Grande is in my well back towards Animas Peak." He waved his hand to an isolated peak which stood up cone-shaped a mile out in the flat from the main range of the divide. " The ground's not rich enough to pay for hauling water and the Gulch hasn't run these eight years back. Do you think I wouldn't have worked those *arroyos* to get cash if they'd been payable ? "

" Anyone else live around here ? " I asked.

" Old Hans lives at the foot of the peak. He came in over fifty years ago when Gutner's Gulch was a real digging. Made a stake out of it too. Then damned if he didn't spend all he'd made driving into Animas Peak looking for silver lodes. Best part of fifty year he's been working on that tunnel of his and got it driven most clear through the mountain now. His money gave out long ago and he's made his living between spells of tunnel driving by operating a bootleg still—that's where you'll get your liquor round here, from old Hans."

" Did he strike any good ore in his hole ? "

The cowboy laughed. " Hans thinks it's the richest ever—the old boy's a bit *loco* you know. When I first came here he was asking a quarter of a million dollars for his mine—this country was alive then, not dead like now. He's been coming down in his price steadily . . . and no offers. Not long ago I heard him say he'd take ten thousand dollars for it, but I bet if you offered him a hundred dollars real money the mine would be yours."

" Anyone else ? "

" Hillsborough town is over there," he pointed south-west. " About eight miles. It's dying on its feet. Down along the Rio Grande there's a heap of Mexicans with truck gardens in the irrigated strip. That's all the inhabitants. There's going to be one less if it don't rain soon." As he gathered up his reins to move his eye once more swept the horizon in its eternal search for a rain-cloud.

I walked to the mouth of the cañon, scrambled through the rough dry wash that floored it and climbed out at the upper end. I was now standing in a small valley whose floor had evidently been washed intensively for gold, judging by the stacks of stones which stood around in all directions. This then was the scene of the famous Gutner's Gulch strike. It had been worked all right. Down to the beginning of the cañon the stones lay piled by hand as they had been picked from the stream-bed by the miners, washed free of any grains of gold which might be clinging to them and piled out of the way in heaps. But at the beginning of the cañon the gold had stopped they said. Why? I set my mind working to try to think of a solution. Some gold must have been carried on by floods into that rocky cleft in the hills because the lighter stuff had washed out into the flats below its mouth. And yet the cañon had evidently not been worked as it would have been had pay-able gold been found. Such an abrupt stoppage of a gold lead was not natural. There must be a solution to the problem and in the solution might lie a fortune for the man that found the answer. Not easy. I knew that. I was willing to bet that most of the veteran prospectors who spent their lives fossicking for gold in the south-west had walked where I was now walking and asked themselves " Why ? " just as I was doing. The problem intrigued me, but I must first establish my position down in the camp. However, as I walked down the cañon I registered one thing worthy of note. While the north wall stood sheer the south wall sloped. The south wall must have fallen in ages back in a landslide. That fall must have blocked the gorge, at least for a time. But whether that fact had anything to do with losing the gold lead I could not then determine.

CHAPTER III

A COWBOY, A BOTTLE OF WHISKY AND A
MINE-SHAFT

I FOUND " Gold Dust " Pete squatted on his heels outside
his tent smoking a pipe.
" Well. What do you think of it ? " he asked, easing
over to make room for me to squat beside him.
" Damned little."
He laughed. " You chaps that aren't miners are apt to expect
chunks of gold to show up on the surface. My claims aren't
rich, but they'll pay any man that works hard thirty bucks a
day on the average. That's a hell of a lot better than working
for wages."
I rocked on my heels as I tamped my pipe full. " Any heavy
gold here ? "
" I guess so. We'll find nuggets when we get down to bed-
rock. Done no more than scratch the surface up till now. But
there's plenty of fine gold on the surface. You can pan colours
'most anywhere in these *arroyos*."
" What kind of bedrock have you got here ? "
He looked surprised. " Don't know till we dig down to it.
What does it matter, anyway ? "
" It matters a lot. A rough bedrock would tend to hold the
gold. A smooth bedrock would allow it to be swept away."
He favoured me with a long stare, but made no comment.
" How deep is it ? "
" I've just said we haven't dug down to it yet, so I don't
know."
" Why is no one working the ground if it is as good as you
say ? "
" I've just thrown it open. Just completed the assessment
work to make my title legal. The men you see in camp are
labourers that have been doing the work for me."
" What about water ? "

" Who the hell are you ? " he demanded, suddenly wrathful. " Is this a Bible catechism or what ? "

" You know my name. I told you."

" It may be a good name for all I know, but it doesn't give you the right to ask if my mother was legally married."

" You want to sell me a claim. I've looked at your claims and I can tell you they don't stack very high with me. I'm doing you a favour if you only knew it. Giving you expert advice free."

" Expert advice ! "

" It ought to be expert. I've been looking at mines for the best part of the last fifteen years . . . and sometimes I've charged people pretty high fees for doing so."

" A mining engineer ? "

" Yes."

" Oh." It sounded like air escaping from a bladder. He tapped the bowl of his pipe nervously against a rock. " Tied up with any of the big companies ? "

" No."

" And you don't think much of our prospects ? "

" Damned little. You may have got the residue of the lost lead of Gutner's Gulch under your feet here, but you've got to shaft to bedrock to find it. Even if it proves to be there it'll have to be a damned sight richer than I think it is to pay for hauling water."

" But they made money working it in Gutner's Gulch in the old days."

" It used to rain in this country then. The Gulch was a running stream. Besides, they worked it higher up, nearer the source."

" But you can get gold right on the surface here. There's gold in every pan."

" Fine gold dust. No weight to it. Colours the size of flour-grains. You can get the same out of any panful of dirt at the foot of any gold-bearing range."

" God Almighty ! How that cow-puncher stuck me." He gripped his head in his hands.

" You don't know much about mining, do you ? "

He shook his head. " Only from what the boys in El Paso used to talk when I kept the Mexican Eagle saloon."

"You just figured on unloading this on any innocents that wandered round, didn't you?"

He jumped to his feet. "I was playing square . . . I swear I was. There was gold in every pan the cow-puncher tried. I saw it and I watched to see that the gold didn't come from up his sleeve . . . I knew that much. I wasn't trying to stick any-one, just to pass it along with a profit." He glared at me defiantly . . . without reason for defiance because I believed him. He was just one more innocent wandered into the mining game. There is as little room for amateurs in mining as there is among horse-dealers and the ethics of both games are about equally low. A dealer will stick his best friend with a spavined horse and brag about it . . . then, in his capacity of church-warden, take the plate around next Sunday with a clear con-science. A mining man will sell his friend a dud mine with an equally clear conscience . . . only mining men don't frequent churches much.

He paced back and forth a moment. "Will you sink a shaft to bedrock for me," he asked suddenly, "just to prove whether it is a dud or not?"

"If you pay me for it."

"But I'm about broke. Paid two thousand bucks for this land. Spent most of what I had left on assessment."

I considered a moment.

"I'm even broker than you are, but I'll take a chance with you. I'll sink your shaft if you board me and my partner free while we're doing it and deed me a fifty-foot claim round the shaft, so that if I find anything worth while at the bottom it will be mine. If I do find a payable lead it will advertise the rest of your ground and you'll be able to sell."

"Right." We shook hands on it. "But in the meantime I can sell claims to anyone who wants them?"

"I don't care how many you sell. The rest of the ground is yours . . . all but my fifty-foot claim. However, I warn you that if anyone asks my opinion of the ground I'll tell them just what I've been telling you. I'm not out to advertise your ground for you but to develop a payable claim for myself."

I selected for myself what I considered a likely site with due relation to the cañon below Gutner's Gulch. After putting four stakes at the corners of a fifty-foot square I ran two diagonals from the corners and placed a fifth stake at their intersection—the centre of the claim and the site for the shaft. By that time the iron triangle at the mess-tent sounded for lunch.

After lunch I took Shorty to the site of our venture and broke the news to him of hard work and calloused hands to come. His face fell. Eating three meals a day and sleeping them off in the sunshine without disagreeable interludes of work seemed to be about his mark.

" How deep does this hole have to go ? " he asked lugubriously.

" To the bottom."

" How deep will that be ? "

" A damned sight deeper than we want. With a bit of luck we may strike pay gravel at twenty-five feet or so."

" Jehoshaphat. What do we do then ? "

" We drive a tunnel underground, from the bottom of the shaft, across the claim to get the average value of the gravel. ' Cross-cutting,' the miners call that. Then if she's rich enough to pay we raise a truck from somewhere, beg, borrow or steal a water-tank to put on it and haul water from a cow-puncher's well to wash the gravel we hoist up."

" I wouldn't mind driving the truck," he remarked hopefully.

" You'll do a hell of a lot of digging before that time comes." I handed him a pick.

He swung it clumsily so that its point struck a rock and twisted the handle out of his hands. " But I've never worked like this before," he wailed.

" Get into it, man. I'll have six inches off your girth and plenty of blisters on your hands before we've been at it a week."

Hard work that was, but it was also what I needed. Ten hours hard labour in that clear air, three square meals and ten hours of dreamless sleep daily. With every shovelful of dirt that I heaved out of that hole I felt my old-time vigour returning. Old I had grown. Old at thirty-five. But every week in that gold camp sloughed a painful year from me.

After we had sunk ten feet or so we rigged up a windlass to hoist the dirt. I appointed Shorty hoisting engineer. Damned glad I was to get him out of the constricted area of the shaft because he was no mole by nature. The amount of dirt Shorty dug in a day would hardly have sufficed to bury a well-fed cat

. . . also he was inexpert with his tools and more than once narrowly missed driving his pick clear through my foot. At the windlass he was better . . . mainly because there was less work to do. His task was to hoist and empty the bucket when I had filled it. I will admit that I used to stand well at the side of the shaft as the bucket was going up for fear that Shorty would begin day-dreaming, forget what he was doing, let go the windlass and drop the bucket on my head.

Before we reached twenty feet Shorty left me. Unknown to me he had sent an S.O.S. to his mother, somewhere in the northern cattle country up Wyoming way. Mother sent Shorty a cheque for a hundred dollars and Shorty went back to mother's apron strings which was undoubtedly the profession he was best fitted for.

"We're not far from bedrock by the looks of it," I remonstrated when he announced his intention of leaving. "Better stick it for a day or two and see what luck brings us. Half of it's yours you know."

"You can have my half of the blasted hole, I've had enough." He kicked the bucket over on its side and walked away and that was the last I ever heard of Shorty.

A few hours after Shorty left, the gravel in the shaft changed. Instead of loose rock and small pebbles my pick sunk into a harder stratum of coarse round pebbles cemented together by a white, limey substance which the local Mexican miners called *caliche*. The same kind of whitened pebbles I had seen stacked by the old miners above the cañon. I had struck the Gutner's Gulch lead below the cañon . . . I was willing to bet the claim on it although it now looked as though the claim might be worth something. That wash was hard . . . devilish hard. The pick-handle stung my hands at every stroke and it took me an hour to pick loose a bucketful. When I had filled a bucket with the new gravel I climbed up the chicken ladder—a couple of two-by-three timbers spliced together. To catch the toes, cleats were nailed on to them. It is the civilised man's adaptation of the savage's notched pole which the savage uses to climb up to his corn-store, built on stilts to keep the grain above marauding animals. After hoisting the bucket I filled my pan with gravel and carried it over to Pete's tent where stood a water-barrel that he filled each day by hauling water from the cow-puncher's well, several miles away. Squatting down on my heels I began to wash my pan of gravel. Pete came over from the mess-tent to watch me and with him a couple of cowboys from a distant range, who had been apparently sharing with him the contents of a bottle. Two wide-brimmed felt hats and Pete's well-oiled brown locks bent over my pan as I worked. Soon there was nothing visible in the pan but a little black sand and a few fragments of odd minerals. But there was gold there I knew. My eye had caught the unmistakable glint, as I had twirled the residue to bring the light sand to the top so that I could wash it clear of the pan.

I held the pan up.

All three faces fell. " Christ ! It's blank," remarked Pete. " The surface gravel's better after all."

" It's the lost Gutner's Gulch lead just the same," I said.

" How do you know ? "

" Look at these big round pebbles with the white stains on them. You'll find the same kind of pebbles where the old miners stacked them when they washed the gulch."

" Criminy, that's right. But where's the gold ? "

With my hand I flicked a few spoonsful of water into the pan from the barrel. Then I gave the pan a twisting jerk—the miners' touch. As though by magic from out of the little streak of black residue shot specks of yellow. Coarse gold it was, quite different from the floury stuff one panned upon the surface of Pete's claims. Two or three jagged little bits like pinheads that have met with an accident and one little round slug about the size of a pea. That one I picked up and let drop into the pan. It sounded. A nugget. That is the miner's definition of a nugget—that when dropped into the pan it is heavy enough for its impact to be heard.

" God, man ! You've got it." Pete's face was white and he clenched his hands. " You sure do know your stuff."

" Ki-yi-yi-yo-kee," howled the cowboy with the bottle pirouetting round and round on the high heels of his top boots till the rowels in his spurs rattled. He grabbed me by the arm and pushed the neck of the bottle into my face. I drank a swig or two.

" Hi-yo-hi-yo-woopee," he howled again, like a drunken wolf. " A strike . . . a strike. Gutner's Gulch has come to life again."

He grabbed his slightly more sober companion by the waist and whirled him away among the tents in a wild dance.

Pete clutched my hand and shook it. "By God, you've saved my bacon. We're made men. We'll both clean up."

I shook my head. "A couple of bits of gold don't make a mine. That was only the first panful out of pay-dirt. If the pay is four or five feet thick and averages like the first pan it's a payable working. But the pay-dirt may be only a few inches thick—not enough to make it worth while mining. Or this may be a freak pan. Can't tell till I've got the whole thing cross-cut. Then the average across the claim will tell us."

I tied the little bits of gold—about a dollar's worth—in the corner of my handkerchief and walked back to my shaft.

Sometime later I was sweating freely at the bottom of the shaft as I drove my pick again and again into the hard cement-like gravel, which I hoped would make for me at least a sufficient sum to give me temporary independence of movement—I had no delusions about making a fortune out of a mine to which one hauled water from a well.

"What-ho there below," came a cry from above.

I looked up to see the drunken cowboy swaying on his heels on the very rim of the shaft twenty feet above me. In one hand he held a bottle of whisky and in the other a revolver.

"Look out or you'll be down on top of me."

"I'm coming down . . . COMING DOWN . . . c-o-m-i-n-g d-o-w-n," he chanted.

"I don't want you down here."

"Why not? Be hosh-hosh-pichable."

"There's only room for one. Besides, you're drunk."

"Not drunk." He straightened up with dignity, or rather with the intention to achieve dignity. "Musht shee shtrike."

"For God's sake keep away from the edge."

"I'm coming." He peered over the edge till I thought he was going to overbalance. Then he saw the chicken ladder. He marched stiffly round the perimeter of the shaft, bottle and pistol still held tightly. To my horror he began to descend the precarious contrivance as though it were a wide stairway. That is, he stepped out on to the almost vertical pole with his back to it—to descend that chicken ladder one should grasp the pole firmly with both hands while one felt for a cleat with one's toes and prayed to God they wouldn't slip.

As soon as his high heel with its projecting spur touched the ladder his feet shot from under him and he bumped his way down over the projecting cleats on his behind. I think he bumped six times, because each time he bumped his revolver exploded and I have a definite recollection of his firing six shots before he landed in a heap on top of me. I was half knocked out for a moment. The shaft was full of powder smoke and the man lying on top of me, an inert mass. I wriggled out from under him, coughing from the fumes that caught my throat. Through smoke-wreaths I saw the bottle of whisky lying on its side and wasting its contents. I rescued it and set it upright out of harm's way. Then I climbed up for air.

How to get my visitor up to the surface was the problem. Knocked out. Mostly from whisky and shock, I guessed, as all his shots had seemed to go up into the air—but I was sure he wouldn't ride in comfort for a long time, the way he'd bumped on those cleats.

I untied the rope from the bucket, dropped one end down the shaft and descended. Put a clove hitch round the inert cowboy's waist, climbed back to the surface and laboriously hoisted, while my home-made winch groaned and creaked under the unaccustomed load. Once I got him up I dragged him clear of the shaft by the heels and left him to sleep off his celebration. Then I retrieved the bottle of whisky and knocked off for the day. I felt I had earned the rest.

CHAPTER IV

A DIET OF JACK-RABBIT AND BEANS

HARD as the pay-dirt was, I got through it all too soon and reached the solid rock below. Bedrock. The lower limits of the gravel. No chance of alluvial gold below that if you were to sink for a mile. It was the rock on which the original stream of Gutner's Gulch had run in ages past, when its waters were wearing down gold-bearing rock in the hills above and depositing gold—the heavier metal—among the pebbles in its bottom. One foot of pay-gravel was all I had to show for the twenty-foot deep shaft I had so laboriously sunk. But there was still a chance that to right or left of the shaft-bottom, in the ancient stream-bed, the pay-dirt would be thick enough to pay. Working alone I drove my little tunnels out to right and left, dragging the loosened gravel to the shaft-foot in an old oil tin, loading the bucket and then climbing the chicken ladder to hoist. Slow, tedious toil. I worked hard . . . I had to because I was broke and hoped to get enough from this claim to enable me to search further afield for something better. But in a couple of weeks after bottoming my shaft I was convinced that the claim was not payable. A stream of water would have made all the difference. Once diverted on to the claim the water would have quickly washed away the dross which I so laboriously hoisted, leaving only the gold and heavier minerals for me to pan, but a mine must be almost fabulously rich before it pays to haul water for its working from a distant well. When I had panned the cumulative results of my labour in Pete's barrel I had a little pile of gold dust and nuggets which I estimated at being worth about fifty dollars. Fifty dollars for six weeks' hard work. Not much. But I had gained something better than gold. I was fit again. My head clear and my body hard. Ready for anything the adventure of life might bring.

It was while I was near the end of my " clean-up " that I

noticed a little wizened-up old chap squatting on his heels and watching me gyrate the pan. Grey as a badger with eyes seamed by the network of wrinkles, which told of peering into far distances through the depths of a sea of bright sunlight over the barren ocean bottom—which is the desert. Ragged overalls and a decrepit slouch hat, the black stains of which bore witness to the number of times it had been used to lift hot, soot-blackened coffee-pots off numberless camp-fires. Around his waist was a cartridge-belt and hooked to it a holstered pistol—a ·22 automatic, it looked, from the size and shape of the butt. The sheen of oil was on that butt. His weapon looked the only modern thing about the stranger.

"Good morning," I remarked as I looked up from my panning.

He did not reply but took a battered pipe from his mouth and waved it genially in greeting.

He sauntered over to me when he could tell by the motion of my hands that only the residue remained in my pan.

"Mind if I look?"

"Not a bit." I knew he was a professional miner by his question. No real miner will look into a stranger's pan without permission. To look into a pan is often to know the value of a mine and there are times when one doesn't want one's goods advertised. In this case my mine was a dud; I knew that by this time and I didn't care who else knew it.

He watched without a word the few specks of gold detach themselves from the black patch of lesser minerals, but his pipe tipped downward between his teeth. I read deprecation in that downward-sloping pipe.

"Poverty-wash," I remarked.

"Doggone nigh it but not quite as bad as that. Pay-dirt all right if this durned country waren't so dry. Looks like the same gravel the old-timers stacked above the cañon in Gutner's Gulch."

"It's the same. I sunk in the flats close by and hit the extension of the lead first go off." There was some pride in my voice. I felt that not every miner could have calculated so accurately the course of that ancient stream-bed now hidden under twenty feet of modern wash.

He laughed. "Maybe a shaft would have struck it just the

same a hundred yards on either side of yours. As I calculate that old stream she widened out soon as she quit the cañon. Spread the gold all about instead of keeping it all in one lead so a man could mine it proper."

"Maybe you're right. You seem to know the game all right. Been at it long?"

"Forty years, nigh on. Old Gable's panned most streams between Alaska and the Straits of Magellan." He placed his pipe in his pocket. "Why didn't you sink in the cañon? That's your best bet."

"Every Desert Rat in the West has tried to find the lead up there . . . and failed."

He laughed. More a physical contortion than a sound. "Here's one Desert Rat that ain't. Like to come and take a look at it?"

We walked across the flat to the frowning wall of the hills and entered the narrow slit of the cañon. It was not fifty feet across and the walls were twice as high.

"I'm willing to bet that the lost lead is right under our feet," I remarked. I had spent a good deal of time thinking about that cañon and believed I had solved its mystery . . . in theory at least. The practical proof I had estimated as being beyond my present means.

He glanced at me curiously. "What do you figger happened here?"

"Both cañon walls were vertical to start with, at the time the gold was deposited. Then one wall slid in, covered up the stream and the gold that was in it. She dammed up, of course, and began a new stream-bed on top of the slide. There's maybe fifty feet of rubble and boulders between us and the pay-dirt."

"God take my shirt!" There was surprise in his exclamation and respect as well.

"What's your idea?"

"Why, Pard, I figgered out the identical same thing a day or two ago."

I must have looked incredulous.

"Come, I'll prove that I'm not hornin' in on your ideas."

I followed him to the head of the cañon. There was a bell-shaped *teepee* tent and beside it the ancestor of all Ford cars. A very early vintage that Ford must have been and it seemed to be held together mostly by baling wire. The tent was old too. Canvas neatly patched here and there with any old material. It was neat inside too. A bedding roll, a frying-pan and a battered and smoked old coffee-pot seemed to constitute all the stranger's household gear, but they were stacked neatly in place and the sandy floor had been recently swept with a home-made broom of sage-brush twigs which lay outside.

" I wouldn't have located here unless I meant business and I never break ground on a proposition till I feel I've got it figgered out. Your thinkin's right.

" How tight are you lassoed to that tenderfoot outfit on the flats ? " he continued.

" I'm about through. That outfit will pack and fade away now that my shaft has failed to strike worth-while ' pay.' They were waiting around for me to prove up their property for them." I explained the history of the business.

" I'm looking for a side-kick. Are you on ? Fifty-fifty."

" I'll barely have fifty bucks out of my clean-up and we'll need a lot more capital than that to sink through that slide."

He rattled some silver in a dirty linen bag which he took from his pocket. " Got about another twenty here. We'll make up in work what we lack in capital. Live on jack-rabbits, if we have to . . . plenty of them jackass rabbits lopin' round these hills." He patted the butt of the pistol at his belt.

I whistled. " God, man ! there'll be boulders the size of a house in that slide. With capital we'd buy drills and dynamite to blast a way through. But picks and shovels won't make a hole through rock."

He grinned. I liked that grin. " What I can't go through I goes around."

Then ensued a couple of months of the hardest physical toil that I have ever laid my hands to. Gable was tough. God ! how tough that meagre body of his was . . . it seemed made of whalebone and steel. I had always prided myself on being a fairly good hand with pick and shovel. A good many holes in the ground I had dug in my time but, even so, my efforts had been desultory except on that tragic occasion when Tom and I had fought to get our prospect holes down on the Ruenya

River . . . and Tom had died. But Gable was an expert. He had had forty years of almost continuous practice to make him so. Hold my own with him I believe I did, but it took all my extra fifty pounds of brawn and muscle to do it.

First we had to dig a well to get water. In a little sandy hollow just above the cañon we dug it, a spot that Gable chose. Good water at nine feet. Water to wash in and water to drink. Also water for the panning of the lost Gutner's Gulch lead when we should find it below the slide . . . we both were sure it was there, just as sure as that I had found its extension in the flats lower down. Fifty feet or so under our feet it was. What I doubted was our ability to get down through that pile of monstrous boulders without explosives. But Gable was just as sure we would get to it as he was sure it was there.

We lived in the little *teepee* set waist-high among sage-brush. On us as we woke was the smell of dew-wet sage-brush—of sun-warmed sage-brush at night when we rolled out our bedding on the ground after a final pipe by the fire. Sweet. It smelt of dew-damped leagues under starlit nights, of clear sunlit days over wide spaces. Queer speckled " road runners " or " chaparal birds " darted out of the sage to inspect us out of their beady bird-eyes, then darted away with incredible speed, running, at our slightest movement. On the ridges great ears drooped, or cocked in alarm, big as jackass ears, where some grandfather jack-rabbit squatted on his kangaroo-like haunches and surveyed us meditatively, or poised for flight.

Not far from our camp the road climbed a spur of the continental divide, the same road Shorty and I had descended a couple of months before. Many stream-lined tourist cars stormed it, roaring and raising a cloud of dust. Full of Eastern people most of them were. Sometimes they saw our tent gleaming patchy white in the valley below them, stopped and walked across to see us. Romance ! Western miners panning gold. Short-skirted women clad mostly in silk stockings screamed with excitement when I rolled out of the baking-powder tin, in which I kept it, the results of my six weeks' work in the flats below. Paunchy stockbrokers or business men in palm beach suits hefted the little nuggets and made remarks they thought were sage in order to impress their women folk. That tin of dust and nuggets was getting lighter every week because from it we bought in

Hillsborough our meagre weekly ration which we supplemented freely from among the jack-rabbits in the neighbourhood.

Sometimes the tourists brought a dog with them and usually the dog stirred up a jack-rabbit, as the place was stiff with the queer mastodon hares. Then there was fun. Generally the dog was a super-civilised dog who fed on a balanced diet with the right number of vitamins in it, got his hair combed daily and had his fleas disinfected for him instead of getting rid of them by the honest dog-method of scratching them on to his master. The jack-rabbit was not civilised. He got his living as best he could out of the sage-brush, and a damned poor living it must have been, judging by the toughness of the meat of all the many jack-rabbits I have eaten. Therefore the jack-rabbit was efficient. He had to be to live. The dog was the reverse . . . a parasite . . . so the chase was hardly fair. The jack-rabbit would usually wait till the dog was almost on to his " form "—a hare's hide-out is a " form," so I suppose a jack's is the same. Jack would establish a lead of about ten yards by dint of a couple of terrific leaps, then he would lope easily around the contour of the hill, keeping his lead. Exploding wildly in a barrage of excited yelps —he had probably never before scented anything wilder than a tabby cat—the dog would pursue. As soon as the dog got into high gear with an initial burst of speed the jack-rabbit would slow down till the dog's nose was almost touching his white scut. Then, in ten-foot leaps, he would sail uphill and over the ridge leaving the dog labouring tongue-out behind. After a few minutes the dog would return shamefacedly and about the same time the jack-rabbit would appear on another skyline and sit on his haunches in plain view, ears drooping in apparent boredom. There's a lot of humour in a jack-rabbit.

Slowly our shaft went down through the ancient landslide. And what a shaft ! A dog's hind leg was straight compared to it. The crookedness of it would have driven a conventional mining engineer to drink. Sometimes it cork-screwed round a boulder. Sometimes it dropped on an incline. And once we had to drive horizontally along the top of a huge slab of rock till we reached softer going beside it. But it went down. As Gable had said, " What I can't go through I goes around." We ate frugally, hoarding my little store of gold—Gable's bag of silver was long since expended, we had used that first. We calculated with luck that my little pile of dust and nuggets would see us through . . . down to the lost lead of Gutner's Gulch which could not now be more than twenty feet below the bottom of the animal's burrow, which we called our shaft.

Then disaster overtook us. A gang of tourists came in a big green car . . . a thing of nickel-plating and upholstered green leather. A man and two women. The man of the "smart Alec" city type. The women clothed expensively and bediamonded. The man squatted on his heels outside our *teepee* and lit a perfumed cigarette.

"Getting anything?" he asked with the wise air of a man who is on a familiar subject, though I was willing to bet he had never even seen a piece of raw gold in his life.

"Not much." Gable gulped the last sip of coffee from his mug and began to tamp tobacco into his pipe.

"Oh, do show us some gold," cried one of the women, clasping her hands and dancing with excitement.

I walked into the tent and brought out my little baking-powder tin.

Taking it from me the man tipped into his left palm a little yellow pile.

I turned to the fire to take the lid off the coffee-pot which was boiling over. By the time I had done so the man was clamping the lid back on the tin. On the ground beside him he placed it. Then he rose to leave.

"Pretty poor," he remarked as they left.

I finished my coffee and we rose to begin work. I picked up my tin. Light it seemed. Hurriedly I opened it and assessed the contents. Two-thirds at least were gone. Our visitor had kept the pile in his left hand. Stolen it.

"God Almighty, Gable! They've swiped half our gold," I cried.

In two strides he was peering into the tin. "The dirty son-of-a-bitch. Swiped it for fun! Souvenir of the Golden West. God rot his guts. There wurn't hardly enough in it to buy one of them bitches a pair of silk stockings they wore clear up to their waists . . . but that bit of dust meant more to us than ten thousand bucks to him." Gable was pale with wrath. All day he hardly spoke. Working savagely as though to make up for our loss.

I was sick. The loss itself was bad enough. But to think of men mean enough to do a trick like that made my stomach twist. If the man had been hard-up, hungry, I would have pardoned him, as I would have expected him to pardon me for theft in similar case. But to steal for a joke. Probably to brag about how the smart Eastern business man put it over on a couple of Westerners. That little theft made the difference to us between possible success and almost certain failure.

" What do we do now ? " I asked, as we sat by the fire that night.

" Up to you," replied my partner, lighting his pipe with a hot coal from the fire.

I considered my reply. " I'll stay with you until the money gives out or until we strike ' pay.' If the pay's rich enough to make a pile out of, I'll stay till it's worked out. If it's poor I'll have to leave you. I've got to be making some real money pretty soon or my wife will be running short."

" Fair enough, Pard." He nodded. " There's many a good prospector spiled by being hitched to a female skirt. Where you aiming to go ? "

" Florida." I had a letter in my pocket from Bill telling me of the beginning of the Florida land boom and asking me to meet him down there as soon as possible. " I can borrow enough on an insurance policy I've got back east to get there with my family.

" What about you ? " I asked.

" I'll sit tight as a sitting hen on this proposition. If the money gives out before we bottom I'll get a job somewhere and save enough to come back and bottom later."

The money did play out two weeks afterwards . . . when we estimated that we were only ten feet from our goal. We debated the possibility of continuing on a straight diet of jack-rabbits, but we unanimously decided to throw in our hand . . . I did not like jack-rabbit the first time I tasted it and I liked it less each time I ate it. I never heard of Gable again or whether he came back to finish our job. A good miner and a good partner.

Within a week after he and I parted I was back in Pennsylvania with Margaret. As soon as we could pack our few belongings, we took the train for Miami, Florida.

PART III

THE GLORIOUS SOUTH

CHAPTER I

A CITY RUN MAD

TAKE a sleepy fishing village of about fifteen thousand inhabitants ; one or two large hotels reasonably infested during the winter season with tourists ; peaceful palm-fringed streets along which the police on duty sauntered idly, leaned against corners and gossiped or sampled locally made pineapple juice from the occasional stand which dispensed it ; a gorgeous strip of outer beach where the Atlantic breakers foamed and to which the few bathers had access by a mile-long causeway across the peaceful blue waters of Biscayne Bay ; bright sunshine all the year round, tempered by the benignant southeasterly trades. Give this little city a singularly energetic and clever gang of City Fathers of the " go-getter " type. Allow these same City Fathers to dip freely into the large accumulated surplus of the city funds in order to finance a nation-wide advertising campaign to extol the desirability of owning a lot in such a delectable place. Time this advertising campaign to break when the nation is nearing the peak of one of its periodical " boom " spending orgies . . . when carpenters, cooks, butlers, elevator boys, miners, mechanics, housewives and their husbands are vying with Wall Street experts in buying almost any kind of security with the near-certainty that in a few days it will be worth more than they paid for it—this does happen for a time in the upswing of a boom . . . till the inevitable " crash ' comes and restores things almost overnight to about their true value. After the crash comes a period of " depression " during which more or less normal business conditions reign till the forced draught of advertising begins once more to push the pressure curve upwards to complete the cycle with another boom. Let the results of the City Fathers' advertising campaign bring to Florida in general and Miami in particular every foot-loose (wheel-loose would be the more modern equivalent of the word) citizen of the hundred odd million inhabitants of the other forty-seven states ; every retired workman, business or professional man with a bit of capital saved up for his old age ; every financier who was out for a land speculation ; every young man out of a job and anxious for advancement ; every promoter (honest or otherwise), shyster or crook whose pickings on his native heath were not at the moment of the juciest ; every woman whose interest in material things was greater than her respect for convention ; every bootlegger whose clientele for illicit liquor was not as large as he thought it should be—the word " every " is not used in its most absolute form, although you would have probably so used it if you could have stood at Miami's northern gates and seen them come piling in. The people with money came to buy land . . . mostly as a speculation. Those who had no money came in hopes of pickings—myself being among this class. Steer enough of this mixed bag of immigration to Miami to increase the population within a few months from fifteen thousand staid, leisurely southerners to three hundred thousand wildly excited speculators. The result . . . Miami, Florida, in the latter half of 1925, chaos, lunacy, pathos, more fun to the minute than any place on earth, the most extraordinary scenes I have ever witnessed in my life . . . subject-matter of the ensuing chapters. I wouldn't have missed the Great Florida Land Boom even if I'd had to pay five years of my life to have been in it. A high price because I've lived my life full, enjoyed most of it, and value every minute of it.

The boom was well under way by the time I got to Miami from the south-west mining country. George Merrick had already put on the first big urbanisation scheme—Coral Gables, and a most beautiful place it was. Fisher's Miami Beach development had added still another suburb to Miami as well as a second causeway and a dozen great hotels. Someone had bought a section of Biscayne Bay and was pumping sand out of one-half of his acreage to make dry land out of the other half—much to the disorganisation of the minor shipping that used to use those waters. Goethals—the engineer who built the Panama Canal— was employed by another development company in building a modern harbour a few miles north of the city. Still another company employed the silver-tongued eloquence of William Jennings Bryan to sell their lots for them. Every vacant piece of land within miles of the city was being snapped up by speculators, at prices which soared overnight as you slept, in order to be cut up into lots to be sold to the long columns of prospective purchasers who were invading the city in everything on wheels from the most ancient of " Tin Lizzies " to nickel-plated Packards . . . on their licence plates the name of every state in the union.

The first result of the Miami real estate boom was a permanent traffic jam. Twenty cars were passing through Miami and per-ambulating its streets for every one that did before. The City Fathers were nothing if not original. They coped with the situation by imposing a speed limit, but not the kind which reads MAXIMUM SPEED TWENTY-FIVE MILES PER HOUR. This one was explicit and revolutionary. ANY VEHICLE PASSING THROUGH THIS CITY AT LESS THAN TWENTY-FIVE MILES PER HOUR WILL BE SUBJECT TO A FINE. The result was surprising, even if it was to be expected. Traffic policemen moved out of their accustomed stands in the centre of street intersections and took their stations on the corners—a simple act of self-preservation for which not even their chief could blame them—whence they urged onwards the mad mêlée like spectators at a football game. At the city limits jaded tourists with thousands of dusty miles behind them pricked up their ears at the sight of the notice-boards ; then, pressing down their caps well over their ears and warning their families in the back seats to hang on tight, settled themselves firmly behind the wheel, pushed their feet down on their accelerators and joyfully barged into the rapids of the traffic stream ; rapids they were. For a while the long column of cars would roar through the sparsely settled suburbs of new developments towards the centre of the city. Then, somewhere ahead, a red traffic light would glow, causing the front cars to jam on brakes to avoid annihilation by the rapidly accelerating cross stream of traffic who were bent on attaining their legal minimum of speed. The result sounded like a mile-long freight train whose engine-driver has incautiously braked the engine to a sudden full stop. The series of crashes could be heard for miles. It was too hectic to last. After a few days the speed regulations were brought to a more conventional form in spite of bitter opposition by the garage interests, who were doing a roaring trade in repairs. So ended a very exciting interlude, just as exciting for dodging pedestrians as for the drivers of cannoning cars.

As the population curve streaked skywards the original easy-going Miami police force became woefully inadequate in numbers to handle the situation, so a number of young farmers were hurriedly recruited in the neighbouring state of Georgia, rushed into uniform, taught to distinguish between their right and left hands, persuaded to shave daily, armed with the usual revolver and baton and placed on point duty. Told to enforce the law, they were. They did their honest best although their methods were not always tactful. There was one of them, for example, who spotted an ancient car driving through a red light by the old post office. His youthful mind ignored the fact that the light was very badly placed among the foliage of a live-oak tree and almost invisible ; that the car had an Idaho licence plate and that its rustic-looking driver was therefore almost certainly a stranger. Quickly the policeman acted. Leaping to the running-board of the slowly moving car he clubbed the driver neatly with his baton. The rustic slumped over the steering-wheel. Car, driver, policeman and passengers crashed through a plate-glass window amid the shrieks of the women and children on the back seat and the wild cries of despair from the Jewish storekeeper. In a minute a mob had formed. The car was backed out by hand. No one proved much hurt except the glass window. A headache and a lump behind the ear were accepted by the driver as a normal manifestation of this paradise he had driven his family three thousand miles to see. But the mob was incensed. Almost anything went in the Miami of boom days, but this was too much. Clubbing in sight prospective purchasers of lots was outside Miami's code. The mob dragged the policeman to a lamp-post with a conveniently outstretched arm, found a rope, tossed one end over the lamp-post, dropped a noose over the policeman and were tailing on for a pull when the patrol wagon dashed up and put an end to the proceedings.

Miami sidewalks were crowded with sightseers who sauntered about and crossed the street as the whim took them, now that the furious rush of vehicles had ceased with the reduction of the speed limit from minimum to maximum. So the City Fathers made a law that pedestrians should obey the red and green lights the same as wheeled traffic. On the morning that this ordinance came into effect a green Georgia recruit was standing on his corner when a man started to wander across the traffic in defiance of the new regulation. The cop shouted at him to return. The jay-walker took on that obviously unhearing air which meant that he intended to be deaf. Being apparently a man of action the cop wasted no more words, but drew his revolver, took careful aim and fired. Missed his mark he did, but hit an un-suspecting citizen in the next street. The cop's bullet drilled the innocent pedestrian through the shoulder and the cop was righteously indignant because he lost his job for enforcing the law he had sworn to enforce.

There was one unforgettable minute during which I watched a cop in difficulties with traffic—it would have taken a good London Bobby to handle properly that horde of undisciplined and reckless drivers. The cop got them properly in a tangle in spite of his best efforts. Being a sport he completed the effort by deliberately waving on the traffic from all four streets at once and walking to the sidewalk to observe the effect. After every vehicle in sight was properly tangled in the snarl he threw his police helmet on to the ground, danced it flat with heavily booted feet and kicked it clear into the middle of the traffic jam. Then, hands in pockets, he sauntered to the police station to resign his job.

The population of Miami was divided into two parts—sellers and buyers. The original sellers were the " Crackers "—native Floridians, resident before the boom—who wisely sold most of their land holdings as soon as the price became fantastic ; when they had sold their own land they went to work reselling it again for the people who had bought it, working on commis-sion. All the newcomers who had any cash were buyers while their cash lasted. When they had bought to their financial limit they too went to work selling for others on commission until their own land should have risen enough in price (not necessarily value) to give them a good profit to reinvest in other purchases, which the flow and ebb of public fancy might make appear more attractive at the moment. Thus almost everyone in Miami was selling real estate except the daily horde of new arrivals of the buyer class whose numbers were large enough to keep the demand hectic and the price soaring.

The usual team for selling numbered three—the "bird-dog," the "contact man" and the "closer." The bird-dog was always a woman, the more attractive the better, who somehow managed to maintain herself at a hotel, the more expensive the better. Her job was to contact the better gilded of the new arrivals, sound their pocket-books, probe them for their fancies as regards districts in which to buy, and pass the tip to the contact man, who would be frequenting the lobby of the same hotel. The contact man would then scrape acquaintance with the prospect, regale him with stories of fabulous profits made by those who had bought early in that particular district—he had no need to invent them, there were plenty of true ones—and finally introduce him to the closer, whose job was to get the signature on the contract and extract the money. Then the split of the commission between the three.

The unbelievable situation was created that while practically everyone sold real estate practically everyone bought. Even the man who made as commission a few hundreds out of a purchaser could hardly wait for the ink to dry on the contract because he was so eager to invest his gains in a lot in Miami Beach, Cocoanut Grove, the Redlands, Sunset Isles, Hialeah, or his particular fancy among a score of others. Most housewives had their daily visit from their real estate agent, just as they did from the baker or the milkman, his wares carried in a brief-case under his arm instead of in a basket. "We've got some lovely bargains in the Redlands this morning, ma'am. Bound to clear you ten per cent. within the week. Or if you'd like it better I've a corner for sale in Miami Beach. Been saving it for a friend but he's overloaded already. Ten thousand dollars, ma'am. Usual terms. Ten per cent. down, forty per cent. in thirty days and the balance on mortgage. Nice south-east exposure." The "south-east exposure" line was worked to a frazzle. If your house faced the south-east trade wind it was cool. If it faced otherwise it was hot. A woman once tried to sell me a grave-yard lot. I refused on the plea that I had no intention of dying just then and never felt less like it. "But it has such a nice south-east exposure, sir . . ." she began.

People didn't worry much about the price so long as they had enough cash for the "binder." The usual terms were a ten per cent. binder which gave you a legal option on the property for thirty days, at the end of which time you had to pay an additional forty per cent. to acquire legal title. If you couldn't make the latter payment you lost the binder. The remaining half of the price was usually absorbed in a mortgage. Gambling on margins with land instead of paper securities, that's what it was. The idea was to secure legal option by a binder and then unload the property at a higher price before the closing payment became due. This often happened. Towards the end of the closing period there was a rush to sell at the best price obtainable to some innocent who would be left holding the baby . . . whoever held the lot under option at closing date would be holding the baby to the extent of putting up the forty per cent. or losing what he had in the deal.

Bill and I once actually sold—this was when we were operating a small commission agency at the beginning—a ten-acre tract of land in the Redlands district four times to four different people within the thirty-day closing period. Each purchaser put up his ten per cent. binder to the seller. The first sale was at one hundred dollars an acre . . . the last at ten times that price . . . all in thirty days. We shortened up the closing period with each sale so that all closings would come on the same date. Our tiny office was bulging with people paying each other large sums of money on each of which we collected our legal ten per cent. commission. None of the buyers had ever seen the land, nor had they ever expressed the least wish to see it nor to know whether it was fit for an orange grove or an alligator farm . . . neither Bill nor I had ever seen it for that matter . . . no one would have expected us to. To all of us that land was just a counter in the game, like securities in a Wall Street gamble. However, some months later Bill and I were driving through the Redlands district—a small farming village surrounded by flats covered with the stately long-leafed pine.

"Let's find that damned lot, Bill," I cried. "It was one of our first sales and I've always been curious about it."

I remembered the landmarks in the legal description and we turned our car towards Biscayne Bay along a woodland trail. Swampier and swampier grew the land as we approached salt water. Finally, when the ground became too soft to drive farther, I got out and hunted up the nearest section corner. Our lot was still half a mile east of us, which would put it well out in Biscayne Bay. Boats sailing over it. I wondered what the final owner—whoever he might be—had thought of it. Surely the ultimate purchaser, the man who had finally got stuck with it at some unbetterable fantastic price, would want to see the land which his paper counter represented. Or would the price have been so outrageous that the kind of land would make no difference and the owner use the paper in an outrageous way and shake the dust of Florida from his tyres in disgust ?

Many people got stuck on land speculation in Florida. In fact most of the speculators got stuck. The original Floridian " Crackers " came out best . . . they had sold their land for hard cash at the beginning. But there was one class that made real money . . . the Rum-Runners. The Crackers had always drunk fairly liberally, as people do in a hot country. Since the prohibition law had prohibited the sale of liquor throughout the United States they had followed the example of most of their fellow-countrymen in drinking a bit more than usual to show their opinion of a law that tries to separate a man from his source of lubrication. As the boom waxed in a *crescendo* the extra thirst engendered by excitement further increased Floridian consumption. Add to that the colossal amount of liquor consumed by the inflowing hordes of northerners—literally hundreds of thousands of cold-country people racing round frantically during their first visit to a hot country. At home the northerner had the long winter evenings in which to concoct his home-brewed beer and " cellar " gin. In Miami he was too busy selling and buying real estate to bother. Besides, money was flowing on all sides like water. In Miami he bought his liquor and bought it freely.

Rum running in Florida took on the mantle of big business. Adventurous souls with ambition would quietly disappear from Miami streets . . . to reappear a few nights later on the dark horizon of the Gulf Stream to seaward at the helm of a fast motor-boat stuffed to the scuppers with half-dozens of bottles wrapped in sacking . . . the rum-runners never ran bottles in cases because of the breakage. A wild and reckless game it was and it attracted adventurers from the ends of the earth. More than once I had an offer of a partnership from one or other of the more successful ones—I could handle a motor-boat with the best of them by that time, and somehow they had sensed or learned that such a profession would fit in with my past better than that of a tame real estate operator. Tempted I was . . . most damnably. If it had not been for the responsibility of Margaret and the children I would have snapped up the first offer made me or, more likely, bought a boat and gone into it to play a lone hand.

From the Bahamas, Gun Key and Cuba came the cargoes. Fleets of fast motor-boats would spend the day loading Scotch whisky, old French wines and brandies or good Bacardi rum, while on the blue horizon, Floridaward, the coastguard cutters lay idly, watching from afar, outside territorial waters. At nightfall the game began. The motor-boats slipped from sheltering foreign shores into the black night, lightless, to land their cargoes in secluded spots along the Florida coast while the preventives did their best—more or less—to prevent them.

At times a truce would seem to exist between the rum-runners and the Government preventive men. The runners seemed to land their cargoes almost openly while the preventives seemed deliberately to look the other way. Then one side or other would break some clause in their unwritten convention . . . and there would be war. When war broke out it was apt to be a grim business. The runners once boarded and captured a Government boat, armed with machine-gun though it was. The coastguard cutter was found drifting empty some days later and no trace was ever found of the eleven armed men who had been its crew. On the other hand, many a rum-runner was machine-gunned on sight by the infuriated Government men when a war was on. I remember one occasion when I was having afternoon tea on the balcony of one of the fashionable hotels which lined the Miami River, a narrow crooked stream which meandered its way through the heart of the city. Suddenly, down near the mouth of the river, a machine-gun started to chatter, coming rapidly nearer. A moment later a fast motor-boat shot round the nearest bend, engine roaring and helmsman crouched low over the wheel. In its foaming wake came the revenue cutter, machine-gun stuttering excitedly as it swung round the curves of the river, peppering impartially the boat ahead, both banks of the river, several busy streets and crowds of gaily dressed people toying with their tea-cups on the verandas of the hotels.

CHAPTER II

A GAMBLE IN REAL ESTATE

I ARRIVED in Miami with my family a few days before Bill and was lucky enough to secure a tiny apartment—accommodation was already becoming scarce—at the not unreasonable rent of fifty dollars a month. By squeezing my whole family into one room we managed to accommodate Bill when he arrived. Both bedrooms were of average size, but the combination kitchen and eating-room seemed to have been designed for Liliputians. Those meals with Margaret sweating at the stove while Bill and I sweated at the table not five feet from it were something to remember.

The boom was daily accelerating its pace and the amount of money one made in the real estate business was governed mainly by the amount of work one was willing to put into it. Bill and I worked . . . this was our chance to retrieve our fortunes and we weren't going to miss it. We usually began with the earliest openers among the real estate fraternity and carried on till the last prospective purchaser had locked his door. After that we frequented the lobbies of the hotels until the small hours on the often realised chance of meeting some newcomer with such zeal to invest that he would not wait till offices opened next day. Selling on commission we were, and the results of our first couple of months of concentrated effort surprised us considerably.

It was about the time we realised what an easy wicket we were on that we both decided we didn't like it. This business of introducing buyer and seller and taking a rake-off for it suited neither of us. Parasites. That's what we were, we both decided. For my part I have always had to be creating something tangible before I was happy. I had been happier sinking that shaft with Gable than I was selling real estate in Florida. I had been broke then . . . flat broke. Now I had money in the bank. But after you have earned enough money to cover necessities and a reasonable amount of luxuries money ceases to count. All I got out of my efforts now was a living and a surplus of money. On Gutner's Gulch I got the living and a hole in the ground as a result of my efforts. I preferred the hole in the ground to the surplus cash. Something tangible, that hole was. Bill was the constructive kind too, only he was content with intangibles . . . power to sway men's destinies . . . the feeling that he was pulling the strings that made things happen . . . whereas for my part I had to have something that men could see, touch, climb over or fall into.

"We've got to get one of these big land developments started," remarked Bill one day while we were sitting on the beach after a swim. "That's the only thing for us. A job one can work on for years. This business of starting a deal after breakfast, finishing it before lunch and starting another in the afternoon is getting me down. Too many mental acrobatics." He drew a big square on the sand with his forefinger and began to subdivide it into lots.

"We've made a few thousands out of commissions but not enough to start us on a big deal." Our little stake wouldn't count for much, I knew, when it came to buying acreage at the outrageous prices already ruling.

"If we could buy a tract of land cheap we could swing the deal on a shoestring." Bill began ornamenting his lots with little sand-houses.

I laughed. "Cheap land ! In Southern Florida you couldn't buy a tract between the Everglades and the Atlantic for less than five thousand dollars an acre."

"True enough. But what about the west coast on the Gulf of Mexico ? No one has paid any attention to that yet. Not the southern part of it, anyway. Land ought to be pretty cheap on the other side of the everglades, Gulf frontage, right across the peninsula from Miami."

I sat up straight. I knew that the coast showed blank on the map sixty miles across the everglades—how blank spaces on a map do always appeal to me—from Cape Sable, the southernmost tip of the Florida peninsula, for about a hundred miles north. That blank space had already fascinated me and I had made a mental resolution to explore it at the first opportunity. No one seemed to know much about the hinterland, but the coastal waters and tidal rivers were reputed to be the best tarpon fishing in the world.

"What do you know about it?" I asked.

"Not much. Baron Collier, the New York financier, had the idea. He bought a tract sixty miles north of Cape Sable and tried to develop it. He's got it going now . . . got a little town there which he called Everglades . . . but he had a lot of trouble with the natives to start with."

"Natives? Indians, you mean."

"No. There are some Seminole Indians living in the ever-glades but they're quiet enough. But they say the white people living on the south-west Gulf coast are tough. Damned tough. They held Baron Collier's people off at the point of the rifle when he sent in engineers to survey."

"God! I didn't know you had any of that sort left in the U.S.A."

"Man, that's the last frontier of the United States over there. Part of it has never even been surveyed by the Government surveyors. Country was too tough for even Uncle Sam's sur-vey crews. It's inhabited by all the outlaws who have got into the swamps one jump ahead of the sheriff. They don't like strangers by all accounts. But they don't matter to us because I expect the country is too swampy to develop, anyhow. If it were any good someone would have snapped it up by now."

I was on my feet by now. "Bill, if that's all the matter with it we can drain it."

"We'd need to raise capital."

"We raised all we needed for the coal business."

"Sales force, offices and all the trimmings."

"That's your pidgin. I'll do the draining and fight the savages."

Bill looked at me and his teeth flashed in a grin. "Let's go, then, you old fire-eater."

"What do you mean?"

"Let's go and look at a tract I know about. Belongs to a Jew named Abelson. We'll talk to him to-morrow about an option and then go and look at it when we have it tied up."

However, it was not till about a week later that Bill and I

chugged down Biscayne Bay in a chartered cabin cruiser on our way to the south-west Florida coast. The Jew had been hard to deal with, as Jews usually are when a prospective purchaser voluntarily walks into their office instead of being dragged in by force with a rope round his neck. But we had got our land at a reasonable price in the end. That is, we had got a week's option on it at a reasonable price. If we decided on our return to purchase, however, the initial payment would absorb about every cent that Bill and I had accumulated and that would hold the land for only another month. In that month we must organise to meet the series of heavy monthly payments which would continue till half the purchase price were paid. A mortgage took care of the other half.

South we moved slowly all the sunny morning, now in wide, open stretches of bluest water, now slipping through narrow channels between low mangrove-covered keys. Then west, through the Bay of Florida, which lies between the blunted end of the peninsula and the crescent of outer keys which sweeps round into the Gulf of Mexico and terminates in Key West. That night we anchored in the shelter of the Horseneck Shoal at the entrance of the Gulf of Mexico, out of sight of land. I would come to know well the Horseneck Shoal during the next year or two. I was to see it many times as I saw it that first night. The shoal itself was invisible except for the slight discoloration of the water to the initiated eye. Endless black velvet water with the stars reflected in it. The only sign of man's habitation of the earth was the ray of the Alligator Reef lighthouse on the outer keys which shone in the sky at fixed intervals of about a minute. The light itself was invisible beyond the southern horizon, but its rays swept high through the sooty texture of the night like the beam of a great searchlight, sweeping the silent untenanted waters as though proclaiming man's domination of them. But there was a night that man's light was dimmed—months later—when I lay alone in my boat anchored in the shelter of that shoal. I saw a sudden blaze of glory in the sky as a great meteor shot past me to plunge into the Gulf not many miles to the westward. So close it was that I could hear the roaring of its passage, and so bright its light that I could have read small print by it. Not before, nor since, have I seen one like it.

Next day the stolid cabin cruiser which we had chartered bore Bill and me northward into the Gulf for thirty miles, till the cocoanut palms on Cape Sable began to waver mirage-like above the blue line of the northern horizon. Still north. Skirting now a mangrove-covered shore with occasional long stretches of white beach. Deserted. Not a sign of human habitation in all its length. Then a great tidal river pouring its waters into a wide bight . . . the Shark River emptying into Ponce de Leon Bay. Still north twenty miles to another river beside the mouth of which a wooden building roosted in the water on long barnacle-covered legs. The Lostman River. Our destination. North and south of us stretched unpeopled white beaches which would be ours if our gamble came off. The mangrove-covered land on either side of the wide river would be ours too as well as the waters of the river itself. It was all ours to win if we were bold enough to dare a financial transaction so far above our means that the thought of it would have made a conservative business man shudder. But we weren't conservative business men. We were a couple of youngsters who had been in the ring already with the biggest of the financial heavyweights and come out undismayed, although they had wrested the prize from us. We owed it to our pride to get back into the fight. Besides, it was Florida in boom time when the big stakes went to the most reckless and daring counted for more than seasoned business judgment.

It was evening and flood tide when we moored our cabin cruiser to one of the stilts of the fish-house. A young man and a girl peered curiously down at us from the little platform in front of the door. They lived here to buy the fish the natives brought in, they told us, representing the Tampa company which put the fish in tins. Once a week the company boat would call with ice and take away what fish they had.

"We want to get up-river in the morning. Can you guide us?"

The young man shook his head. "Never been farther than the mouth. But there's the best man you could get . . . coming out now with a load of mullet." He waved to a small white launch which had just rounded a cocoanut-covered island to the north. "That's Jamie Heddleston's boat. If he likes the looks of you maybe he'll take you . . . he guides fishing parties sometimes. Anyway, he'll say if you can go up or not."

" What's it to do with him whether we go up or not ? He doesn't own this land."

" It's owned by someone in Miami, they say, and I don't suppose the owner's ever seen the place. But Jamie Heddleston is the man who runs things round here." With a glance at the approaching boat he and the girl disappeared inside the building.

The small white launch approached swiftly and lost its way at exactly the moment its bows were nuzzling the pole adjacent to the one we were moored to. A figure rose from the tiller, bounded forward and swung the mooring painter neatly round the post, making it fast with one or two deft movements of his hands. Then he turned and stared at us frankly. A man of middle height with a colossal pair of shoulders and barrel. From under a battered felt hat a small pair of beady blue eyes took us in. A pair of gnarled bare feet gripped the gunwale of the launch. Almost prehensile. The broad sun-tanned face was puckered . . . with curiosity, I decided.

" Good evening." I broke the silence.

The small eyes focused suddenly on me. They moved like the eyes of a fisherman who has been watching a whole shoal of fish floating in clear water and who suddenly focuses his gaze on the first fish to move. We stared at each other in silence a moment, sizing each other up. I liked the man on sight.

" Evenin'," he drawled.

" Mullet must be thick about here." I glanced at the silvery cargo in the bottom of his launch. He must have had a ton of mullet in his catch.

He glanced reflectively at the fish, then at me.

" Middlin' good." He caught expertly the basket-laden end of a rope which the fish-house tender had rove through a block overhead. Then he caught the loose end, dropped it in the bows of his launch and began to fill the basket with the fish.

Barefooted myself, I stepped aboard and helped. When the basket was full I heaved on the rope and raised it to the waiting keeper above.

When we had emptied his launch in silence he turned to me.

" Fishin's good. Seen big tarpon jumpin' up-river yesterday."

He continued to gaze at me, obviously waiting for me to state our business.

" We've no time to fish this trip. Just come to look around. If you could guide us up-river to-morrow we'd be obliged."

His gaze travelled from me to Bill and on to the skipper of our chartered cruiser, whose hinder parts alone were visible as he tinkered with his engine.

" What time ? "

" Any time you like. The earlier the better because we have to get back to Miami."

" Come daybreak I'll be here. We'll take my launch. That herrin'-gutted barge of yourn won't make the tide-rips." Casting a disparaging glance at our cabin cruiser which was of a portly build he cast off his painter, spun his engine and slid out into the growing gloom as soon as I had leaped aboard our own boat. " That goes for you and your friend only," he shouted as he disappeared. " Don't want no Miami tourist conductors learnin' these channels."

" God ! you do make funny friends," remarked Bill. " If you made him a bit more hairy and put him in a cage he'd look quite at home."

I laughed. " Maybe you're right, Bill. But he stacks up to me pretty much like a man."

With some difficulty I got city-bred Bill's breakfast inside of him and Bill himself on deck just as the river waters to the eastward were flushing pink and only a minute or so before the slim white launch slid alongside of us. For a mile or two we slipped easily up the quarter-mile wide river with tall white mangroves lining each bank. Stately they looked with their straight white boles and thick leafy tops of dark green. Once only in that two miles we swerved in our course to pass close in front of a tiny cabin on the river-bank. On the rough jetty before it was standing a tall black-bearded figure, rifle in hand. As soon as he recognised Jamie he gave a cordial wave of his hand and disappeared.

" Winton. My brother," volunteered our guide. Then he took from a locker in the launch a well-oiled rifle which he leaned against the gunwale near him. " The 'gators are swimmin' this time o' day," he explained. "Hides ain't worth much nowa-days, but they're worth the price of a bullet."

Two miles or so up-river a mile-wide lake opened before us. Then another channel and another lake. At the head of the second lake a small island lay in mid-channel.

"Onion Key," remarked Jamie.

"Why the Onions?" A nice little island. About an acre in extent. No undergrowth and just enough shade trees to give it a park-like effect.

"Pa called it that. When he fust come to these parts 'bout sixty years back he made his fust camp here. Planted onions, he did, and grew the biggest onions ever, 'cordin' to his account."

"Where's your father now? He must be pretty ancient if he came in here sixty years ago."

"Pa's 'bout eighty-eight 'cordin' to his figgurin', and he ought to know. Lives off by hisself. Don't mix much with the rest of us since Ma died."

"Is there any open land here?" I asked. "Or is it all man-grove like what we see along the river?"

"Open land! Why there's prairie back of them man-groves."

He headed the boat across the lake and grounded it at a spot where the mangroves were obviously thinner than usual. Then he sprang nimbly from the bow of the launch, his great gnarled feet squelching in the black ooze of the lake shore. I followed, landing ankle-deep in mud. Like a great bear he ploughed his way through the bushes with me behind him. Not twenty yards through the undergrowth we suddenly broke into the open. Before us was a level plain covered with yard-high growth of coarse grass. Dry under foot when we walked out on it.

"It's only the high spring tides that wets these prairies," Jamie explained. "Most times they're dry enough so it shows when you spit."

By noon we had completed the superficial exploration of what I had already determined was to be our domain. Going down-river Bill beckoned me into the bows of the boat for a con-ference : there the steady chugging of Jamie's engine prevented any chance of our conversation being overheard.

"Well?" queried Bill. His brow was puckered, his eyes

fixed on the river behind us where the entrance to one of the lakes was rapidly closing as we receded from it.

" It's all right. We want it." Even as I spoke a great tarpon flashed near the shadows of the mangroves abreast of us. In a silver arc he left the water, flipped his tail in mid-air and disappeared with a splash. A gigantic herring. Five feet long I judged him, with scales as big as a shilling piece. From his post in the stern Jamie's eyes caught mine. He grinned and his hands went through the motion of winding in a reel, while he steadied the wheel with one foot through the spokes.

" I'm afraid of it." Bill's tone was tense. " Too wild. It'll scare people off."

" Like hell it will. They'll flock to it."

" What will bring them ? There's nothing here. Not even a road for them to come in on."

" Roads can be built. We can't be more than half a dozen miles from that Tamiami Trail they're beginning to construct across the everglades. We'll put in a connection with that as part of our development."

Bill shook his head. " But why should they buy in a place like this ? What's to attract them ? "

" That's one thing to attract them." I pointed to where the tarpon's splash of foam still showed on the glassy surface. " Fishing. Then there's miles of beach, miles of river and any number of lakes. Did you see the way the sun warmed the river mist as it rose this morning ? Turned it pink like the inside of a sea-shell. That'll bring them . . . beauty. Plenty of people are still not too civilised to enjoy natural beauty—even in this over-mechanised country of yours. Besides, we'll be selling the cheapest lots in Florida. We can afford to do it because the price of this land is barely one-tenth of the price of similar land on the Miami side of the peninsula. We'll develop a townsite on that open prarie I walked on to. I'll build you a levee to keep the water out, same as they've done in New Orleans. A canal to drain the rainwater off. Once that's done you'll fill the place with retired folk who want to live in peace."

" They'll be eaten alive with mosquitoes . . . to say nothing of the alligators." He pointed to where two black knobs were sliding through the mirror-like water, leaving a wake behind. The knobs were the periscope eyes of a 'gator.

I laughed. " The mosquitoes will go when the land is drained. A few 'gators will add to the attraction."

But still Bill shook his head. Never in his life, I was sure, had he been so far from roads, movies and steam heat.

" Good God, man," I argued, " we can run the most honest real estate show in Miami. Tell the people exactly what we've got . . . swamp land, mosquitoes and alligators. Promise them nothing except that we'll drain it, build a road to it and mark off the lots. They'll be so surprised at our candour after the rosy promises most real estate salesmen make that they'll buy. Besides, the place has got a future. This very lake we're running through would make a first-class harbour with a little dredging inside and a channel cut through the shoals out in the Gulf."

Bill grinned suddenly—I knew I had won then. " Let's take in Key West on our way back and talk to the sheriff there. We're in Key West county here, you know, so he's the chap that'll have to keep law and order. These native chaps will take some handling by the look of them."

Lucky I had already got Bill convinced because the Key West sheriff was not encouraging . . . a heavy bottomed man with a big black moustache in the Victorian style.

" God Almighty ! You boys are crazy. Them Heddlestons'll run you off same as their friends farther north tried to run Baron Collier off. It was only Collier's money that pulled him through. If you boys got a million or so to work with . . . why, go ahead. If not, take my advice and leave it alone. Them Heddlestons are bad *hombres*. The old man come down to the Lostman country 'bout the time of the Flood . . . soon after the end of the Civil War . . . deserted from the Confederates, the story goes. Married a Seminole girl. She died. He went for his next to the Conchs and what with one wife and another bred three wild sons. They all wived among the Conchs too and bred wild children."

" Who are the Conchs ? "

" The people of the outer keys, between here and Miami. In the old days there weren't no lighthouses, only light-buoys to mark the reefs. The Conchs used to pray to God to send a wreck, then douse the light on a buoy and put a lantern in the wrong place to make sure that God did."

"We met Jamie Heddleston. I liked him."

"The sheriff went to a drawer and took out a black bottle and a glass. After Bill and I had sunk a snifter apiece from the glass the sheriff put the neck of the bottle to his mouth and gurgled.

"Jamie's all right," he replied after he had given the conventional shudder at the passage of the fiery spirit. "That is, he's all right as long as he stays on the Lostman River and you stay somewhere else. But just you try horning in on Jamie's country and you'll be out of luck. Besides, there's not only Jamie to be reckoned with. There's his brothers and a scad of cousins. To top all . . . as if that weren't enough . . . there's some bad actors that have drifted in and live under the Heddlestons' protection. Wanted, some of them are, but good deputy sheriffs is too hard to come by to waste them trying to dig criminals out of Jamie Heddleston's country."

"What do you do about them?"

The sheriff spat expertly into a brass cuspidor at least ten feet from where he was sitting. "I leaves them alone as long as they stays there."

"You don't send in to arrest them?"

The sheriff chuckled till his big belly wobbled. "You're damned right, I don't. Two good reasons. One is that the deputy wouldn't go if I sent him. The other is that he wouldn't come back if he did go." He drew up his chair and leaned closer. "Ever hear tell of Old Man Watson while you were in there?" he asked.

We shook our heads.

"Well, I'll tell you the story and then you can forget about the Lostman River and go home like good boys to play at selling lots in Miami. Old Man Watson drifted into the Lostman River country better than ten years back. Just oozed in like. Inconspicuous. One day he wasn't there and the next day he was . . . some trouble up north, he'd had, by all accounts. Lived back from the beach and lay low, did Old Man Watson. Married one of Chief Tigertail's Seminoles and bred a tribe of copper-coloured kids. The Heddlestons let him be so long as he didn't worry them . . . same as they've done to others. Then last year 'King' Jamie suddenly decides that the Lostman River kids need educating seeing that none of them can read and write although some of them's married already . . . or what goes for marriage along the Lostman River. Jamie builds a school house and brings in a young chap from outside to teach. Everything goes hunky-dory till the young chap takes on himself to lick one of Watson's kids. Watson shoots the school-teacher on sight next time they met . . . happened in the trading store at Chuckaluskee, in the Ten Thousand Islands, where all the Lostman River people get their mail. Watson leaves him lying on the floor, finishes his own drink and goes home."

The sheriff rose and fumbled in the drawer.

" Go on. What happened next ? "

" They buried the school teacher."

" Finish the story, man."

The sheriff looked up under his bushy eyebrows. " That's all . . . so far."

" But what happened to Watson ? "

" He went home, I tell you."

" Where is he now ? "

" Home, I suppose."

" Aren't you going to do anything about it ? "

The sheriff waved the bottle. " Like hell I am." He guffawed. " I'm leaving that to Jamie. He's running the Lostman River."

" Then you won't appoint a deputy to keep order for us ? " Bill's forehead was puckered. " We'll have over a hundred workmen in there when we get going."

" Not I." The sheriff poured a double one into the glass and handed it to me. " He wouldn't go in there if I did appoint him."

" Let me appoint one," I pleaded. " I'll find someone to go. We've got to have some official in there."

Bill spoke hurriedly. " I won't have you appointing yourself, Pete. Besides, you can't. You're not an American citizen."

I laughed. " I'm no policeman, but I bet I can find one."

The sheriff stared at me for a minute. Then he took from his drawer a tin badge and a paper. " What name shall I fill in ? " he asked, sitting down at his desk.

" Leave it blank, sign it and give it to me."

He gazed at me doubtfully. " How the hell do I know who you'll appoint ? I'm responsible for him."

"I'll be responsible to you. I'll bet you a bottle of whisky you approve the man. If you don't you can always cancel the appointment."

"Tell me the man's name."

"I've got to talk to the chap first. If he takes it I guarantee he'll keep order on the Lostman River."

"He must be one hell of a man. Seven feet high, weighs half a ton and shoots from both hips."

"Sign the appointment, then."

Drawing a deep breath he dashed off the signature, held the paper before him for a minute . . . hesitating, and then pushed it abruptly towards me with the badge.

"God help you if your man don't stack up," he cried as we left.

"Who is your man?" asked Bill as we walked towards our boat.

"Tell you when I've got him, Bill," I laughed. I did have a man in mind, but getting him to take on the job would be another matter.

CHAPTER III

THE CRUISE OF THE *POINCIANA*

A S soon as we returned from the Lostman River we made our first payment on the property and thereby cleaned out our bank balance almost to the point of extinction. When Abelson had signed the documents which gave us legal title to the land and the waters within its boundaries—subject of course to a number of further payments which loomed colossal in my mind—we rose to go.

"That's a beautiful place you've sold us," I remarked, lingering a moment. "Didn't you like to visit it?"

"What? Me?"

"Yes. Weren't you sorry to let it go?"

"Sorry I sold you so cheap! Yes."

"I don't mean that. Didn't you love that land?"

"Me love land? Two years I owned that tract and never seen it yet. I buy land, then I sell it. But love it? I love my wife, my car, my house. But land!"

"You've never seen it. That's why. I'll take you to see it some day."

"What for?" His fat face looked surprised behind his hooked nose.

"Just for fun. You'll love it when you see it."

"God! I got no time for fun."

"Anyway, will you take a trip with me when we have made all the payments?"

"All right. When the last payment is made I come." He roared with laughter. "The last payment! God! I got all your money already. I done some sleuthing while you were away. Know all about you. The day you bring me that last payment I fall dead from shock."

"You won't live very long then. He'll raise those payments." I jerked my head in the direction of Bill who was waiting for me outside the door.

The Jew stopped laughing suddenly. " You got a smart partner. I'll say that. When you go broke I give him a job. But this deal you can't swing. Too much money to raise for one thing. Too many bad people for another. Them Heddlestons is enough to break you without having to raise payments. Them people are tough."

" The Heddlestons are my part of the job. The payments are Bill's. We'll both come through. In six months all the payments will be over and I'll have the Heddlestons tamed by then. In six months you'll redeem your promise about our trip."

He laughed again but less loudly this time. " All right. But don't forget if you miss one payment the land reverts to me and you lose what you got in it already."

" Bill," I remarked as we walked down the street. " You've bought a load of trouble. Do you realise how much money you have to raise on the first of each month for the next six months ? "

Bill's jaw set square. " The first one is bothering me a bit, I will admit. After that the others will be easy. By the time the second is due we'll be hauling in more than the payment every month by the sale of lots. But I'll raise the first one somehow. What's worrying me more is your part of the job. Those wild men out there will take some handling, although I admit you made a good start with the gorilla that took us up the river."

I laughed, but just the same I didn't feel too sure. I knew that I could drift into the Lostman River country as a freelance, live with the Heddlestons, drink with them, fish and hunt with them, even run liquor with them—by all accounts they were among the most daring rum-runners in Florida—and be received into the bosom of the clan. But to come among them as the owner of the land on which they had lived for generations ; to take in gangs of workmen to drain the swamps and forests in which they hunted ; to settle among them a horde of north-erners ; to destroy the wilderness in which they lived and from which they derived the greater part of their livelihood ; to bring law and order into a community which prided itself on open defiance to authority : that was something else. As tough a job as I had ever tackled. But done it had to be. The antagonism of the clan would break us just as surely as a failure to meet the payments on the land. How could we sell lots to people unless we could guarantee them peaceful occupation?

No. It was a case for diplomacy. To force ourselves upon the Heddlestons would be sheer lunacy from a business point of view, quite apart from the fact that an appeal to force would probably result in a premature demise on my part. I must get to know those people better before they became aware of my true status as part owner of the land. Gain their confidence. Get them working with us, instead of against us as their neighbours had against Baron Collier. Visit them alone. Drift into the Lostman River in a small boat and live some weeks with them. That was the scheme. I started out at once to look for a seaworthy boat which I could navigate alone to the Lostman River. I little thought of what delightful companions I was to have on that voyage which I intended to make alone.

Meantime Bill moved fast. Within a week he had dug up a pair of brothers named Untel. Amos and Patrick Untel. With a moderate amount of capital the Untels had arrived in Miami from some city of the far north-west about a month before. Pushers. As full of energy as a pair of fox-terriers. In that short month they had bought a small orange grove near Coral Gables, cut it into lots and sold them out, doubling their money. They hadn't made a fortune out of it but just enough to whet their appetite for a big development . . . it was also more than enough to meet the first of our monthly payments if we could induce them to come in with us. Furthermore they still retained their force of trained salesmen, just what we wanted as a nucleus for our larger sales organisation.

We offered them a half interest in the property for the price of that first payment and a bit over for working capital. They hesitated. Wanted to see some photographs of the property.

So Bill and I chartered a seaplane for a day, borrowed a press photographer from one of the big Miami dailies and flew over our Lostman River tract taking photographs, our crazy pilot diving and swerving on the way back as he chased portly-flying pelicans which jettisoned themselves into the blue water below with unearthly squawks as though scandalised at the interruption to their fishing.

When we had pieced the photos together we had a bird's-eye view of our ten thousand acres. God ! what a piece of country it looked as seen from the air. Twisty rivers winding between mile-wide lakes. Black patches of mangrove forest alternating with wide green prairies. Leagues of white sandy beaches cradling the sleepy blue Gulf of Mexico.

The photographs did it. They fetched the Untels into the deal and we made our first payment a couple of weeks ahead of time, almost to the consternation of the Jew . . . payments on time he understood . . . defaulted payments he could deal with . . . but payments before time ! Loss of interest !

Then we rented a suite of offices and stuck our big composite photo in the window.

What to call our development ? We each thought up a name and stuck them in a hat. My choice was drawn. POINCIANA. The gorgeous red flame-tree of the tropics which lines so many of the Miami streets.

What plan to follow ? We would lay out a townsite in the wide prairie Jamie and I had visited. Two thousand of our ten thousand acres to be divided into lots and sold off for enough to cover the expenses of the whole development. We would take our profit in land. The remaining eight thousand acres, situated as they would be around a growing township, would be prize enough.

Meantime I had found my boat . . . a twenty-four-foot life-boat. Built of zinc sheeting instead of wood. Nothing but a tin-opener could have sunk her. No beauty. In fact she looked disreputable, in keeping with the part I wanted to play. Open decked. I had her flush decked fore and aft, leaving a six by six-foot cabin in the centre. To get head room in the cabin the sides of it had to protrude three feet above the deck like the ventilator in the roof of a building. Two wooden lockers in the cabin provided a pair of make-shift beds and ample storage for supplies.

When she was finished I proudly tooled her down the Miami River to try out her paces in the wider reaches of Biscayne Bay. I had never had much to do with the sea up till now—although once I had been partner in a ship—but I had always imagined it must be in my blood from a series of naval ancestors. In my blood it might have been, but I soon found it wasn't in my hands. The *Poinciana*, as I had christened her, steered like a drunken sow, and the whole river was barely wide enough to accommodate her gambollings. A flash-looking cabin cruiser treated me to a dose of profanity as I missed her snow-white paint by inches, and an opulent-looking steam yacht pushed me ignominiously away with a mop when the *Poinciana* evidenced every intention of climbing on board. But once out in the wide waters of the bay I did better . . . it was acreage I wanted. There was sea-room there . . . miles of it. I tried out the old scow's paces. Six knots per hour. That was all she had in her with her toy engine wide open. But she could roll. Even in the tiny chops of the bay she rolled like a man in bed with the itch. She was seaworthy though. I judged her fit for any weather we might meet. With her metal sides and bottom I could ram her full speed on a coral reef without damaging more than her paint. Poor old *Poinciana*. A hurricane did sink her in the end . . . filled her with water at her moorings where she never had a chance . . . but that was after she had left me. I never saw another boat of her construction before or since, and I was to handle many boats within the next year or two. On this first occasion of our acquaintance I tried her paces in Biscayne Bay until I felt I had learned the rules of the road and learned to steer her approximately in the direction I wanted her to go. After a few such trials I sat for a licence. That was easier than I expected. The answers to a few simple questions obtained me a document LICENCING CAPTAIN RAINIER TO COMMAND AND NAVIGATE IN COASTAL WATERS OF THE UNITED STATES ANY CRAFT UP TO ONE HUNDRED TONS BURTHEN.

All this time the northerners continued to flock to Miami and the *tempo* of the boom was rising to the *crescendo* it was to reach a few months later.

Margaret and I were comfortable enough in the somewhat restricted apartment we had rented after our arrival and the two children were flourishing in the Miami sunshine. We were both content. She had her home and children and she always was a great home-lover. For my part I had now something constructive to occupy my mind. A tough job by most standards, but I knew I should see it through somehow, although I wasn't sure how things would develop. Making friends with the

Heddlestons and winning their confidence, that was what I had to concentrate on for the time being.

But a week or so before I was due to leave on my voyage to the Lostman River our landlord appeared unexpectedly one morning while we were having breakfast. A decent chap I had always considered him. Helpful. One of the old Florida residents who was rapidly getting rich through the appreciation in value of the local property he owned.

"I've come to raise your rent," he greeted me.

"Go easy with it then. I'm paying fifty a month now and that's all this little place is worth." But I knew that rents were soaring and I had been expecting this visit for some time.

"It'll be two hundred dollars a month from the first of next month." He gazed earnestly at a piece of mud he was scraping from one shoe with the toe of the other.

"Great God, man! Be reasonable. That's four times what I'm paying now. This is a hold-up."

"I'm sorry." He looked me in the face at last. "I can rent the place for that. Got an offer for it last night. This boom won't last for ever and when it's over all you drifters will be moving out and leaving us locals flat. We've got to get ours while the getting's good."

"Give me time to think it over then."

"I'll give you till to-morrow morning. You can bring me the first month's rent at the new rate or consider yourself given a month's notice to vacate."

Boiling I was. I jumped into my car at once to hunt another place to stay. But all day I hunted in vain. Every house was full. Every apartment. Whole families I saw living in verandas. All the vacant lots in town were packed with jerry-built tar-paper shanties. The tourist camps on the outskirts were full of cars in which whole families pigged it. Hundreds of thousands of people were crowded into a fifteen-thousand village which hadn't grown fast enough to accommodate them in spite of the hectic building boom. Crestfallen, that night I paid the two hundred dollars and signed a lease for a year in case some crazy new-comer should offer the landlord a still higher rent.

Wednesday was the day on which I had planned my departure. The moon would be about right then and the tides full just after dark. For effect I wanted to time my arrival in Poinciana just after dark and had no wish for the sea-wise Heddlestons to find me in the morning aground on one of the numerous shoals and sand-bars I had noticed outside the mouth of the Lostman River. With high tide I could float over most of them, I was sure, and trust to luck to miss the rest. Dramatic. But first impressions are valuable on a job like the one I had in hand. To win the heart of primitive peoples you must do the things they take pride in a little better than they can do them themselves. There was no hope for me to beat the Heddlestons at seamanship, but at least I should get credit for some seamanship if they found me safely moored to the fish-house some morning, come in during the night through shoal water.

It was on the Sunday prior to my departure that I met two people the thread of whose lives was to be woven with mine at least until this time of writing, nearly fifteen years later.

"Met a man called Chesbrough yesterday," remarked Bill that Sunday. "He might be interested in our proposition. Let's go and see him."

We found the house in Coral Gables easily enough. Chesbrough was a tall red-headed man with an Irish look about him. Aristocratic. Polished. Then a girl came in with whisky and glasses on a tray. God! how long since I had been served with a drink in African style. Long whiskies and sodas, not neat spirit poured into a glass or drunk from the neck of a bottle which had just been wiped with the host's sleeve. Ruth, the girl was. Ralph Chesbrough's wife. Black hair, tall, brilliant and charming. Bill—with business uppermost as usual in his mind —had to sit back as the three of us all began to talk at once. Chesbrough had been a consular official in Constantinople . . . they had lived for years in Egypt and the Levant. They drew me out on Africa. Drunk I was . . . and not on whisky either. They made me tell them stories . . . the German South-West African campaign . . . Chief Gungunyana's diamonds . . . the time when Malachi ran *amok* and had to be quelled with a pick-handle. They were interested. Not like most of the people whom I had met in recent years, who had no interest beyond their own little circle and promptly became bored when I mentioned any experience out of their ken. I was in love with both the Chesbroughs before I left that morning.

" Come back next Sunday," they chorused as we rose to leave.

" Next Sunday I'll be on the Lostman River."

" He's going to tame gorillas over there," explained Bill. " He'll probably have been eaten alive by next Sunday." Then he explained why I was going to the Lostman River.

I saw Ruth and Ralph exchange glances. There was a look in her eye which made me uneasy.

" We are just about due for a holiday," she remarked innocently.

" This isn't a holiday trip." I refused to rise to the bait.

She seated herself primly in a chair with a hand on either knee, a " school-marm " attitude which, I was to learn later, meant that she had made up her mind about something and would not relax till she got her way.

" We love boat trips and roughing it."

" Not on my boat, you wouldn't. It's not built for passengers."

" I'm sure we should love it and we'd really be no bother. Besides, you need someone to cook for you."

" I'll take you both on a trip when I get back and have a better boat." I gave Bill an imploring glance but the devil was grinning.

" But we want to go with you now . . . unless you really don't want us."

" Of course I want you . . . but I'd want you to enjoy the voyage. You don't understand. I'm going out to make friends with a lot of rough men. Outlaws. Live with them. Get drunk with them."

" I'm awfully good at taming wild men." She cast a glance at her husband who promptly subsided into his chair, convulsed with mirth. It was plain I had to fight my battle single-handed.

I played my trump card. " All right. We'll leave it open till to-morrow morning. Come and look at my boat then and if you still want to go I'll take you." The old *Poinciana* wouldn't let me down, I knew. One look at the interior of that scow would scare any woman off.

When they arrived on the dock next morning I took them into the cabin which barely gave standing room to three fair-sized people. Ruth looked around and sniffed audibly at the odour of bilge . . . nothing subtle about the *Poinciana*, she fairly heaved her smell at you. Then Ruth gulped several times so that I could see the Adam's apple move up and down her throat.

Striking while the iron was hot I opened the door which led into the tiny engine compartment aft. Dark. I turned a flashlight inside. A lake of greasy bilge swayed and lapped oilily with the rocking of the boat as we moved about. On its viscous surface cockroaches floated.

Ruth moved back hurriedly and stood with her nose close to the mosquito gauze skylight.

"Where do we sleep?" she asked.

I pointed to the lids of the lockers on either side of the cabin. Six feet long and two feet wide they were. No upholstery on them. Plain wood.

"You two will have to share one. I'll take the other."

"Why can't we sleep on deck?"

"Those Lostman River mosquitoes would just about pick you up and carry you away."

"Surely one of us could sleep on the floor?"

"Of course. But when she rolls at night that bilge will ooze up through the deck-boards."

She shuddered and I felt that my battle was won. But little I knew the lady. She turned to her husband.

"Ralph. Our pneumatic mattress will just about fit the locker. The two of us can squeeze in somehow."

They turned to go. "We leave at noon sharp on Wednesday," I reminded them. "If you're not here by then I'll know you've changed your minds. You've got to dress up like vagabonds too if you come. Bond Street clothes will spoil everything."

Well before the appointed hour on Wednesday my guests arrived. I had donned ragged old khaki clothes myself . . . the same which I had worn when prospecting with Gable. But they had me outvagabonded. Utterly disreputable. None of the Heddlestons could ever say that the crew of the *Poinciana* were toffs. Ruth seemed to have selected her wardrobe from the old clothes-bag, while Ralph sported a Homburg hat with a grouse feather in it, a ragged khaki shirt, a torn pair of tennis flannels and a hefty pair of mountaineering boots whose caulked soles quickly liquidated any air of respectability which poor old

Poinciana's newly laid deck might have boasted. On his back was a *ruksak*.

We did try to sleep on deck that night but the mosquitoes soon drove us below to our narrow locker tops.

There was a stiff breeze blowing next morning when I started the engine and began to thread a narrow waterway which led to the open reaches of the Bay of Florida. Calm it was in that twisting passage but the tall tops of the mangroves on either side were bending and clashing. When I spun the helm hard over for the final sharp bend of the channel the open waters of the bay seemed to leap towards us. Foam-flecked waves raced to break on the bar almost under the boat's fore-foot. Straight into it I headed . . . nothing else to do . . . not even time to shout a warning to my two passengers peacefully sleeping below. I braced my bare feet on the deck and gripped the wheel as a great grey comber reared wickedly under our bows like a snake about to strike. Crash. We took it over the fore-deck and a flood of water swept us half-way to my knees. Crash, once more. We were across the bar now and into the smother of choppy seas beyond. Gripping the wheel I peered down into our home. The bilge had sprung from its hiding-place on the keel and invaded the cabin, swollen by the water we had taken aboard. Black, foul and greasy. Fore and aft the viscous mass slid with the wild pitching of the boat. Ankle deep. Wallowing in it with horror-struck faces were two scantily clad forms . . . pitched clear from innocent slumber into that obscene liquid without a moment's warning. Only a glance I took because the *Poinciana* needed all my attention. Unsinkable, I believe she would have weathered a hurricane, given sufficient sea room, but she was pitching so heavily that I should have been shot overboard had I not clung tightly to the wheel. Rapidly I changed my course to get under the lee of a long mangrove-clad island. With the seas now abeam she changed her pace from pitch to roll . . . how that tub could roll ! From the clatter which rose to me from the cabin every-thing out of the lockers seemed to be shifting ground. Then the companion door opened and a bedraggled female form crawled feebly on deck, bilge-soaked night-clothes tucked into dilapidated riding breeches. On her stomach she wriggled slowly to the side and remained contemplating the wonders of the deep, holding by one hand tight to my ankle to save being rolled overboard . . . the *Poinciana* did not boast a railing. Another glance I gave below. A forlorn female shoe—once dainty—floated disconsolate. In one corner a manly form in smeared and dripping pyjamas held tightly to his bosom the sooty oil-stove on which I hoped some time to have our breakfast cooked.

CHAPTER IV

THE TAMING OF THE HEDDLESTONS

THE Gulf of Mexico was like a sheet of rose-pink glass as the sun rose over the mangroves which fringed the Lostman River. The mist-wreaths mingled with my pipe smoke as I dangled my bare feet over the side of the portly *Poinciana* . . . painted a garish yellow she was, with her name picked out in black . . . about as much in keeping with the quiet beauty of that scene as a chorus girl at the King of England's garden party. Below was silence. I had left my guests asleep . . . our two previous anchorages had been choppy and the outer sleeper seemed to me to have spent most of those nights in climbing back into bed after the *Poinciana* had rolled him out of it. Low tide. The piles of the fish-house to which we were moored were encrusted to the high-water mark with small oysters and barnacles.

Somewhere in the dark line of mangroves the engine of a motor-boat exploded, chattering like a machine-gun in action, after the first few hesitating bursts. Then another and another from different points along the shore. The Heddlestons had finished their night's mullet fishing and were bringing their haul to the fish-house. One after another the ghost-like shapes of their white launches slipped towards us through the mist-wreaths which the sunrise waters were breathing.

Jamie came first. At several hundred yards range I distinguished his stocky figure, standing up and peering under his hand at the gaudy apparition which he could not know had taken sixty hours to round the Florida peninsula . . . twice the time of an average boat. When he finally recognised me he bent double with laughter.

" Knowed you'd be back sometime," he remarked as he made his launch fast to a pile. " Seen your eye when that tarpon jumped up-river that time I guided you."

" Got fed up with the city."

"Don't blame you none. Them tourists done got Miami spoiled."

Meantime his expert eye was roving over the corpulent lines of my boat, over my bare feet and the frayed ends of the khaki slacks I had resurrected for the voyage. His innate delicacy must have prevented him from commenting on my ragged attire for he returned to the boat.

"P-O-I-N-C-I-A-N-A," he spelled out haltingly. "Queer name for a boat."

"Name of a tree."

"Sure is. The one with the red flowers. How come you named it that?"

"It's pretty near the same colour."

"Sure is, but most boats is painted white. Is she your'n?"

"Yes. Bought her."

"Brought her in to the fish-house at night too. We all heerd a strange motor outside last night. Couldn't 'magine who it could be. Looks to me like that *Poinciana* boat would roll awful in a sea." Hoisting himself alongside of me he drummed his heels against the metal side of the boat.

The other launches were arriving now. Jamie introduced me to their owners as "Cap'n Rainier" . . . my dubious feat of navigation had apparently stamped me as a boat-master in his esteem.

There was Winton, the great black-bearded giant whom Bill and I had seen standing by his cabin on our first trip and whose Indian mother peeped out through his coal-black, beady eyes. Lean in the flank and broad in the shoulder was Winton. With his bearded face and rangy build he reminded me of a Boer of the elder generation. Three brothers there were. Jamie, Winton and Dicon. "Pa" Heddleston was their father. With their wives and children, divers cousins and in-laws, they made up the Heddleston clan to which had attached themselves several "wanted" fugitives from justice from other parts of the country.

Dicon Heddleston was as large as Winton or Jamie. Jamie's breadth and Winton's "Greek God" build seemed to have combined in Dicon's burly figure. Huge and blond. More than one wife had the old man had in those earlier, wilder days, at the close of the Civil War, when he had wandered southward into the Florida wilderness.

"Get them goldarned mullet up, Jimmy," cried Jamie to a gangling youth who had accompanied him. But hardly had he spoken when I saw his mouth open as though in consternation. Staring behind me, he was. When I turned my head I saw a tousled head looking out of the door of the cabin. Ruth, curious to know whose were the voices which had awakened her.

Jamie was on his feet in a moment, pulling his fore-lock in best nautical style—I seldom saw him wearing a hat and seldom wore one myself during the years I spent in Florida.

"Goramity, Cap'n. Whyn't you tell me you done got your wife down below. Here've I bin swearin' like all get out and a lady listenin' all unbeknownst." He was evidently framing an apology to the lady when her head disappeared.

I explained who the lady was. Jamie was about to say something when the stutter of another approaching motor-launch claimed his attention. He barely vouchsafed the launch a glance . . . knew the owner at once by the sound of the motor. The sound of that launch changed the genial tone of the gathering just as a sudden lie thrown across the table changes a friendly group of card-players to a circle of potential enemies . . . tense and watchful. Jamie's face hardened . . . became grim . . . as though a mask had dropped over the smiling friendly features of a moment before. Young Jimmy's face paled and his lips compressed. Winton and Dicon moved silently and swiftly to their launches and dipped their hands into the lockers where I knew their rifles reposed.

Jamie watched the approaching launch under beetling brows. He seemed to be weighing some course of action in his mind. Then I saw the light of resolution in his eyes. He shook his head slightly at his brothers, who removed their hands quietly from the lockers, although they left the locker lids open and stood by, obviously keyed to a high pitch of alertness.

The oncoming launch slid smoothly to the other side of the fish-house, and nuzzled a shell-encrusted pile while its occupant moored it with quick, jerky movements of his hands. A short, active-looking man whose square jaw was ill concealed by a bristle of stubbly black beard. On his hip swung a heavy revolver, the only short gun I ever saw carried on the Lostman River as the rifle was the weapon the Heddlestons loved, carried out of sight in the lockers of the boats from which they were seldom separated by more than a few yards. As the newcomer waited for the fish basket to be lowered he swept the obviously hostile clan with a defiant glance, then turned his back on them contemptuously while he scooped silvery mullet into the basket. Watson, it was, I surmised. It could be no one else. Watson, the killer of the young school teacher whose death the Key West sheriff had described. I remembered too that the sheriff had foretold that Jamie would see the crime avenged. But none of the Heddlestons made a move. For at least fifteen minutes Watson worked within a few yards of his enemies, seeming to disregard them entirely. Then, his fish loaded, he received without a word the tally slip which the fish-house keeper lowered to him, spun his motor, swept his launch in a defiant curve and headed shoreward. Not until he had disappeared into a narrow bayou among the mangroves did the tension of the Heddlestons relax. Then their hands moved away from the lockers and the eyes of each one turned on Jamie.

"What fur no?" queried Winton. "It wur a chance, Jamie. Nary a better will we get from him."

Jamie frowned in reply and jerked his head slightly in my direction. Then he rose from his sitting posture beside me on the deck, sprang into his launch and left without another word. In quick succession the white launches sped shoreward behind their leader.

There was a smell of coffee and frying bacon emanating from the cabin, so I went below. Ruth handed me a plateful which she scraped from the frying-pan which sizzled appetisingly on the little oil-stove.

"Are those your wild men?" she queried. "I never saw friendlier people in my life."

"You almost saw a shooting, or would have almost seen one if you'd been on deck." I told them of the silent aftermath to my meeting with the clan. "They'll take some taming," I added.

"But they wanted to shoot Watson, not you. They seemed to like you."

"They like me all right as a drifter, but the rub will come when they find out we're going to push in a crowd of workmen here to drain and develop the place under their feet."

Past Onion Key we slid and into one of the upper lakes—

Jamie called them "Bays." Two miles across it was, or there-abouts. Two miles of blue mirror across the face of which white cloud shapes drifted, duplicated from the Gulf Stream clouds which glided overhead. The borders of the mirror were an apparently unbroken line of mangroves topped by the high leafy heads of cabbage palms.

"Where are we going to-day?" asked Ruth, surveying rue-fully the rapidly fraying knees of the dilapidated pair of riding breeches she had been wearing ever since leaving Miami three weeks before.

"I ain't agoin' to tell you yet, Ma'am." Jamie's face was alight with the pleasant anticipation of a child about to surprise its elders with an unexpected treat.

Straight at the farther shore he held his course. Nearer and nearer it approached without disclosing the slightest sign of an opening which might lead further into this network of lakes and waterways where a city-bred man could wander for weeks without finding his way out. That was how the Lostman River got its name, according to the Heddlestons. Generations before, soon after "Pa" Heddleston had arrived, some unknown stranger brought a boat through the entrance from the Gulf. Weeks after "Pa" found the boat in a far-back bayou. The man was never found.

A flight of white cranes took wing from the shallows as we approached the shore. A pair of ducks scuttered across the water and alighted behind us. Jamie cut his motor down as we slid silently to the wall of green, leaped to the bows and checked the way of the launch by catching an overhanging limb.

"'Fraid you'll have to lie down, Ma'am, while the rest on us manhandles her through," he cautioned. Then, to the rest of us: "Don't break no branches to mark the passage. This here's my private hole. Mine and my boy Jimmy's. Even my brothers ain't found it yet. 'Pa' may know it though. Ain't no waters round the Lostman River strange to him."

For probably a couple of hundred yards we heaved and tugged at branches, mangrove roots, dead and decaying semi-submerged trees and anything else that gave a hand-hold. At times the waterway was so narrow that we had to literally force the slim launch through the matted obstructions, but after a while we saw bright daylight ahead and a minute later were floating on the placid surface of a long, narrow strip of water. A couple of hundred yards wide and a mile long I judged it. Fringed with cabbage palms which raised their heads above a sea of saw-grass . . . we were in the everglades proper now, having just penetrated through the last of the mangrove belt which fringes the coast. After we had cleared the fallen leaves and twigs from the bottom of the boat Jamie stood erect.

"Cabbage Bay, I calls it." He surveyed it proudly. "The Seminoles that lives in the 'glades knows it, I suppose. Ain't nothin' about this country they don't know. But Jimmy and me, we're the only white folks what ever sot eyes on it . . . 'less it be 'Pa.' You, Ma'am, you're the fust white woman what ever seen it and there's the purtiest fishin' here you ever did see."

The boat drifted in silence. Then from the shore came a crashing crackling sound, like the branch of a tree being torn off by the wind, only there was no wind. The day was still.

Jamie smiled, almost the proud smile of a father showing off his child. "That's b'ar. An ole b'ar done climbed up a cabbage palm and ripped out the heart with his paw for breakfast."

White egrets sailed above the cabbage palms. A 'gator slipped easily into the water from a mud-bank and periscoped his way across, only his protruding eye-shades visible, a faint wake behind him. Peace. Unutterable. Unspoilt. Truly this was the last frontier of the United States as Bill had said, and there was nothing else in the United States like it . . . or elsewhere as far as my experience went. Then and there I registered a mental vow that this bit of Paradise would remain unspoiled if I could keep it so. When I returned to Miami I began a campaign to dedicate this section of the everglades to the nation as a national park. The seed I planted fell on barren soil for a time . . . people were too busy making money in Miami during the boom to worry about anything but the price of lots. The seed remained, however. Later it germinated . . . when normal conditions once more reigned and the fever of gambling had died for the moment. That section of the Florida ever-glades is a National Park now and if it should ever be my fortune to see Cabbage Bay once more I shall find it as I first saw it on that unforgettable day . . . unspoiled.

Jamie rummaged in a locker, produced and jointed a rod

with a reel like a miniature windlass and carefully knotted a silver spoon. Then we trolled, slowly. Dead slow. The gentle purring of the engine seemed to blend with the silence.

" S-K-R-E-E-E-E-E," the rod almost leaped from my hands as the line streaked out. A hundred feet behind us a great silver shape leaped high from the water, turned end over end and crashed in a fountain of spray. I was on to him. The thrill of a new sport ran through my veins. Never had I fished for sport since I angled for cat-fish in the Natal streams as a boy. My fishing hitherto had been for the pot . . . a damned empty pot too, sometimes. But this was a sport—comparable to stalking big-game on the veld—this playing of a big-game fish with a slender line that looked to me no thicker than a silken thread. Over an hour I worked on him under Jamie's direction—almost tearful at times, he became, when my incompetence endangered the capture of the monster—till I brought him within range of Jamie's gaff. One hundred and forty pounds he weighed on the fish-house scale. One hundred and forty pounds of shining silver enjoyment.

The others seemed to lapse into a dreamy state on our way back to the *Poinciana* from Cabbage Bay, but as we slid smoothly over the still water I was busy debating in my mind the proper time for me to have a showdown with the Heddlestons and reveal to them my true status of part-owner of the land and waters on which they lived. The situation was ripe now, I felt. They liked me. The object of my sojourn among them had been to win their confidence and I felt that I had done so. Even the scowling Dicon had ceased to scowl at me—stories of big-game hunting in Africa had broken down his resistance to a stranger, for Dicon spent much of his time hunting in the ever-glades and was a famous shot. Winton already treated me like a member of the clan, even to the extent of showing me the primitive still where he distilled the fierce corn liquor which the clan loved. Although they handled dozens of cargoes per annum of the finest foreign liquors, the Heddlestons seldom drank any but their own fiery vintage, fresh from the still. " Pa " Heddleston approved of me, I felt. One day he had emerged from the fastnesses in which he lived alone like some old bull driven from the herd . . . I believe he had been literally driven out some years before over a family argument and Jamie had assumed command thereafter, but the old man still seemed on quite friendly terms with the rest of his numerous family. Well into his " eighties," " Pa " was tanned by the sun to a dark walnut colour. Dark brown skin, white hair and moustache. He had rowed a skiff seven miles the day he came to see us in the *Poinciana* and refused with scorn our offer of a lift back. Ruth had entertained him with tea which he had obviously drunk only as a social duty and he had sat for the rest of his stay, saying little, elbows on knees, gnarled brown hands steady and devoid of any nervous movement, dark eyes roaming restlessly over every item in the little cabin. When he left he gave us an invitation to visit him in his cabin on Plate Creek.

" Why is it called Plate Creek ? " asked Ruth.

" Well, I done lost my plate in it when fust I come here. Plates was hard to come by in them days. Every time I ate my victuals without my plate I'd mind me of the creek where I lost it, so it got to be Plate Creek in my mind."

Jamie. Well Jamie and I were already friends.

I was still debating as to how and where to break the news to the clan when I saw a 'gator swimming parallel with our course. Two hundred yards away he was, I calculated. Just his little eye-knobs showing. A sporting shot. While beside me, glistening on its rack in the open locker lay Jamie's rifle, and it occurred to me that I had not fired a single shot at game with a rifle since I left Africa seven years before.

" Lend me your rifle for a shot, Jamie." As I took the weapon from him my fingers were itching for the feel of the stock.

My first shot was over. I had over-estimated the range. Carefully I timed the second while Jamie held the boat to a straight course. At my second shot the 'gator gave one convulsive writhe and floated motionless, white belly upward.

" Gorramighty . . . dog my cats ! " Jamie looked at me with startled eyes as he swung his launch from its course to pick up the kill.

I was almost as startled as Jamie. A reasonably good shot, I am. Could hardly help being that considering the amount of shooting I have done. But to hit a moving mark the size of a tennis ball from a moving launch ! It was the kind of shot a marksman dreams of and succeeds in pulling off only once or twice in a lifetime . . . unbelievable luck that I should pull it off just at this time, when I wanted my prestige to be at its highest. Only a small 'gator, about six feet long, but my shot had hit the base of one of his periscopic eye-lids and lifted his brain-pan clean off.

Before Jamie spoke again he watched in silence as I cleaned his rifle carefully and returned it to its rack in the locker. " Cap'n, dogged if that warn't the best shot I seen on Lostman River. There ain't but one man among us mought equal it. That's Dicon . . . an' I bet he couldn't do it often. If you'd sculped that 'gator first go off I'd 'a thought it wur a fluke. But you missed your first one and cal'lated the second one just right."

" I bet I couldn't do it again in a hundred tries, Jamie." That was true enough. So true that I never again used a rifle when the Heddlestons were around . . . having acquired a high reputation by a lucky shot I didn't want to lose it. That lucky shot decided me. I would break my news to the clan the very next day. Never would their psychological reactions be more favourable than after Jamie had done telling them the story of that shot.

But my plans were due for interruption although I did not connect young Jimmy with them when I saw him waiting at the fish-house as we reached the *Poinciana* just before sunset. He beckoned his father aside and they conferred together for a moment in a low tone. I saw Jamie's smiling face assume the same grim lines as when he had restrained his brothers from shooting Watson a few weeks before. " Chukaluskee . . . tell the others," I caught the disjointed phrases in what appeared to be a discussion of moment.

In his preoccupation Jamie spun the motor of his launch and was about to leave us without a word, but I sprang into his boat just as he was to throw in the clutch and get under way.

" Jamie, I want to talk some business with you and your brothers to-morrow."

The hard granite of his face seemed to soften with a conscious effort as he replied, " Sorry, Cap'n. Not to-morrow. We got a bit of business on to-morrow that jus' can't wait. At Chuk-aluskee tradin store it is."

It was two days before I met Jamie and his brothers on Wood Key where Jamie lived—a delightful little island, the most southerly of the Ten Thousand Island group which littered the

Florida shore of the Gulf of Mexico between the Lostman River and the Baron River, thirty miles to the northward. It was in Jamie's rough timber cottage that I found them waiting for me. There were several women about. Jamie's wife and in-laws. A horde of barefooted children scuttled underfoot. One of the women brought a bottle and tin mugs. As she was pouring for us a baby began to cry from what looked like a pile of old clothes in another corner of the room. The woman set down our bottle hurriedly, took one of the drinks she had already poured and fed it in sips to the child as a more conventional mother would feed a yearling child milk. The little devil's face puckered but it took its liquor manfully, turned over and went to sleep . . . no wonder . . . the product of Winton's still was potent enough to make a Highlander drunk.

"Is that good for children, Jamie ? " I asked.

"Dogged if I know, Cap'n. The women gives it to them an' it keeps them quiet. Good corn liquor never hurt no one."

"I've got something to tell you people. The business I spoke about." I was feeling nervous now the crisis had been reached. My future and that of my partners would depend very largely on how I handled my cards during the next hour or two.

At a glance from Jamie the women disappeared and took the children with them. The three Heddleston brothers sat on a wooden bench facing me across the table. Even Jamie looked formidable to me now as he sat with his elbows on the table and his hands rumpling his sun-bleached mop of hair. Winton was sitting upright stroking his black beard with long regular sweeps of his hand. Dicon sat hunched up . . . scowling.

As briefly as possible I explained the situation to them. We had bought the ten-thousand-acre tract through which the Lostman River ran and intended to develop it. I went into some detail.

The three exchanged glances. "Figgered it mought be somethin' like that," remarked Jamie, laying his huge paws on the table before him. " We bin certain all along you and your friends wasn't drifters. We done talked it over, the three of us, and figgered you'd be puttin' your cards on the table when you got ready."

"I wanted to get acquainted before we talked about it."

"We figgered that way. You was right, too. We'd take

more from you now than we would from a stranger. You've kinder fitted in."

But Dicon jumped to his feet, his great fists clenched. "Dog-goned if I'll see a lot o' furriners in these swamps. It'll be shoot on sight fur's I'm concerned."

"If shoot's the word I can shoot as well as the next." I turned hot. Dicon always had the faculty of making me bristle. "But there's no call to shoot unless you want to. What I'm going to do will be the best thing that ever happened to all of you."

Jamie frowned at his brother. "Go easy on the shoot talk. The Cap'n's a shootin' man same as we are. There's been 'nough shootin' round here for a bit, anyway." I had the impression that all the tenseness in the atmosphere was not due to the business in hand. I had felt it before I broached my business to them. They were worried by something apart from the news I had just broken.

"Just what do you aim to do when you talk about developin'?" Jamie turned to me, his face puckered with thought. Winton was twisting the end of his beard into tangles and Dicon still scowled although he had subsided into his seat.

"We're going to dig canals round that prairie you and I walked on near Onion Key . . . to keep the water out of it. Then, when we've got the land dry we'll cut it up into lots and sell it. Some of the people that buy the lots will come here to live. A town will start. It means prosperity for you. A market for everything you can produce. The original squatters round Miami are rich men now."

Jamie scratched his blond head with a fixed grin . . . a way he had when perplexed. "What about the land we live on? It ain't much by city standards but we done worked hard to fight the forest for it."

"What kind of legal title have you got?"

"That's the reef we're goin' to wreck on, looks like. We ain't got no title. Bin fightin' for a title these years past, but them Key West lawyers is just money sharks."

"I can easily fix that for you."

"How?" His voice was eager.

"If you have no title the land is mine. My partners and I have clear title to the whole tract without reservations. I'll give you a free title deed to all the land you are using now and as much more surrounding it as you can reasonably expect to cultivate in the future." The few score acres these people would want were a cheap price to pay for their good-will. We had plenty of land.

"You say you'll give," sneered Dicon.

I opened a bundle of papers I had prepared and tossed them across the table. "There are the deeds . . . they only need the boundaries filling in. I'll fill them in and sign them now . . . as soon as we've come to an agreement."

Winton reached for the papers and began to scrutinise them. He was the best educated of the three.

"What-all do you want us to do?" asked Jamie.

"Leave my people alone. In return for your promise to live in peace with us you'll get clear title to your land."

Winton laid the papers down on the table. He nodded in reply to the silent query of his brothers. He had approved the documents evidently.

"We got more stake here than land," he remarked.

"What else that wouldn't automatically go with the land?"

"There's my still. Bin runnin' good liquor since 'Pa' done turned it over to me. Wouldn't want no revenuers snoopin' round my still."

"I don't give a damn about your still. I'm no revenue officer."

"But if furriners come here to live they'll want protection. Police."

"That's years ahead yet. You'll be so rich by that time you won't bother about your still. But I am going to appoint a deputy sheriff in the meantime, to keep order while I have workmen in here."

Once more Dicon was on his feet. "Deputy sheriff . . . hell. I don't give a God-damn what Jamie says. I'll shoot the fust son-of-a-bitching deputy I sees . . . run the bastards off."

"You won't run my deputy off."

"Like hell I won't."

"Bet you a dozen out of the next cargo you run that you won't."

"I'll run him off or plant him."

Jamie intervened. "Them deputies is no good, Cap'n. All

they does anywhere is make trouble. They gets good men in bad with the law for shootin' them."

"The one I appoint won't bother you. I guarantee that."

"Is it someone we know?"

"Yes." I stepped forward and pinned the nickel plated shield on Jamie's shirt front.

He glanced at it down his nose, then pulled forward his shirt front to better examine it.

"You're it, Jamie."

He cast a swift glance at his brothers. Their mouths were open. Wordless.

"Will you take the job on? Only I warn you that Dicon is going to run you out or plant you."

Jamie rubbed the shield with his finger-tip as though to assure himself that it really was there. "Dog my cats, Cap'n. Where'n hell did you steal this . . . this bit of joolry?"

"The Key West sheriff gave it to me to pin on the deputy I should appoint."

"Goramighty!" Jamie still squinted down at the shield. "The sheriff'd have a conniption if he knowed who you'd pinned it on."

All three laughed uproariously. "Bet you he'd never sign my appointment," added Jamie.

"I bet he would."

"Dogged if I don't take the job on if you can get him to sign it." Jamie thought he had me in a hole and his face lit up accordingly.

I took the appointment from my pocket, unfolded it and handed it to my new deputy sheriff after filling in his name.

Jamie's face flushed as he read it through carefully—he examined the signature thoroughly first, then read the rest of the short printed form, his lips moving as he spelt out each word laboriously like a child conning a school lesson. His brothers, reading over his shoulder, burst into roars of laughter at his discomfiture. Jamie joined their mirth after he had finished. I thought my battle was won. But they sobered simultaneously as though a thought had struck them all at the same moment. Their faces grew grave. They exchanged glances.

Jamie leaned back on the bench and gazed for a moment at his feet under the table. "Can't do it, Cap'n." I could hear his horny feet shuffle on the rough board floor. "Hate to go back on my word but there's somethin' we'd forgotten. Call me a liar if you want to and I won't fight."

"What's the difficulty?"

Jamie glanced at his brothers and remained eyeing them from the corner of his eyes.

"Tell him," suggested Winton. "He'll hear it sometime, anyway."

Jamie turned his head to me, his hands clenched on the table.

"Well, Cap'n. There was a bit o' trouble yesterday at Chukaluskee."

"What's that got to do with it?"

"Ole Man Watson done got hisself killed."

"Who killed him?"

"All on us."

"Tell me what happened."

"You seen Jimmy waitin' for me when we come back that day you shot the 'gator. Well, Jimmy tells me Watson is goin' to Chukaluskee next day ... found it out, he did, from one of Watson's kids. We all been waitin' for Watson to go there to fix him for killin' the young school teacher ... you done heard 'bout that I suppose?"

I nodded.

"Well ... we fixed him."

"Killed him?"

"Dead as that 'gator you shot."

"Who did it?"

"All on us."

"How many?"

"Twelve on us was there."

I evidently looked my surprise.

Jamie frowned. "I know what you're thinkin', Cap'n. One to one is all right for a hot killin'. But this wur cold. None on us was scairt of Watson. If we'd 'a been hot any one on us three could 'a taken him on easy. But this wur punishment ... we ain't plumb lawless in here even if we does keep the Key West sheriff's deputies out. Yes. There was twelve on us waiting in the Chukaluskee tradin' store. Watson seen his time was come soon as he cleared the door and he goes for that short gun he totes. We all fired at once and all on us hit him

. . . except young Jimmy and his gun missed fire. Then we put Watson in his launch and towed it to Rabbit Key . . . that bit of an island with a white beach, way out in the Gulf. Buried him on the beach and sunk the launch." The narrator unpinned the sheriff's shield from his chest and laid it on the table where his fingers continued to toy with it as though reluctant to let it go.

" Did Watson fire ? "

" We'd 'a been fools to let him."

" Then he never had a chance ? "

" Neither did the school teacher."

" Watson's killing is none of my business, but the Key West sheriff is bound to hear of it." I was cursing that killing just the same. It had upset my plans just when they seemed to be going favourably.

" We ain't worrying none about the Key West sheriff. He dasn't send deputies in here to take the lot of us." Dicon's voice was like the growl of a beast and his scowl once more hung heavy across his brows.

" But he'll have to this time or else the federal authorities will take the matter up. You may be able to scare deputy sheriffs off but Uncle Sam's soldiers will be another matter." I was racking my brain for a solution. To bring workmen and settlers into the Lostman River I must have some official protection. It was unthinkable to try and plant any outside law-enforcer on these wild people. Jamie himself was the one man in the world who could control the Lostman River country. Unless I could get Jamie for my deputy sheriff job my plans would flop.

" There's been killin's before in here and nothin' happened," remarked Winton quietly, stroking his beard.

" But this is different. It's one thing for a man to disappear quietly in the swamps. It's quite another to have him riddled in a public place. Chukaluskee store is a post office too, you know."

" We know that," admitted Jamie gravely. " That's why I got to turn this deputy business down. It'd 'a tickled me kind-of to take it on, but being deputy sheriff will make this Watson business harder on me."

Suddenly I saw light . . . a blinding flash.

"Read the date on that appointment of yours, Jamie."

He scrutinized the document again. "Dogged if it ain't a month old."

"You've been a deputy sheriff for a month. You took the others to Chukaluskee to assist you in arresting Watson. Watson went for his gun . . . resisted arrest . . . so you shot him. That let's everybody out . . . including the sheriff."

Their jaws dropped. Then they rocked on their seats with Gargantuan mirth. Somehow a bottle appeared. Four tin mugs miraculously filled themselves to the brim and we drank the fiery stuff. Choking with combined alcohol and mirth Jamie stuttered. "But the sheriff . . . he may not see it like you does."

"Don't worry about the sheriff. I'll see him on my way back to Miami and get things fixed up."

From the sheriff's remarks about Watson last time I had seen him I didn't anticipate any trouble on his part and I was willing to bet that he would approve my choice of a deputy sheriff.

CHAPTER V

AN AMPHIBIOUS SURVEY

THE accurate survey of such a vast country as the United States is a colossal undertaking. Uncle Sam's surveyors —technical descendants of George Washington who was a surveyor by profession—had made a rattling good job of dividing the country into square miles with a monument at each corner, but they hadn't quite finished it, as I found when it was time to begin the survey of our property. To legalise the townsite in which we proposed to sell lots it was necessary to file in the county record office of Key West an official map— " plat " is the technical term. In order to make it acceptable this plat had to be " tied in " by survey to two Government monuments in two different directions. Somewhat to my consternation, when I examined the old government survey records, I found that the nearest government monument to the northward was about forty-five miles away . . . forty-five swampy miles too, across the everglades. In the 'nineties, when the survey had been made, the government surveyors had apparently worked down the west coast of the Florida peninsula, southward, to the edge of the almost impenetrable everglades and there stopped. Those old surveyors had compiled a log, in shipshape form, of which the pertinent paragraph read about as follows— " Discontinued survey as land to the southward too swampy to set up instruments and was not worth surveying anyway. Furthermore no stones were available for monuments. Our last monument was a wooden post marked . . . Also marked three witness trees to facilitate location . . . an oak, an ash and an elm." Then it gave the distance and bearing of each tree from the monument.

This was a problem. That monument would have to be located and a survey made from it to some fixed point in our property. But the wooden post which constituted the monument would surely have rotted and disappeared in the thirty years since it was erected. There remained the trees as the only clue to the monument's location. Those trees must be found. Three trees with hatchet-cut gashes on their boles. Three trees out of the thousands that might be growing in the vicinity. An oak, an ash and an elm. That puzzled me because none of those varieties grew so far south. Then I evolved a theory about the trees. I could easily visualise a hard-bitten party of northern surveyors gradually, month by month as they took their sights and recorded their figures, working their way southward through a strange tropical vegetation. Month by month their familiar northern trees would have been gradually replaced by queer exotic growths. Then, finally, hatchet in hand, standing before the last three trees they had to mark before they returned to their cooler northern homes.

" What the hell kind of a tree would you call that now ? " one of them might have queried as he stood before a mangrove growing on its stilts or the buttressed trunk of a swamp cypress.

" How in God's name would I know ? " would be the reply. " Let's call the blasted thing an elm and get to hell out of here before these cursed mosquitoes eat us alive."

Yet to make our survey of the property legal we must find those trees forty-five miles across the swamps to the northward. We must also find a second government monument which apparently lay thirty miles east of us. That would complete our " tie in " and put us on the map. This latter monument had been erected by a second party of government surveyors at about the same time as the other, a party which had worked down the east coast of the Florida peninsula to the end of it and then turned westward with a view to meeting the first party, but they too had bumped against the " saw-grass hell " of the everglades and stopped. I did not anticipate much trouble in finding their monument as it must be situated on the edge of settled territory, for that part of Florida was inhabited right up to the edge of the swamps. Some local native would soon show us where the monument stood.

All these details should be borne in mind because the fact that the two government parties never met and thus never had a chance to correct an error which might have accumulated in their work was the cause of our being faced later with an extraordinary predicament.

I began to organise a survey party and to look for an experienced leader for it. As luck would have it, Sabe just then walked into my office in Miami unexpectedly, as though in answer to some unspoken prayer . . . tall, grim and looking every drop of his dour " State of Maine " Puritan blood. Sabe had been superintendent of our Moshannon mine in the days when Bill and I had been powers in the coal business of the country. Better still, before he came to work for us he had been a surveyor for one of the big railway companies.

I put our survey problem up to him at once.

Reaching into his breast pocket he extracted a cigar of unbelievable blackness, clamped it into his anvil-like jaw, lit it with a stinking sulphur match and puffed a cloud of evil-smelling smoke that caused my elegant secretary to look up from her typewriter and cough pointedly.

" Maybe we'd better smoke outside," he suggested, with a glance at the offended lady.

I laughed. " She's about got used to my pipe. She'll get used to those filthy weeds of yours in time."

His eyes twinkled although the hard lines of his jaw showed no relaxation. " That sounds like you were going to offer me a job."

" I'm offering you this one if you think you can handle it."

" Never seen a survey job that beat me yet. There's nothing you can't survey on the earth's surface as long as you've got something steady to set your ' gun ' on."

" That's the trouble. Uncle Sam's surveyors would have finished the job if the land had been solid enough to set their instruments on. The country's neither land nor water. The blasted stuff's all mixed. You can neither swim nor walk."

With a mobile twist of his lips he shot his cigar from one side of his mouth to the other and cocked it jauntily upwards. " When do we start ? "

" Soon as we can get a crew and equipment together."

" Got the beginnings of a crew already."

" Who are they ? "

" Baldy Troop and Art Bender."

" How come ? "

" Well, after you left Moshannon . . . or the Moshannon left you "—there was the suspicion of a grin now—" we all stayed on although we didn't like the new owners much. Then a while back we heard you had a job of work on here in Florida. We waited a bit for you to send for us. Then when you didn't send we came to have a look-see and maybe give you a reminder."

" Would more of the old crowd come if I sent for them ? "

" Dad-burned right they would. A telegram would bring them running."

I was relieved at that . . . flattered too. On Poinciana we'd need at least a hundred workmen . . . two hundred more likely . . . before we were through with our development.

That afternoon I ran Sabe down Biscayne Bay in the *Poinciana* for a breather.

" For Land's Sake ! What kind of a tree do you call that ? " He was gazing in astonishment at a mangrove which stood high on its stilts above tide-level.

" A mangrove."

" Many like that where we're going ? "

" Millions."

Then Sabe chuckled. A rusty, mirthless sound, which it took strong emotion to produce from him.

" What's the joke ? "

He removed his cigar and held it between his fingers. " You remember old Jack McKechnie that used to run our clearing gang on the Moshannon . . . the old coot that used to brag about how quick he could down a three-foot pine ? "

" Yes."

" Well, I was just picturing old Jack's expression if we ever set him up against a tree like that and told him to cut the legs off it."

About a week later we left for the Lostman River with a survey crew, equipment and several portable houses of the tropical mosquito-proof variety with which we proposed to establish a bee camp on our property from which to run the survey. We had chartered a small sailing schooner for transportation. The *Isabel*. Ted Collins was the owner's name and the schooner was his home. Up and down the coasts of Florida he plied for a living, getting cargoes where he could. Precarious his living must have been, and my six months charter was probably a windfall. Ted was a good man. He gave us first class service and once—much later—he showed great bravery in trying to warn us of danger. For some time the *Isabel* was to be our only link between the Lostman River and our Miami head office.

Ted's wife was his crew—the schooner was named after her. A pleasant young couple they were. Normal, except for one kink in Ted's make-up. His religion. Both he and his wife belonged to some obscure sect—something like an off-shoot of the Seventh Day Adventists it sounded to my uninitiated mind. Like most people who suffer from an overdose of religion Ted was burning to pass some of it on and soon made an attempt to proselytise me.

Laughingly I shook my head. " That sort of thing's not much in my line, Ted. The only religion I've got is to do the best I can with whatever job of work I've got in hand."

" But it's your only chance."

" Chance of what ? "

" Salvation. Only those who believe will be saved."

" What will happen to the rest of us ? "

" Hell-fire. I like you and want to save you from that."

" Do you really believe that everyone but your own particular brand of religion will roast in hell ? "

" Absolutely."

" How many are there in your sect ? "

" Only twenty-three believers as yet."

I shook my head again. " Heaven would be too sparsely populated for even me at that rate."

It took us three days of softly-fanning trade-winds to get to the Lostman River under sail. There was only one tiny cabin in the ship so the crowd of us passengers slept on deck. When Ted hoisted the anchor at daybreak we all tailed on and helped him hoist the big mainsail . . . all but Baldy Troop whom we discovered, after we had made all fast, sleeping among a pile of stores in the scupper. A roll with the foot sent Baldy overboard, pyjamas and all, to wake in the tepid blue waters of Barnes Sound. His bald head emerged, blowing like a grampus, with a horror-struck look on his round moon face. Then someone pitched him a rope's end and we hauled him aboard.

Baldy was a mechanic by trade and I had engaged him to care for the engines of the fleet of small boats I could envisage as forming the transportation of our future working parties.

Baldy was unique in my experience. Always the butt of every camp he lived in and always seeming to be happy about it, his ever-smiling face fronted a very keen intelligence and his slightly bulbous figure concealed a very loyal heart.

Art Bender was a young college-trained engineer who, early in the history of our northern coal developments, had attached himself as a sort of *aide-de-camp* to Sabe and had followed him from job to job as the course of our progress dictated. Blond and effervescent was Art—a proper foil for Sabe's dour New England character.

On Onion Key we established our base camp and prepared for our plunge into the everglades to make the " traverse " which would connect our property with the Government beacon up north . . . when we found it. Our first step was to build a fleet of light flat-bottomed skiffs out of the timber we had brought with us. Shallow draft and light enough to be dragged overland when necessary. Next we drove an iron stake firmly into the soil of Onion Key. This was our starting-point. Our traverse would connect this stake with the monument to the northward. Another traverse would connect the stake with the easterly monument. The iron stake would then be accurately and legally located on the map of Florida and the detailed survey of our property could be based on it.

Our survey began at daybreak one morning, a long line of loaded skiffs being poled up-river. Just before we turned a bend, and so got out of sight of our stake on Onion Key, we cut piles from the forest, drove them down to solid rock below the mud and nailed a platform on the top of them. The platform was made out of the boards we carried with us in our skiffs and on it we set the instrument for our first sight. From the second platform we would sight back on the first. And so on through the everglades till we made the last sight of all on the monument we were bound to find.

I remember seeing in a geography book when at school an illustration of the everglades which used to fascinate me. Great trees arched over gloomy-looking stagnant pools on the edges of which reposed somnolent alligators. Panthers crouched among thick underbrush and fearsome serpents of unbelievable dimensions festooned themselves from twining creepers overhead. But the real 'glades aren't a bit like that. Vast flat plains.

Six to twelve feet of black muck soil . . . rich once drained. On top of the black ooze is six inches or so of tepid, sun-warmed water. In crossing the 'glades you sink each step from knee to waist deep, depending on your skill as a swamp-walker. Over all is the saw-grass. Thick it grows to the height of a tall man, each blade edge a row of almost invisible saw-teeth which cuts a hand to the bone if your grip is insecure when trying to pull yourself clear of the mud of some narrow, sluggish bayou where you are quite liable to have stepped on a hibernating alligator, squirming beneath your feet and making your impulse to reach the bank dynamic and overwhelming. Here and there in this saw-grass sea rise little islands covered with low timber. "Hammocks" the natives call them. Their inhabitants are scorpions, rattlesnakes and mosquitoes . . . myriads of mosquitoes. Bears live on them also and an occasional panther, although none of those we perforce visited boasted of such congenial inhabitants.

Day by day we forced our passage northward, poling, wading and sweating under the Florida sun as we stood waist deep in ooze to build the platforms upon the solidity of which would depend the accuracy of our survey. Two miles a day when the going was bad, double that if we were lucky enough to strike a few solid hammocks on our line and so obviate the necessity of building platforms. But the nights were the worst. Our skiffs were eight feet long and three feet wide, but in them we had to sleep unless we had found a hammock within reasonable distance. Even on the hammocks the nights were bad enough, God knows. To fight off the mosquitoes we plastered our arms and faces with mud and huddled in the lee of green brushwood fires.

One night we found a hammock already occupied by a family of Seminole Indians. The copper-faced, hawk-nosed brave in a multi-coloured pleated skirt stalked over to where we were settling in. Surveyed us impassively.

"Wi-no-na?" he queried with a suspicion of eagerness. Whisky.

When I explained by signs that we had no whisky he turned his back on us and stalked back to his side of the hammock where a squaw, bulky in numberless petticoats of the same cloth as her husband's skirt, and a couple of papooses were grilling some boney-looking fish over a fire. They paid no more attention to us . . . not once did I catch them glancing our way. At daybreak in the morning they left silently in a narrow dugout canoe.

For food we ate the tinned stuff we had brought with us and we drank swamp water for lack of better. Filthy, tepid stuff, but it didn't seem to hurt us. When we could we took it from the sluggish moving bayous rather than from among the saw-grass stems . . . it seemed to taste a little less of decayed vegetable matter where the water was moving.

More than two weeks elapsed before we noticed the lowering of the water level among the saw-grass. Where it had been calf-deep it now barely covered our ankles. The ground, too, was firmer under foot. One day we *cached* our skiffs and splashed through the last few miles of swamp to the edge of solid ground beyond, where the Government surveyors of thirty years before had stopped their survey and turned back. That night we set up our instrument on dry land and took the elevation of Polaris. Luckily the night was clear and we got an excellent sight of the north star as he made his nightly circle round the polar ice-cap—God ! how we could have done with some of that ice that was going to waste up there. Our observation told us that we were almost exactly on the latitude of the last monument . . . the one we sought. Somewhere either east or west of us it lay, within a mile or two. For two days we searched and then we found what we had set out to find . . . three trees on which were blaze marks, faintly visible under the moss and lichen which clothed the boles. Our quest was ended. Lucky that the three trees stood apart from others, isolated on a lonely hammock and visible from afar or else we might have been searching yet.

" They look as much like an oak, an ash and an elm as they do like wheat-sheaves," I remarked to Sabe as we stood, bedraggled and filthy, before them. Mangrove, swamp cypress and bog-myrtle were the trees.

He scratched his head and wrinkled the several weeks' growth on his face. " What would you expect a white man to call them ? I'd maybe have called them the same, likely as not, if you hadn't taught me the names of lots like them on the way here. One tree grows on stilts, one has buttocks and the third is no tree at all. If those old coots hadn't put familiar names on their survey log their boss up north might have sent them back to check up . . . they didn't want that, not if they felt like I do."

Our homeward journey was a holiday by comparison because our platforms were all built and our skiffs riding light, mostly empty. We checked each sight as we returned and found no errors. Three days it took us. When we broke at last from the saw-grass hell in which we had been submerged for nearly three weeks and glided out into the clear waters of the Lostman River we gasped. So good it looked. A burnished mirror in which the mangrove fringes eternally admired their dark green heads. Calm after the stormy seas of the endless saw-grass waves and the infernal rustling of their stems in the breeze. Like frogs off a lotus leaf we dived in. One splash after another. Clothes and all. Not till we had washed the mud of the everglades from us did we climb back into our skiffs and pole forward to Onion Key and the camp which we had left Baldy and a couple of helpers preparing.

It was a comparatively simple matter to tie in with the other survey. This done, we had now connected the two independent surveys of east and west Florida. When we projected the length of our own surveys from the respective Government monuments they should have reached the same point. But they didn't. To our dismay, when we plotted them on paper, we found a gap between them. In technical terms a *hiatus* had developed . . . surveyors, like men of other professions, are not above disguising their errors with high-flown language.

" What does she amount to, Sabe ? " we were poring over the big drawing table in the canvas house we had erected as a drawing office.

The black cigar in his mouth rolled from side to side wildly. " I've met some *hiatuses* in my time, but this is the grandfather of all of them."

" How much ? " The gap between the ends of the two lines looked unbelievably wide to me.

He scaled the distance off carefully. " Three miles and a bit." The cigar glowed violently and a puff of evil-smelling smoke enveloped both of us.

" Great God, man! You must have made a mistake in plotting."

" Christ ! " Sabe seldom swore. " I've checked and double-checked the plotting. I'll swear there's no error like that in our survey, either. We were too dad-burned careful."

But there it was. Either we had been three miles out in our survey—a hundred yards or so I might have admitted, but not three miles—or the Government survey was wrong, one or both of them. That must be it, I was willing to swear. Those two Government survey parties had started hundreds of miles to the northward and crept down the peninsula independently of one another. Somewhere a cumulative error had crept into their calculations. A foot or two to the mile would be enough to account for the three miles—a tiny error become cumulative means a big one. That was the cause . . . I knew it just as surely as if I had checked their figures and found the mistake. The result was that to the western half of the Florida peninsula was added a strip of land about three miles wide and thirty miles long. That land did not exist officially. Nobody owned it. The state of Florida was that number of square miles larger since we made our survey. It was a head-scratcher. I took the problem across to Miami and laid it before my partners.

" The gap cuts through our land so that part of it must be ours. We'll cut it up into lots and sell it." Patrick Untel ruffled his red hair. As sales manager his mind ran on selling lots. The lots in our Poinciana townsite were selling like hot cakes under his direction.

But his brother Amos leaned back in his chair and pressed his finger-tips together—he always reminded me of President Wilson when he took that attitude. " I don't like it," he pronounced. " May make a flaw in our title."

" Lie low and say nothing about it," Bill crossed his slender legs and his face set in the sanctimonious lines which usually presaged some daring raid on the fellow pirate craft of the sea of business.

Amos shook his head judicially. " Can't be done. Some day some sharpshooter would get hold of the story and blackmail us. He'd threaten to invalidate our title because our survey didn't agree with the official one. We'd be in a pretty pickle then with thousands of lots sold. We'd either have to let him hold us up or we'd have lot purchasers suing us by the score for selling land we didn't own."

I had had longer to consider the problem than the others during the sunshiny days of my voyage back from the Lostman River, so I voiced my opinion boldly. " Why not file a claim against the State of Florida for the whole *hiatus* ? "

My three partners glanced sharply at me. The Untels in surprise. But Bill slapped his hand against his thigh. He knew better my processes of thought than the others. He'd known me longer.

" We'd never get it," objected Amos, swivelling his chair towards me.

" Of course we wouldn't. But the State of Florida would immediately check our survey to see whether the error was ours. If we are right and the *hiatus* really exists they'll change their maps to conform with ours and our title will remain legal. If the error is ours, on the other hand, we'll change our maps accordingly and they'll have corrected our survey for us. Our title will still be all right."

" Why don't we check our survey first ourselves ? " suggested Patrick.

" Nothing doing as far as I'm concerned," I exploded. " I've wallowed in everglades mud for the last few weeks and I've hardly got the saw-grass seed out of my ears yet."

Bill left a few days later for Tallahassee, the state capital, to file his claim. The business turned out about as I had expected. The State checked our survey—I did not envy the surveyors, having had some myself—and found it reasonably correct. The error was in the old Government survey and the *hiatus* really did exist, but the State of Florida had no intention of giving away a large tract of land for that reason. They declared the strip in question to exist just north of our own tract so that our development should not be divided by someone else's land. This was all we hoped for really and our title remained sound. So at least that month of hardship had accomplished something for our business. Besides, I felt like a minor creator. I had caused land and water to exist where none had been before. Furthermore I had completed the survey of the United States of America. Left my name on it too, because, when the time came to make a detailed survey of our property it fell to me to name the topographical features. On the plat that I filed appear the names of lakes . . . Lake Rainier is there, to match the mountain in the State of Washington which was named after my great-great-grand-uncle, the Admiral, by the explorer Vancouver. Lake Margaret and Lake Ruth are there too. So are Plate Creek, where " Pa " Heddleston lost his plate and Onion Key where he planted onions and all the other local names which the Heddlestons had given. So they appear on the plat and they are the official names which can only be changed by act of legislation.

CHAPTER VI

ALLIGATORS, SHARKS AND A SCHOOLMARM

NOW that our tract of land was legally and precisely located on the map, we could begin its development without the fear that someone might lay claim to it. Rows of portable canvas houses began to grow like rectangular mushrooms on Onion Key. Gangs of northern workmen began to cut long swathes through the mangrove forest, while survey parties sighted through instruments and drove in pegs—in the mysterious way survey parties have—marking the course of drainage canals and streets.

For myself I worked out a schedule of one day a week in the Miami office to keep in touch with my partners and the business side of the development. The rest of the time I would spend in Poinciana development, or travelling to and from it.

One of the first things necessary was to buy a faster boat than the old tortoise of a *Poinciana*, well as she had served her purpose. I now relegated her to the weekly mail service of the camp. With Baldy at the helm she travelled once a week over the blue gulf waters, skirting the mangrove-clad Ten Thousand Islands, to the little wooden-built town of Everglades thirty miles up the coast, the nearest point on that side of the peninsula where one encountered civilisation.

I consulted Jamie about boats. Seated on the gunwale of his launch I found him, whittling horn from the soles of his bare feet with a sheath knife.

Jamie considered the question. "Last time I wur in Miami on business . . ." I surmised that the business had to do with payment for a cargo run. I had a suspicion that Jamie still engaged in the nefarious trade of rum-running in spite of the shiny tin badge he wore proudly, pinned to the bosom of his ragged shirt front. But I didn't care how many cargoes he ran. He was keeping the Lostman River country quiet. That was enough for me.

"Last time I wur in Miami I saw a boat for sale."

"What like, Jamie?"

"Cabin cruiser. Got an injin in her the size of a sea-cow. Fitted like a yacht, she is, with state-room and galley. Dogged if she ain't got a privy that does things when you pull a string. Sixty-footer and timbers sound as a bell."

"How fast?"

He twisted up a foot with one hand and pruned carefully at a callous under the joint of his big toe. "That's why they're sellin' her," he admitted. "They built her double-ended . . . starn sharp as her bows. When they opens up that doggoned great injin she just squats on her behind and paws the air like with her bow. Reckon they don't get ten knots out'n her, for all the six hundred horsepower they put in her. But if I had her I'd make her do twenty or better."

"How would you do that?"

"Put skid-boards on her."

"Put what?"

"Boards on either side her starn. Aquaplanes they calls them. Bring her starn up out of the water when she gets up speed. Gor'amighty! how that cruiser would travel fixed up like that."

"Will you put them on for me if I buy her?"

He shook his head as he slipped his knife back into its sheath, his pruning job now completed. "Ain't got the tools. But there's a man in Miami that'll do a good job for you." He told me his name.

So I acquired the *Corsair* and I never regretted it, except for a fleeting moment each month when the petrol bill came in . . . six hundred horses harnessed to a heavy boat do eat petrol. Twenty-four knots per hour she logged on a trial run after her boards were fitted. Comfortable and seaworthy too.

Miami, by now, was fuller than ever with northerners come to invest in building property. The numerous development companies were asking such fantastic prices that they drove into our fold those prospective purchasers whose capital could not stand the strain of three thousand dollars for a building lot on a back street or ten thousand dollars for a corner in a suburban development. For our part we were selling lots at about one-tenth of the price asked by our competitors . . . we could afford to do so because we had bought our land so cheaply.

It was about this time that I got the opportunity of buying, at a comparatively low price, a newly built house in Coral Gables. I closed with the offer. The rent we had been paying for our tiny apartment was outrageous and this represented the first chance of getting clear of the burden. We moved into our new home at once and I set out to make the best deal I could with our landlord about the apartment we had vacated. I expected to drop a bit of cash in dealing with him . . . any man who will jump his rent four hundred per cent. at once is a hard man to deal with. But things went by contrary in the Miami of those days. The landlord was obviously overjoyed when I hinted tactfully that I might consider getting out of my contract. His pleasure was so obvious that—mindful of our previous dealings—I became hard-boiled and managed to screw him up to the point of returning me my last month's rent if I would call the contract off . . . a deal that left me two hundred dollars the richer instead of considerably poorer as I had expected to be. It seemed he had another tenant ready to move in.

"What's that poor devil paying you?" I asked him after we had torn the contract up.

He winked usuriously. "Never you mind. I'm getting it while the getting's good and you'd better do the same. This pace can't last much longer."

I was inclined to agree with him. The race to buy Florida building lots had acquired such a pace and prices had gone so high that it could not last long. But in the meantime our business was prospering exceedingly. Only a few more months, at the rate we were selling, would see us with the land paid for, a sufficient sum in hand to complete the development and a good cash profit for ourselves as well. Once we had reached that point the boom could crash when it liked as far as I was concerned. The land we should own around our townsite would steadily increase in value as time went on and constitute our profit. But, on the other hand, if the boom crashed before we reached the safety-point we should lose all reward for our efforts. Our project would die.

By this time on the Lostman River we had acquired quite a fleet of small power launches for the use of the working parties. No walking to work through feet of ooze until the place was drained and the ooze became rich black soil capable of producing several crops a year. The engines of the launches were Baldy's responsibility. His shiny dome bent over a work-bench was usually the first thing I noticed in our camp at Onion Key as I cut the roar of the *Corsair's* six hundred horses to a contented purr and eased her gently to her berth alongside one of our numerous small jetties.

Like most places—however pleasant—the Lostman River country was not perfect. If you caught all the mosquitoes in Africa and loosed them in the restricted area of southern Florida I believe that the native variety would still far outnumber them, during the summer months at least. I have seen my bare forearm literally black with them . . . then bright red with blood as I wiped my hand down it. At times I wondered whether they wouldn't drive our purchasers away when the time came for them to occupy the lots for which they had paid us in advance.

But Jamie reassured me when I mentioned my doubts to him. " Gor'amighty, Cap'n. Don't let them skeeters worrit you. A bit o' drainage and some clearing will fix them little bastards. Miami wur every bit as bad as this in the old days . . . not so long since, neither. Why I mind me laying on my bunk in a bit of a schooner I used to own in the Miami River. The skeeters wur that black on the ceiling I couldn't see the boards."

Nevertheless, the mosquitoes constituted a problem. Half a dozen of our survey parties were working in the forest and a surveyor can hardly be expected to do accurate work if mosquitoes are boring into his eyes, nose and ears while he is squinting through his instrument. My first anti-mosquito measure was to buy a supply of citronella which everyone said would keep mosquitoes away. However, the Lostman River variety of mosquitoes refused to conform to the popular theory. They seemed to love citronella. My men in the swamps swore that the mosquito swarms redoubled at the first whiff of it. My next experiment was more successful. I tried oil of tar, a black, viscous, evil-smelling liquid which looked somewhat like the tar itself. My men didn't like smearing their faces with it at first, but they became enthusiastic when they found that the mosquitoes hated it. From then on each workman in the field carried in his shirt pocket a small bottle of oil of tar. Black as niggers they looked when they had used it. It was Baldy's job to see that all bottles were replenished every night after the crews returned to camp. Being a wag, Baldy once chose to replenish the bottles with the black asphalt paint one uses to stick tar-paper on to roofs. The asphalt dried and refused to be washed off. Until it finally wore off the camp looked like a darkey labour battalion. Baldy got a ducking for his pains, clothes and all, at the hands of a half-laughing, half-enraged mob of black-faces.

Baldy was always getting into trouble . . . he was that kind. As I have already mentioned he ran the mail-boat to Everglades. One day he came back twenty-four hours late from his trip, just as I was beginning to organise a search crew for him.

"What the hell happened to you?" I asked.

"I ran aground," was his explanation. It was easy enough to run on to a sand-bar on that treacherous coast. We all did it. I should have thought no more of the business but Baldy evidently had more to say. He stood looking at me sheepishly, sweat breaking out and standing in dewdrops on his bald head.

"I'd like to get off that Everglades run," he got out at last.

"What for? Don't you like Everglades?"

"I like Everglades all right, but there's some there that don't like me."

I laughed. "What's her name, Baldy?" His amorous propensities were well known.

It seemed that on his weekly visits to the settlement he had become acquainted—intimately acquainted—with a young married woman there and had developed the habit of taking her for a spin in the *Poinciana* while her husband was at work. On this last occasion he had had the misfortune to run aground and stay there twenty-four hours before he could get the old scow afloat. He had found the husband sitting on the door-step on their return and explanations had apparently been embarrassing.

"Was she worth it, Baldy?"

"So far she was, but if you send me back there she'll come too high."

We changed our mail-carrier.

But Baldy's amours are a digression.

Once I noticed a member of a survey party carrying an empty nail keg as he ploughed his heavy way through the swamps.

"What do you want to clutter yourself up with that for?" I asked.

"Well, this belongs to the gang and it's my turn to carry it to-day."

"What for?" I could see that the keg had neither top nor bottom.

"If you tuck your shirt tight round the top when you take your pants down you can do it in comfort without the mosquitoes feeding on your behind."

Over a hundred men now lived on Onion Key. A cook and several flunkeys ministered to their appetites and dumped the kitchen garbage into the river where the tide swept it away. The local colony of 'gators soon learned of this and took up their quarters among the over-hanging mangroves on the opposite bank. When the garbage was dumped there would be a race for the choicest morsels. One of the 'gators finally became civilised enough to swim over at a whistle and take a ham-bone from your hand. "Archibald" we christened him, and it became a favourite Sunday diversion to lasso Archibald, drag him ashore and put a tape measure on him to see whether he had grown. Archibald didn't seem to mind and was always ready for a tussle with the rope the following Sunday. The Florida alligator appeared to be pretty harmless, although I had an instinctive dread of them . . . they looked too much like their deadly cousin, the African crocodile, for my liking.

I opened a trading store in Poinciana, mostly for the convenience of the Heddlestons. It saved them a twenty-mile run up the Gulf to Chukaluskee whenever they wanted to buy a bit of baccy or any other of the few luxuries they used. One day Chief Tigertail of the Seminole tribe came in to trade . . . stately in his multi-coloured petticoat, standing erect in a dugout canoe barely wide enough to accommodate his feet side by side.

He strode up to me and shook hands.

"Wi-no-na?"

I shook my head. "We don't sell whisky."

"Ugh." He grunted his disappointment. However, I persuaded him into the store and made him a present of some cheap mirrors and a length or two of cloth. After that he and his people often came to trade. They would bring 'gator skins, fish or wild turkey and take tobacco and knick-knacks.

There were about four hundred wild Seminoles in the swamps —the unconquered remnant of the once powerful Seminole nation which had fought the United States Government in the 'nineties. At that time the main body of the nation had surrendered and been transported half a continent away to waste land in Oklahoma where I had lately seen them, rich on oil royalties and addicted to driving their families about in hearses and expensive cars. Tigertail headed the unconquered remnant which still regarded itself as being at war with the United States —technically they were right, I suppose, as they had never surrendered. At any rate they displayed no animosity to white men of any kind. But they had their pride. Some time before my arrival in Florida the Government had created, to avoid white encroachment, a Seminole reserve comprising that part of the everglades where Tigertail's people had their hunting grounds. As soon as Tigertail heard of it he moved his people off and lived elsewhere. "No favours from the enemy" seemed to be his motto. Tigertail's remnant was rapidly being depleted. The fleshpots of civilisation were drawing members of the tribe away to join the band of Seminole hangers-on at Miami and pose for photos to tourists for a living.

When our last payment to Abelson, the Jew, was due I made a point of taking the cheque to him myself and held him to his promise to visit the property with me. My motive was admittedly vindictiveness, as I didn't anticipate any pleasure from several days of close association with him. But I wanted to make him pay for those remarks of his about "having got all our money" when Bill and I had paid him the first instalment of our debt. I stocked the ice-box for our voyage with pork.

We started early and had breakfast as the *Corsair* roared down Biscayne Bay. Abelson rubbed his hands with anticipatory gusto when I brought to the cockpit a savoury smelling platter—he had relieved me at the wheel while I cooked.

But his face fell when I took the lid off and revealed a mess of ham and eggs. "God! How good it smells," he remarked wistfully. But he shook his head when I began to heap a plate for him.

"Why not?" I pried my face into the semblance of concern.

"I am Jew. Orthodox."

"Good God! I'm sorry."

"Perhaps you have something else?"

"Sausages . . . but they're pork too. So are pork chops."

" Nothing else ? "

" Eggs and bread."

He smiled cheerfully and breakfasted on poached eggs on toast. He lunched on poached eggs and toast with almost the same cheer. Such a game sport he seemed that my heart misgave me for punishing him . . . I consoled myself with the thought that we should be in camp by dinner-time. But, as luck would have it —it was a genuine accident, I swear it—by careless handling I ran the boat aground on a shoal in the Bay of Florida and we stayed there for twenty-four hours before I could get her floated off . . . for some reason I do not understand there was practically no tide in the Bay of Florida at any time I navigated it. Both bread and eggs ran out and my guest supported himself altogether on hope while I ate the rations for both of us. But he did dine well on arrival.

My opinion of him had risen during the voyage, but he remained completely uninterested in what we were doing with the wilderness which we had bought from him. To him land was a counter in the business game . . . something to make a profit out of, the same as stocks and shares. Once his profit was taken the land ceased to exist as far as he was concerned, even though thousands might benefit from its development.

About this time our son was born. We called him Peter William after his father—Peter was a family name which the eldest born son had carried for many generations, ever since the last de Regnier had left France after St. Bartholomew's Eve one short jump ahead of his Catholic pursuers and changed his too-French-sounding surname to the still older but more English-sounding one of Rainier. Our son was the first child born in Doctor Tallman's newly opened maternity home in Coral Gables, and the Doctor made him a present of a five-dollar gold piece as a souvenir. As I first looked at him in his mother's arms I hoped he would be lucky enough to break free from Suburbia and to experience as big a share of the fullness of life as his father.

I was continually worried with misgivings about our business in spite of the phenomenal success it had shown up till now. It seemed to me that the Florida real estate boom was already passing its zenith and would crash before we had accumulated sufficient funds to complete our development. But my partners did not agree with me. The three of them were unanimous in giving the boom several more months before it would end. With many misgivings I bowed to their more experienced business judgment, although my own reaction was to accept one of the several attractive offers we received to purchase our business as a going concern . . . offers which would have left us with a substantial return for the effort we had expended. When our views diverged my partners tactfully pointed out that the business end of our affairs was their concern, while my responsibility ended with the development and engineering department, so I carried on with it, hoping that they were right and that the sales department would continue to raise enough money to cover the large expenditures which the reclamation of swamp land entails.

A good life it was in Poinciana, meanwhile. Sport in plenty. Fishing for sharks at high tide was one of them. The tide rips in the narrow entrance to the Lostman River from the Gulf was the place for that. A big hook coupled to a stout rope by a yard or two of chain was the tackle. Once hooked the shark would travel like blazes for a mile or so, towing a light skiff at a high rate of speed. Then he would turn sulky and the run was over. Exciting. I imagine one got all of the excitement of holding a wild buffalo by the tail without the risk and exertion. The first time I tried it I got defeated. At first all went splendidly. I hooked my shark and got towed well out into the Gulf, the light skiff sliding over the ripples like an aquaplane. Then the shark stopped and I hauled my skiff towards him, being the lighter vessel the skiff moved instead of the shark. Right up to his ugly nose till his rough skin grated on the side of the skiff. Then stalemate. I had neglected to bring anything more lethal than a pocket-knife with which to kill the shark. There was no question of hauling the shark aboard. He wouldn't have fitted in that small skiff, anyway, and if the shark had come aboard I should have jumped overboard and swum for it . . . I wanted no live sharks as fellow-passenger. I looked at the shark frustratedly. The shark regarded me malevolently out of his little eyes and gave a warning switch of his tail which rocked the frail skiff violently. Hurriedly I cut the rope and made the shark a present of a piece of pork, which he had swallowed already, a hook and several feet of good chain. After that I carried a hatchet with me with which to kill the shark and cut the hook free.

Seeking variety, I once tried the same kind of tackle on an alligator, but the 'gator didn't know the rules of the game. As soon as he felt the bite of the hook he rolled over and over in the water, winding up my rope as though he were a windlass. Within half a minute of hooking him I was cooling my rope-burned palms in the water while a well-corseted 'gator was splashing his way furiously ashore.

We had our own wireless transmitting station too, for communication with our Miami office. At the Miami end we made a contract with an amateur operator to tune in for us every evening so that I could communicate with my partners. Our wireless was also a source of news, although broadcasting the spoken word was a science still in adolescence and far from being as perfect as it has since become. We got our news in code from ships mostly, sitting in the canvas house with Sparks, while he translated the gossip of ships' captains, thousands of miles apart and hundreds of miles away.

Old Man Watson's demise from lead poisoning had rid the Heddleston clan of the most virulent of those unrelated outlaws who had taken sanctuary in the Lostman River swamps, protected by the resentment to intrusion by authority on the part of the Heddlestons. But a few minor undesirables still clung to the Heddleston coat-tails and were tolerated by them so long as they did not interfere in clan affairs. One of these was a poisonous little man with the puritanic label of Jonathan Barr. A comparative newcomer to the Lostman River, he had squatted on some land just north of our boundary, set up a still and made a living by selling liquor to Tigertail's Seminoles. It was when he began to sell his rot-gut to my workmen that Barr and I clashed. First I warned him. At his second offence I forbade him to set foot on our property. At his third I sent young Jimmy Heddleston with a message to the effect that I would have him hog-tied and delivered to the Key West sheriff if he caused me any further trouble.

It was only a few days later that I was standing on one of our jetties. As I was on the point of stepping into a launch to inspect one of our working parties I heard the beat of an unfamiliar engine coming up-river. A few minutes later Barr moored his boat loosely to the jetty on which I was standing and walked truculently up to me, a shot-gun held in the crook of his arm.

"You're the bastard that's going to run me off, aren't you?" His swarthy brows beetled over shifty little eyes and his mouth worked nervously.

"I'm going to throw you off the property as I said I would." I didn't like the look of that shot-gun, but he was still too far off from me to do anything about it.

"Let's see you try it, you . . ."

All the time he was speaking he was coming closer, shifting his gun into his hand and cocking it ostentatiously . . . the click of those hammers being cocked sounded as loud to me as the trumpet on Judgment Day. Ratlike the man's face looked, with stained teeth showing.

When he shifted his hold on the weapon the end of the barrel came within reach. I grabbed it promptly and turned it away from the line of my body. All the time I had been looking at that confounded gun the holes at the ends of the barrels had been growing larger and larger. Now, with a jerk, I snatched the weapon from his feeble grasp and threw it into the river. Then I felt better. Next I caught Barr and threw him after the gun. After that I untied his painter and set his boat drifting up-river on the incoming tide. It was laughable . . . after it was over. The man had the impulse to be dangerous but lacked the technique. Ludicrous he looked, swimming after his boat.

Even as I watched him came the roar of a wide-open engine from downstream. Jamie's launch swept round the bend, reversed opposite me and kept its place against the current.

"Seen anythin' of Barr, Cap'n?" Jamie's face looked grim, just the expression it had worn that day when Old Man Watson had flaunted defiance at the clan beside the fish-house.

"Yes."

"Gor'amighty. He come up-river filled up with his own corn liquor and swearing to blow your guts out with his scatter-gun. Where is the bastard?"

I pointed upstream to where Barr was slowly overhauling his boat.

"Dog my cats." Jamie calmly depressed the rifle-barrel of some zealous relative who was drawing a bead on the swimming man. "How come he got in the water?"

"I threw him in."

The occupants of the launch gazed at one another. Then they exploded into a roar of laughter.

Jamie straightened himself, tears still in his eyes. "Doggone it, Cap'n, but I like you. If you and me was ever to get into a fight and I had to kill you I'd be sorry because I'd still like you."

The Heddlestons caught Barr just as he was clambering into his boat, towed him down-river and sent him chugging out into the Gulf, free to land anywhere he wanted except, on pain of instant dissolution, in clan territory. Outlawed.

During one of the summer months—June I think it was—a curious phenomenon appeared along the Lostman River, lasted a few weeks and disappeared till the same time the following year. Flies. Not the harmless-appearing little fellow who washes his face peacefully on the windowpane—although these mammoths of the species were built on the same lines as the common house-fly, but larger. So large that one just fitted neatly into a "Lion" match-box. In fact, the combination of fly and match-box conceived in the nefarious mind of Baldy a scheme. Placing a live fly in a match-box he made it into a neat parcel and addressed it to Sabe's wife in far-away New England, marking it "A present from Florida." From all accounts the fly arrived safely and full of energy. I could imagine the commotion in the speckless New England household where an ordinary house-fly would be cause for a chase until it were killed. Baldy's present, buzzing round the room like a demented aeroplane, must have caused enough excitement to feed the village gossip for a month.

For a while we had a school in Poinciana—this was later, after Ruth and Ralph had come to live with us there because the famous Florida hurricane had so damaged their home in Coral Gables. Ruth volunteered as school teacher and Jamie undertook to make the younger generation attend. Twenty-three of school age there were. The eldest pupil was a buxom wench of twenty years or so, nursing a baby. The youngest was about six. All were in the same class . . . the lowest. Due to the late Watson's difference with the previous school teacher the Lostman River children were illiterate, to say the least.

At Ruth's request I once inspected the school soon after it opened. With Art Bender to keep me company I stopped my launch at the little wooden building we had erected on the river-bank. Moored nearby were half a dozen launches in which as many families had come to school.

Ruth began on history. "Now, children, tell me who discovered America?"

There was silence in the class. Vacant stares. Pupils suddenly discovered things of great interest in their desks. The eldest pupil fished out a very meaty-looking bosom and began to nurse her child although the child appeared to me quite happy.

At last a hand shot up.

Ruth looked relieved. "Well, Johnny?"

"Jesus Christ." The child's voice was triumphant.

Ruth gulped twice and swiftly changed the subject to geography.

"Tell me the capital of the United States?" Ruth's eyes pleaded.

This time there was no hesitation. Several pupils jumped to their feet and the eldest hurriedly pushed her dairy under cover and tucked her baby under one arm with a view to following suit. There was a unanimous cry of "Chukaluskee."

Poor devils. That tiny trading-post was the nearest approach to civilisation they had ever seen.

But Ruth was a good teacher and her class really began to make progress before very long. Her main difficulty was to keep them from fighting during break. No ordinary school fights were these, with a ring formed and rules observed. When the Heddlestons fought they did so with a purpose, to maim or kill the enemy with the utmost expedition, regardless of rules. Any argument was apt to turn in a few seconds to a biting, gouging mass of children as each family would immediately spring to the support of any brother or sister who was attacked. If you fetched one clear of the scrum by pulling on his leg he was liable to come to the surface with his teeth locked in some opponent's calf. There was complete equality of sex in these affrays. The girls gave and took as much as the boys and asked no quarter.

It was a girl who was the cause of the school's final closing. Dicon's fourteen-year-old daughter. She smuggled her father's rifle into her launch and tried to pay off a grudge by sniping her enemy through the schoolroom window after excusing herself for a moment from class. It was nearly a tragedy. At the moment Ruth was explaining something at the blackboard to the intended victim. The bullet passed between them. After that I closed the school down permanently as I didn't want a second school teacher buried on the property.

CHAPTER VII

TOWING A DREDGE ACROSS THE GULF OF MEXICO

TO drain our land we should need canals and to dig canals a dredge. That had been foreseen early in our scheme for the Poinciana development and a dredge had been ordered from a northern manufacturer : of the dipper type. A conglomeration of heavy machinery floating on a wooden hull with a dipper of two cubic yards capacity which would tear its way through mangrove roots and swing three tons of muck clear of the canal cut at every one-minute cycle of its work. The acquiring of this dredge would have been quite simple in the ordinary course of events. The machinery would have been shipped by rail to Florida and the hull built there. But there was no such thing as an ordinary course of events during the Florida boom. Such was the onrush of northern people and their belongings to Florida that the state's only two railway systems became swamped with goods which it was beyond their capacity to transport. Snowed under. Timber, building material and all kinds of freight piled their goods yards high. Congestion. Frantically they set about double-tracking their single lines which meandered southward through the pine groves, but in the meantime, to avoid being completely swamped with business they had no hope of handling, they declared an embargo and would accept no more freight for Florida destinations. So, when the time came to ship our machinery, the manufacturers wired that no railway would deliver it in Florida.

I took what seemed the next best alternative. Build the dredge in a neighbouring state and deliver it from there by water. So the machinery was shipped to Mobile, Alabama. When the dredge and its attendant barge were afloat I would charter a tug to tow it to the Lostman River, a matter of six hundred miles or so. In charge of the dredge erection I put a man named Sam Shooter. A good dredge man, but his great defect was a fiendish temper. Sam was hard on hats. When annoyed about some trifle he would dash his hat to the ground and dance on it.

When the dredge and barge were ready to be towed Sam sent me a telegram to that effect.

I replied :

CHARTER TUG AND COME DOWN WITH TOW. ADVISE PROGRESS.

There was a week's silence. Then :

NO TUG AVAILABLE.

Unbelievable. On all that busy Gulf coast, comprising such ports as Galveston, New Orleans and Pensacola, that no tug should be available for a tow. We needed that dredge desperately as the date when she had been scheduled to begin digging had long since past.

I wired :

TRY AGAIN. WILL PAY EXTRA RATES IF NECESSARY.

After some days' interval Sam replied :

ONLY CHARTER AVAILABLE TWO MONTHS AHEAD.

I chucked a clean shirt and my shaving gear into a small suitcase and boarded the first northbound train.

A few days among the Gulf ports convinced me that Sam was right. There was not a tug charter to be had. Some flurry in the oil market had tied them up for months to come. This was serious for us. My partners were counting on me to carry the development through on a pre-arranged schedule and, at some considerable trouble, had accumulated quite a respectable " development fund " to cover the expense. That dredge must go south. At once. If I couldn't charter a boat to drag it down to the Lostman River I must buy one. But to buy an ocean-going tug was beyond our means and we wouldn't know what to do with her when that one tow was delivered. If we bought a boat to tow it must be one that we could use afterwards for other purposes. Like a good cabin cruiser with a heavy duty engine in her. That might do the trick and handle the tow in good weather. I could handle that kind of boat myself, and we could always do with another boat of that type in Poinciana. True, I had never handled a tow, but I could handle motor craft with the best of them by this time, and I could learn to tow as I went along. I did learn. My God! What I learned about tows between Mobile and the Lostman River!

It was in Biloxi, Mississippi, that I found the boat I wanted. A rum-runner's boat that had been confiscated by the authorities . . . a sixty-footer. Good she looked, sitting on the ways where she had just been overhauled and painted. I liked the lines of her. Her fore-foot was shaped like a duck's bosom and looked as though it would ride over any sea. Decked in all the way with a turtle back that would shed blue water. When the companion was closed she was almost hermetically sealed. You could have rolled that boat over and over without sinking her. Below decks she looked as good as above. A heavy duty Dorman engine looked as though it would run for ever . . . an honest-looking work-horse of an engine, looking like new. No name was painted on her so we called her the *Ada* after a wife Sam had just married.

I cabled to Miami for funds and bought her outright for a fraction of her real value. Sam could act as engineer while I would be skipper, but we needed a roustabout deck-hand, someone to handle tow-rope and anchor. I picked up a rat-like little man by the name of Diggles, who claimed he had worked on tows down the Florida coast and knew the inland waterways which we could use wherever possible. I wanted all the sheltered water I could get for such a top-heavy craft as a dredge. March was the month. The season of equinoctial gales. I didn't want to be caught by a blow in open water with a tow hanging to my tail.

The first day's run from Biloxi to Mobile confirmed my good opinion of the *Ada*. She handled nicely. Not fast. Ten knots was about her best, but she was sturdy and took the water as though she liked it.

The following morning at daybreak we headed out into the Gulf from Mobile River, having picked up the tow in Mobile. At the end of a two-hundred-foot hawser was the top-heavy-looking dredge, floating low in the water, her towering steel superstructure looking as high as the top-hamper of a battleship. Two hundred feet behind that was the barge, equally clumsy if not so top-heavy.

In my ignorance of the freakish disposition of towed craft I had not been wise enough to wait for slack tide on which to take my tow down the river. The full force of the ebb tide swept us seaward and I had all I could do to keep the tow-rope tight enough to maintain control over those diabolical craft behind me. First to one side and then another they careered. At times each tried to veer in a different direction. The devil himself seemed in them. Sirens shrieked and hooters blared as the river shipping scurried frantically out of our way. I heard more outspoken nautical language in that half-hour than ever before. But luck was with us. We cleared the river with no more damage than a bit of paint scraped off the barge as she endeavoured to butt —a farewell gesture—a great range beacon which towered at the river entrance.

A mild swell on the bar made the *Ada* bob a few graceful curtseys and the tow plunge wildly, a mild augury of what that tow would do if we ever struck a real sea. Then we were in blue water, grinding our way westward along the Alabama coast. Four knots an hour I calculated our speed. No wind. Towing twelve hours a day it would take us the best part of two weeks to get to the Lostman River. Two weeks ! We'd have been lucky. Times were coming when we should pull for hours against a head-wind and barely hold our own or even be dragged by the wind resistance of our clumsy tow. Once in open water I shed the coat of my best suit—the one I had been wearing when I came aboard and my sole equipment for the voyage—kicked off my shoes and took the wheel, clad only in shirt and trousers.

All that morning I watched the slow procession of white beach recede on our port side. Curve after curve. Dune after dune. A wicked coast with deep water right up to where the breakers foamed on the shelving sand. No holding-ground should we be caught by an on-shore wind.

That afternoon a revenue cutter ran alongside to look us over.

" Where the hell are you taking all that ? " queried the officer on the bridge as the long wicked-looking craft wallowed in the swell alongside of us.

" Lostman River."

" Where in the name of God is that ? "

" Thirty miles north of Cape Sable."

He whistled. " You'll be there by Christmas with a fair wind.

But you'd better make all speed you can to Pensacola. There's a blow coming from the south."

In our cabin hung a huge bunch of bananas. We shared them with the revenue boys who were out of fruit.

"If you're not in Pensacola by midnight we'll come out and look for you," was their parting shout as their propeller churned white and their craft shot forward.

When dark fell I sent Diggles in the dinghy to hoist lanterns on the tow. Still calm. But the ocean heaved, as though drawing breath for some effort. There was a long oily swell which caused the dredge to roll drunkenly. The *Ada* forged ahead steadily. All day her engine had been throbbing like the heart of a strong man.

After dark Sam came up for a breath of air and sat beside me. "How deep is it here?" He looked over the side and spat into the dark shoulders of a swell that showed for a moment in the circle of our binnacle light.

"Chart shows two hundred fathoms. Are you thinking of getting out to walk?"

He lit his pipe and flicked the lighted match overboard. "Two hundred fathoms is twelve hundred feet. Our tow-rope to the dredge is only two hundred. What would happen to the *Ada* if the dredge capsized and sunk? A hundred tons of dead weight on her stern would pull the *Ada* under."

God! I hadn't thought of that. "You're right. She'd sink like a brick unless we could cut the hawser in time."

Without a word Sam went below and returned with a hatchet, which he lashed to the wheel-post within my reach. "In case it turns bad and you have to use it." Below he went with a long glance to the southward where the starlight seemed obscured by a dark curtain.

Now a fitful breeze began from seaward. Like breaths of the sea, inhaled by the deep heaving of its bosom and now expelled. The breeze grew stronger. The line of whitecaps to port came closer—I could now hear them crashing on the beach above the beat of the engine. The breeze was blowing us inshore. I altered course a point or two to seaward and the white line of the breakers crept away.

Still stronger grew the breeze. Continuous now. The swell increased. Lightheartedly the *Ada* leaned against it, let it tilt her keel and leaned the other way. Not so the dredge. Her gantry light was swinging in an arc which startled me . . . like a drunken star.

By eleven o'clock we were having a rough time, but by then I could see a glow on the horizon far ahead which could only be the reflection of the lights of Pensacola town. That heartened me although the stars were gone. Only the lights of the tow swung wildly against the scudding cloud wrack overhead. It was not a storm. Hardly a stiff breeze, although already I was steering at a wide angle to our true course in order to keep us clear of the breakers that were pounding the beach with a clearly audible crashing. Without the tow the *Ada* would have laughed at that weather. She had my complete confidence now. I felt that I would be willing to take her out in a hurricane, although I little dreamed that I should one day have to do so. It was that dredge that worried me . . . a hundred tons of metal sinking to the bottom and dragging us down with it. I felt that I must cut loose if the weather got much worse. But I hated to do that. The dredge would be a total loss. To lose it would be letting my partners down.

Just as I was trying to arrive at a decision the companion opened and Diggles' insignificant form appeared against the glare of light from below. Not a word did he speak, but when I glanced at him I saw that his one hand had grasped the handle of the hatchet while the fingers of the other were undoing the lashing. In the dim light of the binnacle his teeth showed white like the teeth of a cornered rat. His eyes were turned towards the stout towing hawser which creaked and groaned at our feet, stretched tight by the pull of the tow. The little swine was going to cut us loose !

Holding the wheel with one hand I grabbed the hatchet with the other and threatened him with it. " I'll use it on your head next time you come on deck," I shouted. " Get below until I ring you up." I was hot with rage. One stroke with the hatchet on that tight hawser and the dredge would have been adrift with no hope of hooking on to her again in that sea in the darkness.

Diggles ducked hurriedly below.

A moment before I had been indecisive, but that little rattle-snake Diggles had stiffened my resolution. I swore to myself that I would not cut the hawser until the dredge light actually disappeared. Thereafter I steered with one eye on the compass card and the other on that wildly swinging light astern.

Slowly the weather stiffened, but the glow ahead was nearer now. Another hour or two, if we could weather them, would see us in the sheltered waters of Pensacola Bay.

Then the lights of a vessel appeared ahead, red and green, coming towards us. Soon the glare of a searchlight blinded me for a moment, then switched off. The long lean shape of the revenue cutter slid abeam of us and lay rolling fifty yards away.

" Are you all right ? " The voice from the dim figure on the bridge was the voice that had spoken to me that afternoon.

" Yes." I was all right. I knew it now. The glow of light which had indicated Pensacola beyond the horizon was above the horizon now. Something made me certain that we would reach shelter before the wind became too strong.

Then the searchlight flashed again . . . showing the dredge this time. I gulped. That cursed beam showed how wildly the dredge was wallowing, the great square wooden box of a hull dipping its edges under each incoming swell . . . the swells were beginning to wear their white caps now, racing in and out of the illuminated circle like children playing follow-my-leader.

" Hadn't you better cut loose ? " There was an anxious note in the voice this time, since its owner had looked at the dredge.

" I'll be damned if I will." Only a little longer to stick it and we should have won the fight.

" We'll stand by, then." Stand by they did, until an hour or so later I saw the two range beacons at the harbour entrance swing slowly into line. I spun the helm over. The *Ada* swerved, headed shoreward and leaped forward with the wind at last astern. Four o'clock in the morning it was when we reached smooth water that reflected the lights of the nearby town. Twenty-two solid hours I had stood at that wheel. I rung the engine down, gave the anchor sixty feet of rope and dropped it overboard. Then I staggered below and into my bunk.

It must have been about ten in the morning when I once more came on deck. There was still a stiff breeze blowing from the southward, the first thing I noted. Then I looked for the town in front of which I had anchored, but the town was not there. No land was in sight. I blinked and looked again. Far to the southward was a smoke smudge which must denote the town. We had dragged our anchor and were somewhere in the vast landlocked expanse of Pensacola Bay. When we raised the anchor it was polished silver. A glance at the chart—a more experienced mariner would have taken it before he anchored—showed sixty feet of water, the exact amount of rope I had allowed the anchor when I dropped it. Instead of gripping, the anchor had been burnishing itself on the sandy bottom as the wind drove us along. It took us a whole day to drag the tow back to Pensacola against the wind.

I called the others and we held a council of war. Inside water was what I wanted. I'd had enough towing in the open Gulf for a while.

"There's an inland passage about twenty miles farther along the coast," remarked Diggles.

I pored over the chart. "The chart doesn't show it."

But Diggles was insistent. "The chart wouldn't. It only shows the coast. We have to go inland about fifty miles up the St. Andrew's River. Then we take a canal for a long way. Finally we come down another river to the coast. It'll save us two hundred miles of open water. I know the way. Worked on a tow that went that way once."

Open water was what I wanted to avoid. That night coming into Pensacola had shown me the danger of our tow in anything like rough weather.

The following night we were well up the St. Andrew's River before we tied to a tree for the night. All the following day we travelled up it against the slight current. Suddenly, about four o'clock, Diggles waved excitedly from his position as look-out in the bows. "Starboard. Hard a-starboard. Take the narrow bayou. It'll lead us to the canal."

No time to think, as the entrance to the bayou was right under our bows. I swung the tow and headed into it. For about a mile we went. Then we grounded in soft mud. A swamp had taken the place of the narrow bayou. We were aground somewhere in the middle of the State of Florida with an ocean-going tow.

All next day we pried and heaved, waist deep in ooze. Not only was the *Ada* aground, but the dredge and barge had slid up on to the mud behind her. Diggles was unpopular. Finally, like souls passing from purgatory to paradise, we swung once more into the clear water of the river. Hardly had we steadied on an up-river course when the canal opened in the bank. Straight as a crack in a table it pointed south-eastward . . . the direction in which we wanted to go. Without consulting Diggles I dived into it. Eventually it led us to another river— I forget the name—and the river led us to the sea. All I remember of that river is that we reached the mouth of it on a strong ebb tide which swept us sideways and wrapped the tow neatly round a buoy at the entrance. Five days had we been away from salt water.

Now fifty miles of open water to cross the northward-thrusting arm of the Gulf of Mexico. Fifty miles. That meant a day out of sight of land. The weather remained calm, but hardly had we reached land once more and begun to coast southward along the west coast of the Florida peninsula when a real blow came up. In the teeth of an on-shore wind we staggered into the lee of a sand-bank and anchored. Three days we lay there while great seas crashed on our low sheltering whaleback of sand and sent spume flying over us.

South was our course now. The dangerous part of our voyage was over. True, we were in open water, but it was shallow and the bottom coated with weed . . . like cruising a foot or two above a field of oats, but the weed broke the swell and made the water calm. Day after day the sun rose over the low coastline, swung overhead to make our decks sizzle and dropped into the Gulf in a riot of rose-pink light. Day after day the *Ada's* engine throbbed without missing a beat. I grew to almost worship that engine. Our being revolved around its sturdy persistence as the being of a home revolves around a wife's love.

Off Tarpon Springs the sponge fleet lay. Greek divers sprang naked overboard. Bronzed skins, blue sky and water, white sails of the schooners of the sponge fleet.

Below Tarpon Springs we entered the inland passage that would take us south as far as the Ten Thousand Islands, almost to our destination. Both sides of the southern half of the Florida peninsula are so guarded. An outer beach takes the onslaught of the open sea. Between beach and mainland is a mile-wide lagoon, navigable for small craft. That night it was almost dark when I anchored. There seemed to be a lot of stakes about . . .

marking lobster-pots, I supposed. To my consternation when daylight came I found we had anchored in the middle of a real estate development. As I gazed around I noticed that the stakes were in geometric pattern marked with the names of streets and avenues. When enough lots were sold to provide the capital the developer would buy a sand-dredge, pump sand in and make dry land of it. We moved out of there hurriedly, before the owner should appear and note the damage caused by the swinging of our tow in the night. Dozens of stakes were floating about. We had ruined his town lay-out.

I had hoped to get into the Lostman River before dark on the last day and swing my tow to anchor proudly in full view of the camp on Onion Key, but a head-wind and a choppy little sea held us back. Seeing we had only twenty miles to go by dark I held on through the night. By midnight I spotted the slight break in the mangroves which indicated the entrance and headed in. Hit the channel fairly and navigated its ramifications perfectly until the last shoal of all. There we ran aground, hard and fast. But what did we care? We were at our destination and in sheltered water. The morning tide would float us off. We went below and slept. Still sleeping, long after sunrise, Sabe and his crew found us when they came down-river in a launch. They drew alongside and hailed us.

I walked on deck. Still clad as I had thrown myself down on my bunk the night before.

From the launch there came a startled gasp, then a shout of laughter. Even Sabe's impassive face split wide. It took me a moment to realise that they were laughing at me. Barefooted. Naked down to the waist. My best trousers had eroded badly . . . nothing but a tattered remnant round my crutch remained. And I hadn't shaved for weeks.

But I had brought the dredge.

CHAPTER VIII

THE HURRICANE

WE got the first whisper of it from the wireless room when Sparks gave me a message he had decoded . . . from some ship down near the Sargasso Sea, many hundreds of miles away. The ship's captain was reporting weather, winds of hurricane force. He gave their direction. Somewhere down there in that breeding ground of hurricanes a great circular whirlpool of wind was spinning over the open ocean at an unbelievable velocity, which would be the greatest round its central core. The actual centre of the hurricane would be windless. Windless but not calm. In that sinisterly windless centre mammoth waves would be ravening—not the orderly attacking lines of combers which a ship can meet bows on and fight, but huge undisciplined masses of water charging madly in all directions and just as like to board a vessel from stem, stern or beam, whatever her course.

After an hour or two came another message, from another ship, several hundred miles from the first. This one reported hurricane winds also, but their direction was almost exactly opposite to the first. It was evident therefore that the two ships were on opposite edges of the invisible whirlpool of the tempest and that somewhere between them was the dreaded centre. That centre and the spinning cataclysm round it would be slowly moving towards us at the rate of ten to fifteen miles an hour. Many hurricanes brewed down there and most of them took a north-westerly course towards Florida, but few arrived so far north as the United States . . . something to do with a high-pressure area which, like an invisible fence, barred the way and sent them back to vent their fury on the Caribbean Sea and its islands.

For diversion Sabe and I got out a big chart of the Caribbean and stuck a pin in the centre of the hurricane. Such a disturbance sets ships gossiping and from their gossip we'd follow that hurricane on the chart till she slowly died in mid-ocean or flung herself lustfully to rape some palm-fringed island, snapping stout cocoa-nut palms like match-sticks, flinging fisher craft crashing far on to dry land and whisking the flimsy native huts to sea. Terror and destruction.

For a couple of days we watched that hurricane. A little line of pins upon the opened chart marked its path. So far it had followed its appointed path . . . north-westward . . . directly towards us. At any moment now the high-pressure area which guarded Florida would fend it from us and send it whirling south-westward. Like Spaniards at a bull arena we watched. Impersonally. Till suddenly it dawned on us that the high pressure area wasn't working this time. The barrier was down and the bull was coming straight for us. The hurricane was approaching. Already only some three hundred miles distant from Miami. At its present rate of progress it would strike Miami sometime that very night and us a few hours later. Furthermore we were right in the path of the deadly centre, around which revolved the wind of the highest velocity.

The hurricane could not have caught us at a worse moment for, a few days before, the Miami wireless operator who was our Miami link had left for the north on a couple of weeks' vacation and we were therefore out of touch by wireless with that city. All we could do was take precautions for our own safety and trust that our friends and loved ones there would do the same. I wasn't really worried much about them. Miami boasted of an up-to-date Government meteorological station and I was sure the authorities would give the people warning and proper instructions regarding safety measures. But I was wrong. All the notice of that hurricane that Miami got was a small paragraph in the paper which mentioned that a hurricane might strike the city. As most of the inhabitants of Miami at the time were northerners who didn't know what a hurricane was, they paid no attention. I believe that the heavy loss of life was mostly due to this.

For my part I immediately issued instructions to pack up all our movable equipment and load it on the boats, something like a score of which were moored to the jetties round the island. Those boats could seek safety by running up the many narrow bayous which opened into the river. There, protected by the willowy mangrove growth of the upper river, they would be reasonably secure. By dark that night everything the boats would hold had been stowed aboard and the men told off to their respective craft so that there would be no confusion when the order should be given to embark—probably in the dark hours of the night.

I considered sending warning to Jamie but he saved me the trouble by appearing in his launch to warn us. His weather-wisdom was as accurate as our wireless.

"There's a whale of a starm comin', Capn," was his greeting, with a glance to the eastward where the evening sky was already assuming a dull, metallic appearance. Threatening and oppressive.

"We're all ready. Better get your boats loaded up and move inland." I gave him what particulars I had of the approaching tempest.

He shook his head. "We-all done weathered these starms before. She won't sweep our beaches high enough to harm us none."

"This is going to be a bad one."

"Don't worrit none about us. It was you-all we was worriting about." He turned his launch and sped homewards.

No sleep for anyone on Onion Key that night. Black. That night was black as the mouth of hell and there was the hint of hellish force, too, behind the gusts that rose ever stronger and stronger.

By midnight there was a full gale blowing and, with it snarling at her heels, the *Isabel* came winging up-river, Ted Collins at her helm. Come down the coast to warn us. Run through in spite of being continually swept by seas in the open Gulf. Plucky. Ted was considerable of a man in spite of his freak religion. I was glad to see him. The schooner would hold the remainder of our stores which our own boats had no capacity to carry. Through the black hours we loaded the *Isabel* while the wind rose ever stronger.

By three in the morning we were ready to embark. Every single thing in camp was loaded and waterborne . . . all but our canvas houses. These must be left for lack of space in which to stow them. They were stoutly built and well anchored, but I knew they would not stand against the terrific wind pressure to come. A mental calculation told me that the centre of the hurricane must still be at least a hundred miles distant. That the wind velocity near the centre would be at least twice what was striking us now and yet already the light buildings were swaying dangerously and already boughs were being rent from trees and whirling past us . . . augury of the peril of being caught on that open island by the full force of the storm.

In reality it was time to go . . . and yet I hesitated. In a dilemma. So black the night that I was afraid to venture. True, each boatmaster knew the bayou allotted to him and was thoroughly familiar with the waters around camp but, even so, it would be easy for the most experienced to run aground on a sandbar in the darkness and the fate of a boat aground and exposed to the tempest to come would be a perilous one. I would wait, I decided, either till day broke or the island became absolutely too dangerous to remain on. There was still an hour to go before daybreak. Flashlight in hand I went the rounds and checked each boat's quota of men. Then we waited. Nerves tense.

The gusts grew stronger. The menace of the comparatively calm pauses between them intensified. I felt oppressed. Explosive. My responsibility sat on my shoulders like a pack. If I delayed our departure too long we might all perish. On the other hand, if I chanced a move in the darkness some of us almost certainly would. But if daylight should come before the wind made our launches quite unmanageable I believed that every man would survive and all our valuable equipment be saved.

Still we waited. No one spoke because conversation was useless . . . the wind whipped the words away from the speaker's mouth.

At last I could stand it no longer. We must chance the darkness. Already the wind was so strong that it was difficult to stand erect. Then, even as I prepared to flash the embarkation signal on my flashlight, I glanced to the eastward whence the storm was approaching. There was light there. An ominous yellow light . . . lowering . . . brazen . . . sinister . . . like the reflection of hell's fires smouldering. It seemed to illuminate a bilious yellow pall in the direction of Miami, which the centre of the storm must be now approaching. Evil that pall looked. But there was reflected light on the water now.

One by one the motors started, their roaring almost inaudible against the roaring of the wind, and the white shapes of the launches shot from their berths into the yellow reflection on the water.

When all were on their way we slipped the *Ada's* painter and let the wind sweep her clear of her berth. As the churning propeller gripped the water and the boat plunged forward it took all my strength on the wheel to hold her head against the blast. A quarter-mile spurt up-river, holding her bows well into the gale to keep from being swept ashore, a quick turn of the helm to port and she shot into the dark mouth of a mangrove-shrouded bayou like a rabbit into a hole, ran on a few yards, then grounded in soft mud. Safe as a nail in a board. No big trees near to crush us when they fell. Only a low willowy growth of pliant young mangroves which the wind was already pressing down on our awning like a roof. That narrow tunnel of a bayou was windless as the underground earth of a fox . . . and it stank about as badly . . . stale mud instead of musk. All our launches were safe, I believed, as the other bayous selected for their shelter would be just as windless as mine and I had seen them popping one after another into dark holes in the river-bank as we came upstream. Only the *Isabel* worried me. Her mast precluded her seeking the same kind of shelter and she had anchored in the wide reach of river just opposite the opening to our den. In full view of us, her forefoot deep in the water, she tugged and worried at her anchor cable like a puppy at a rope's end. I judged her safe as long as her anchor held—no seas could rise to breach her in the narrow limits of the river. I prayed her anchor would not drag.

The round score of men I had aboard the *Ada* with me watched the tempest from the deck awhile. Silent as though awed. Then they turned in below to make up for the sleep they had lost the previous night. But no thought of sleep came to me. Only once in a lifetime—if as much—would it be given to a man to view the full fury of the elements unleashed, himself in safety. I would not have missed a moment of that opportunity. I was watching the demons of hell at play while safe, myself, outside the portals.

Overhead spread a sulphurous dome which looked as though its rim were resting on the horizon. The spasmodic gusts of wind had long since ceased and a continuous droning roar testified to the strength of the invisible force which was sweeping sheets of spray along the surface of the water. Yet when I lit my pipe the flame of the match burned steady, so sheltered was I.

The roaring of the wind steadily increased as the centre of the hurricane moved nearer. The *Isabel* was still holding her ground, but her bare mainmast bowed with the wind pressure, quite stripped of canvas though it was. The blast was sweeping in from the Gulf, from the opposite direction to the forward movement of the storm. With the wind pressure behind it the water began to rise. The *Ada* floated and pressed against her living roof which eased upward to give her room as the spring of a bed would rise to the back of a man crouching beneath it. The force of the wind was sweeping the Gulf of Mexico upon the western Florida coast and raising the water level. God help Jamie and the dwellers on the outer beaches if this went on long. The rising water and the terrific waves which must be running out there would be sweeping the low sites upon which they lived. Their houses would be washed away even if they withstood the wind. Worse. The salt water would pervade the cisterns in which their drinking-water was kept—caught from the rain—and there was no fresh water in the tidal Lostman River . . . even as far up as Onion Key it was too brackish to drink.

Still the wind increased in force and the water rose higher. There were local swirls of air I noticed within the wide sweeping circle of the main hurricane. Miniature, but deadly, whirlpools of air within a greater. Their force must have been terrific. When they struck the flattened surface of the river they pulled great chunks of water from it with a spout of white spray like the strike of a shell from a naval gun, leaving for a perceptible moment a great hole in the water.

Across the river from us I saw a great mangrove tear loose. A lusty giant of a tree with wide-flung branches and a spread of roots as big as a cottage. It soared from the ground like a rocketing pheasant, rising, spinning and shedding gobs of muck from its ooze-encrusted base. Still rising it sped towards us and passed high overhead with the speed of a modern bombing plane. Fear clutched me then, in spite of the safe retreat in which I sat.

I learned in that moment that man lives only by sufferance of Nature. Her ragings awed me.

For hours the roaring onslaught lasted. My senses dulled as though I were in a dug-out, suffering an intensive artillery preparation.

Then suddenly the wind stopped. At one moment it was bellowing at me. The next moment was dead calm. Startling. At the abrupt cessation of the noise through which they had been sleeping the men awoke and came on deck.

" God ! that wasn't so bad," remarked one. " I guess these hurricanes aren't what they're cracked up to be."

" You'd think different if you'd watched it." I felt irked at the lack of appreciation of the spectacle. Just as though it were something I had staged myself. " Besides," I added, " that's only the first half of it."

" But it's over. There's not a breath of wind. Look." He held out the cigarette he had lighted. Its smoke rose straight up. A tiny grey column.

" Because we're in the centre, you fool."

" How long will it be calm like this ? "

I shrugged my shoulders. " An hour, maybe. Perhaps only half of it."

The calm lasted almost an hour. Ominous. Brooding. Most oppressive of all was that respite from the tearing wind. When I studied the barometer on the *Ada* it was registering below 28—I have forgotten the exact reading. At any rate it checked with the official records of the storm in Miami and was the lowest barometer reading ever recorded in the United States up till that date. The mercury was pumping up and down like the pulsing of blood in an artery. The smooth surface of the river outside reflected the brassy glare of the dome overhead and seemed to pulse also with the rhythm of the mercury in the glass. My nerves were taut. Something terrible was upon us. Worse than we had experienced before.

At last it broke upon us. With a shrieking roar, worse than the bellow of a locomotive in a tunnel, the blast sprang at us from the opposite direction to before. No warning. One second it was calm and the next mangroves were rending and crashing while the air was thick with flying wreckage. Worse than the first half was the second. The mangrove growth seemed almost to have been bracing itself against the westerly onslaught and to have been caught unawares by the sudden change in direction of the storm's attack. On us humans, too, the second half made more impression. The first half of the tempest had begun with a breeze and steadily increased till the wind reached an unbelievable force. So our nerves had become gradually attuned to it. But the second half struck us with its maximum fury just after we had experienced a calm. It felt almost as though an unexpected artillery barrage had burst on us. We cowered on the deck although our roof of willowy mangroves still protected us.

"Christ!" the blasphemy was almost a prayer from the man who had sneered at the first half of the storm. "Christ! . . . and I thought it was over."

But after an hour or two the wind began to perceptibly decrease. By three o'clock in the afternoon it had stopped sufficiently to manœuvre a powerful boat in it.

I ran the *Ada* out into the river, transferred most of the men on board to the *Isabel* . . . the top of the schooner's mast had been snapped off by a flying mangrove branch but she was otherwise staunch and unharmed . . . and headed down-river with only Baldy and Art Bender aboard. The Heddlestons would be in need of help as soon as we could bring it to them.

The run down-river was easy enough, although the wind was strong enough still to enforce our steering a quartering course. As we passed Winton's cabin I brought the *Ada's* head into the wind and paused. I could see that the cabin was down and across it lay the bole of a cocoa-nut palm. Winton's launch lay high on the bank, splintered against the stump of another palm. But Winton emerged from some shelter behind the ruins of his home. He waved me on, excitedly, shouting something which did not carry to us against the wind. With the throttle wide open I continued downstream.

The bar at the mouth of the river was a white smother of foam. Great grey combers were rearing in from the Gulf and hurling their grisly shapes upon the shallows. Vindictive they looked. They frightened me and my knees felt weak but the job had to be done.

"Get below and batten down," I screamed in the ears of the

two beside me. "Keep giving me all the engine's got till I ring you down."

Baldy's lips pursed in an inaudible whistle as he gazed at the mess we were headed into. Blowing a kiss to the waters ahead he disappeared. Art Bender followed him, but he returned in a second with a rope and lashed me to the wheel-post with a couple of quick turns, then dived below. I heard the companion door slam behind him. I was alone. Riding the *Ada* into battle. The bark of the engine quickened. The boat gathered speed. Hard I gripped the wheel and my bare toes splayed over the deck boards, almost prehensile in the urge to find firm footing. A snarling grey shape towered before us, hooded and evil like a cobra about to strike. Dirty grey, it curled over the bows and struck with the impact of a shell-burst fair on the turtle-backed fore-deck. A flood of sand-burdened water swept over me, waist deep, while spray stung my face and almost smothered me. The *Ada* paused, plunged into the trough and shore clean through the next breaker, nearly drowning me. To the third she rose before it could break, kicked her heels triumphantly as she cleared it and jazzed her propeller in the air to show her contempt. Then we were out in the Gulf in what was no worse than a full gale of wind. Well out to sea we ran. Then a quick turn of the wheel spun us round and we were racing down-wind towards Wood Key, the island where Jamie lived. Long before we arrived I could see that the waves were breaching the island. Jamie's house had disappeared and most of the cocoa-nut palms were snapped off. The mangroves were standing though and in them the shapes of men. Women and children too I could distinguish as we rapidly drew closer.

When I had brought the *Ada* as near to the edge of the surf as I dared, I spun her round again and rung the engines to SLOW so that she would just about keep her position against the drive of the wind. A ticklish position and one I didn't want to hold longer than necessary. While I jockeyed the helm as a rider jockeys a horse the others paid out a long rope to which they had attached an empty petrol drum as a float. God! How I hoped that line would prove long enough to reach the shore. It was. A wave dashed it up among the mangrove roots. Jamie and Dicon dropped on it from their perches like leopards on prey, held tight to the mangroves while another great smother swept over them, then carried the end of the line aloft. That part was done. Well done. But it was all we could do. By rights we should have had a bo'sun's chair and another line to haul them along with. But that single long rope was the only one long enough among our stores in camp. The rest was up to the Heddlestons and they were equal to the task. They were men, the Heddlestons. Women and children on their backs they worked their way along that rope in a continuous procession. The cabin filled as we hauled them aboard. Thirsty. Since the night before they had been roosting without a drink. Jamie came last, shaking the water from him like a great shaggy dog as he clambered on deck. He looked round and grinned.

"Gor'amighty, Cap'n. I seen some starms, but dogged if that warn't the grand-daddy of all on them. I never did think I'd be as glad to see anyone as I wur to see you-all when you come over the bar. Thought you wuz goners once but you sure did handle her fine."

"Anyone else need help, do you think?" There was not much more room. We already had about a score of refugees on board.

He shook his head, water spraying from it. "Them that lives inland is all right anyway and all the beach-livers come to my place before she started. They're all here."

By the time we got our living cargo to Onion Key the launches were beginning to come out of their refuges and nose into the places where their berths had been. The wind was a whisper now, but what a mess it had left! A few tattered shreds and bits of timber were all that was left of the camp of which I had been so proud. Shade trees snapped off short. But there was one blessing. No debris to clean up. The wind had done that for us very thoroughly. Above all we had saved all our boats, stores and equipment and not a single life had been lost either among our own men or the residents of the perilous outer beaches.

Food and water. In addition to our own men we must feed the Heddlestons we had rescued. A quick assessment showed that with care we could live for a week without outside assistance, but that assistance must be asked for at once. Someone must go to Miami and notify the authorities of our plight.

It seemed to me useless to attempt a voyage to Miami by sea

. . . those narrow waterways along the east coast would be blocked by fallen timber. Only one course remained : to cross the Florida peninsula. Sixty miles separated us from Miami of which the first forty was mangrove swamp and everglades. Miles of saw-grass country such as we had encountered on our survey. The last twenty miles was pineland and carried the semblance of a trail over which it was possible to drive a car. But it would all be flooded now, with the amount of water the storm had pushed inland.

"Jamie, I've got to get across to Miami . . . overland."

He scratched his head. "Too much water. The starm will have piled the Gulf of Mexico clear across to Biscayne Bay."

"I know that. I'll do it in the Canadian canoe." We had a small canoe with a kicker motor. Light enough to drag over fallen timber or to carry on your back for a short portage.

At daybreak I started. The upper river seemed fairly clear of timber as the young mangrove growth up there had resisted the wind well. Even in the saw-grass it was easy for a while. The water level was several feet above normal and I buzzed merrily along wide stretches of water which had been narrow bayous before the hurricane. All went well until I struck the pine country. Higher ground. But there was still enough water to float my light craft and I carried on. From that point my troubles gradually increased. Down timber. Those pine trees lay in swathes and tangles where the wind had hurled them. They stopped my progress finally. After many failures to get the canoe farther I was forced to halt. Knee deep in water. Half the day gone and forty miles to go before I reached Miami, my means of locomotion gone. God ! What wouldn't I have given for dry land to walk on instead of that amphibious stuff. I sat down, lit my pipe and considered the situation.

As near as I could judge I was due south of a little construction camp on the rough trail which led from Miami westward and which was afterwards to become the famous Tamiami Trail—streams of cars slide easily across it now, traversing the peninsula from Atlantic to Gulf in an hour. Straight and level it cuts through the swamps. Asphalt. Civilised. If the tourists who frequent it could have only seen me then. Eight miles or so to the camp I guessed. On foot I started. Abandoned the canoe. It is there yet for all I know. Anyone that wanted it could have it as far as I was concerned. Not for a fleet of canoes would I have returned to that wreckage of a country.

Knee deep in water and splintered debris I ploughed my way forward. Where the water deepened I had to swim at times. Bodies of dead birds showed bedraggled heaps of feathers among the tangled wreckage of the pine-tops. Warm the water was under the stinging sun. Like a perpetual tepid bath, enervating my body and making my knees sag. But I dare not tire. I must reach that camp or lie down and die. No one would ever find my body in that lonely place. Plunging, wading or swimming I progressed slowly and finally staggered into a clearing where was the wreckage of some wooden huts.

But the men were alive and they lent me a car. The oldest of Model T Fords. Splashing water right and left it wallowed along the trail towards Miami.

About half-way to my destination I met another car coming in the opposite direction. Stopped the driver with my outstretched arm. Haggard his face looked. His dirty overalls those of a mechanic or some such trade.

"Much damage in Miami?" I queried.

He shook his head mournfully. "There is no Miami," he stated solemnly.

"What?" My family was there.

"Miami's wiped out. Don't exist no more."

"Many killed?" I tried to keep my voice steady.

"Thousands. The tall buildings all went. The Biltmore Hotel in Coral Gables is flat." He drove slowly past me.

My soul rocked on its foundations. It had been worse even than I had feared. Then a doubt crept in. It could not be as bad as the croaker had made out. I pushed the throttle forward and sped on.

Night fell before I reached the outskirts of Coral Gables, Miami's westward suburb. There was a bright moon. As I drove along the road something in the distance caught my gaze. A tall silver tower that seemed to shimmer in the moonlight. I stopped with a jerk and gazed again. There was no mistaking it. The tower was the Biltmore Hotel that the man had said was flat. My heart leaped. He had been just a croaker then. If the Biltmore stood, many other buildings would be standing too.

At the city limits I was held up by a man in plain clothes who pointed a revolver at me.

" You don't go no further," he remarked almost casually.

" What's the idea ? "

" No one allowed inside city limits after dark."

" But I live in Coral Gables."

" So you say. There's been looting and no one gets in. That's my orders." He flashed a nickel shield in the moonlight . . . a deputy sheriff.

I got out of the car and walked over to him. " Look here." I kept my voice calm with an effort. " My house is not two blocks from here. I don't know whether my family is alive or dead and I've crossed the State of Florida to-day to find out. The only way you can stop me is to shoot me but I'M GOING IN."

" What's the address of your house ? "

" Number 159 San Miguel Avenue."

He scratched his head. Then his face brightened as a heavy tread approached.

" There's a reg'lar cop coming. Tell him your story."

I told it to the uniformed policeman when he approached. He considered me for a moment. Flashed his lantern over me.

" I'm going down San Miguel Avenue," he pronounced finally. " You can come with me. If your story's all right you're all right. But if it ain't, God help you."

In a few minutes we were standing before my door.

I knocked.

The door opened. With a shriek of joy Margaret had flung her arms round my neck.

" I guess that's proof enough for me," remarked the cop as he tramped away grinning.

For a week I was busy with every other able-bodied citizen cleaning up the wreckage of the storm.

A few instances of the force of the hurricane will suffice to supplement the account I have already given.

We picked up the body of a young girl and carried it to the morgue. An ordinary three by three timber had been driven right through her chest and protruded several feet behind. We shouldered each end of it and carried her, transfixed, because we couldn't fit her into an ambulance.

I saw the back end of a big Studebaker seven-passenger car which protruded from a second-story window on Flagler Street. Blown through the window by the wind. The window was at least twenty feet from street level. The picture of that was in many of the illustrated papers.

In the middle of Flagler Street, several blocks from the water front, a hundred-foot revenue cutter reposed, high and dry. It had to be dismantled as it was too far from the water to launch.

A two-thousand-ton schooner, the *Rose Mahoning*, lay neatly across Bayshore Drive and effectually blocked traffic.

Later I was gossiping with some friends in the Government meteorological station on Miami Beach.

" What wind velocity did your instruments register ? " I asked.

They laughed. " Our anemometer registered one hundred and fifty-three miles an hour before it blew away, and that was before the worst of the blow came."

CHAPTER IX

A "SHINDIG"

IT was in the upper river that Jamie and Winton caught me, just as I was going out fishing with Ruth and Ralph . . . the Chesbroughs had come to live on Onion Key after the hurricane of the month before had wrecked their house in Coral Gables and ruined his real estate business in Miami. It seemed to me that the hurricane had arrived at the culminating point of the Florida land boom, just as the curve had reached its zenith and was stationary, undecided as to whether it should climb upward another notch or begin its downward course. The hurricane settled the point. Sudden as the fire from Heaven of old and a good deal more effective, it " busted " the boom as the charge of high explosive bursts a bomb. Miami real estate in general was dead. True, we ourselves were still selling a fair volume of lots. Enough to keep our development going. But that was straight commercial business with no hysterical boom psychology in it. People bought our lots because they considered the price low enough to be a good long-term investment. If only enough of them kept on buying we should still be able to realise our plans.

I cut down the engine of my launch to allow Jamie's to catch up. He slipped a boathook over our gunwale and pulled his craft alongside.

" We was huntin' you, Cap'n." He perched on his engine-box, drew his sheath knife and began to whittle his feet.

" What have I done wrong ? " I glanced at the tin badge on his chest. He kept that polished like a soldier does his buttons.

Jamie grinned. Stopping whittling he began to hone his knife on the leather-hard sole of his foot. " We-all wants to tell you thanks for what you done for us in the starm . . . and afterwards." He tested the edge of his blade with his finger-tips and his face flushed.

" You'd have done the same by me, Jamie."

"Gor'amighty, yes. But then the sea's our business. We been fightin' it all our lives. If you wuz caught out in a starm any man that lives by the sea would help you. But the sea ain't your business. An' yet you helped us . . . took a long chance to do it . . . dogged if you didn't . . . an' you a furriner. 'Twarn't just what you done in the starm, neither. After that you goes wallering across Florida after help. We done hardly see the last of your splashing through the 'glades when there comes a relief boat up from Key West with food and water. Food and water you'd sent us. We hardly done got the food and water unloaded when there's comes another boat. Red Cross this time. Carrying lumber to rebuild our cabins. You got us that lumber too. Every time I eats victuals or walks into my house I owes it to you . . . dogged if I don't." Jamie stood up and sheathed his knife.

"We-all's goin' to have a bit of a shindig on Wood Key come Wednesday," he continued. "We-all would admire for you to come along. Bring Ma'am and her husband too."

"Thanks, Jamie. We'd be glad to come." I had heard of the Heddleston shindigs. "Furriners" weren't welcomed as a rule. Strictly family affairs the Heddlestons had always kept them. When the clan relaxed in a carouse they didn't want any strange witnesses present.

The full moon was just rising that Wednesday when I grounded our launch on the white sandy beach of Wood Key. Jamie and a detachment of the clan ran our boat up above high-water mark and moored her to the stump of a hurricane-snapped cocoa-nut palm.

Jamie led me aside.

"We been talkin' about this, Cap'n. We-all would admire if you'd serve the drinks for to-night. The boys all respects you and maybe there'll be no knifin' nor shootin' if you takes charge of the liquor."

"If you want me to handle the bar I'll do my best."

Guiding me by the elbow he edged me to a small clump of palms about fifty yards from the beach, miraculously survived from the storm. Here two broken stumps had been sawn off square and a board nailed across them. On the board were row. of tin cups, ordinary tin pannikins of about a quarter of a pints Behind the improvised counter were the supplies of liquor for the party. Six great stone demijohns I counted. Beside them were a pile of packages done up in sacking. Those bundles would contain half a dozen bottles each, run in from the Bahamas, Gun Key or Cuba. Scotch whisky, old French wines and cognac, peach and cherry brandy would be there—enough first class liquor to make a company of regulars tight—while the stone demijohns would contain raw spirit from Winton's still, so new and crude that it would be almost warm.

" How do you work it, Jamie ? "

" Looks like there'll be enough liquor." He surveyed the pile with pride. " The idea's to make 'em all happy. It'd be a shame if they wurn't all skewed before the liquor guv out."

"'God ! That quantity of liquor ought to make the whole United States tight."

He puckered his face. " It'll do if it's mixed right. It's the mixin' does it."

" How do you usually handle it ? "

" Give 'em that stuff of Winton's first so's they get a foundation of good liquor. After they done swallowed them demijohns you can pile all the furrin rotgut you like into 'em and they won't know no different."

" How much to a drink ? "

He gazed at me in surprise. " Full cups. They'll feel they're cheated if the cups ain't full. It's fair and square drinkin' here."

He wandered off to get his fiddle. I took stock of my customers. About sixty there seemed to be, of which some were children.

Dancing soon started on a square wooden platform on the white beach, swimming in moonlight. Old square dances they danced. There was a touch of the Elizabethan about it. Jamie played the fiddle. " Pa " Heddleston had emerged from his lonely fastness to play a mouth organ. The third of the orchestra was a woman. Ruth's eldest pupil . . . the one with the baby. She played a concertina, and her efforts to suckle her baby without interrupting the music would have turned a conjurer green with envy. She finally got her blouse open so that her meaty bosom dangled just above the baby's face as it lay on her lap. To and fro her body swayed in time with the music. To and fro the bosom swayed with her, eluding the baby's two-handed efforts to grab it. Just then the first dance ended and I had to dash to my post at the bar.

After each dance the men solemnly brought their partners to the bar and quaffed, unblinking, a pannikin full of crude liquid fire, undiluted. Nor were the women lacking in stamina . . . they downed their drinks as rapidly as the men. No one seemed to swallow. There was a visible swelling of the throat as their practised muscles held the valves open, they tilted their cups and laid them back empty on the bar. I was awestruck. Astounded. Even though I had seen them give the same spirit to a young baby to keep it quiet. I had seen some drinking in my time, but nothing like this . . . a lesson in the proficiency reached in training from childhood.

Meantime the children whispered and scurried in the bushes behind me. An argument broke out among them and all the symptoms of a free fight drifted down the breeze to me, but I was too busy with my duties to settle children's troubles. Soon the noise of fighting gave place to giggles. Then a little girl emerged into the moonlight. Staggering. Tight as a lord she looked. Instinctively I looked down at my stock to see if they had filched a bottle. One of Winton's demijohns was missing. Back among the bushes I found it . . . more than half empty. Around it lay the younger generation. Sozzled. The little devils had celebrated a shindig all on their own.

Dance after dance. Drink after drink.

> " Swing your heifer . . . do-see-so.
> Ladies right, gents to left . . . do-see-so."

Jamie's flat feet kept time to the dance-master's chant.

All the demijohns were empty now. I reached for a bundle of bottles and slit the sacking with my knife. Cognac. Aged . . . I tried some myself. A slight look of disappointment was evident when the dancers tasted it and I caught a regretful glance or two towards the derelict demijohns which lay on their sides with their stoppers out. But so far no comment whatever had been made on the liquor I had served. Solemnly they marched to the bar, downed their ration and solemnly marched back to dance where little moonshot waves of light rippled happily against the beach.

Jamaica rum this time. Good liquor. Potent. I sampled it

generously. Then Scotch whisky. After that a heathenish sort of cocktail by mixing everything in sight . . . I did not dare to try that one. Still there was no sign of a stagger among the dancers.

The pile of bundled bottles was visibly diminishing and I racked my brains to think of all the potent combinations a varied career had brought my way.

At last an inspiration struck me. In Jamie's cabin was a large jar of red pickled peppers. Red hot they were. At his wife's request I had sampled them not many days before. Between drinkings I slipped across to the new, neat hut and brought the gallon jar back with me.

I mixed the next round in the proportion of one of pepper sauce to three of whatever else I could lay my hands on. The little red peppers glowed garishly from the surface of cupsful of potent liquor.

Then I got some comment. At last I had stirred them. The first to taste the new concoction promptly lost the bored expression all had worn since Winton's liquor had run out. He took his empty cup from his lips with a flourish. "Tastes like Winton's, but it ain't," he remarked, expelling a redolent breath from the depths of his chest.

Another seemed to choke on something solid in his drink. Hastily he lowered his unemptied cup, ruminated, bit on something and spat hurriedly and audibly.

"Gord, ain't them cockroaches in Winton's liquor hot?" he commented fervently.

It worked. There was a distinct stagger apparent as they marched back. Then one after another they fell out of the dance, reeled away from the platform and subsided on to the beach, asleep before they hit the ground.

The shindig was over. It had been a good show, we decided. About as good as we could stand although our potations had been comparatively moderate.

But the beach looked terrible. Untidy. For a few minutes the three of us worked furiously. Laid the defunct out in rows, face upwards with their hands crossed on their breasts. Then we went home to Onion Key.

Jamie and Winton looked quite cheerful when I saw them a day or two later. It took more than a shindig to give the Heddlestons a hangover.

"We-all wants to say how much we enjoyed havin' you at our party," remarked Jamie scratching his bare shin with one horny toe while Winton stroked his black beard with a caressing motion. "Finest party we ever did have. Nice and quiet. Nary a shootin' and nary a knifin'."

"We enjoyed it too, Jamie."

He laughed. "Dogged if you didn't put the fine touch on it, Cap'n. When I woke up in the morning I thought I wur in a morgue."

CHAPTER X

THE LAST VENTURE

FOR some months after the hurricane we continued the Poinciana development although the funds received from sales were dwindling steadily. Miami was rapidly changing from a wild boom town to a stereotyped winter resort . . . half empty in summer, crowded in winter. At this period came a divergence of opinion between my partners and myself. They were unanimous in maintaining that the coming winter with its influx of visitors would see a resumption of the boom. But I held the opposite opinion. Land sales in Florida were going to be off for years, I felt. The place was oversold.

My partners wanted to shut down the development for the summer, trusting to winter sales to enable them to resume.

For my part I advocated an attempt to obtain financial backing for our project—a sound project it was—in New York. If we gave up half our interest, I argued, we could secure sufficient capital to complete our development. Half a loaf seemed to me better than the "no bread" which I could see looming ahead. I sensed that once the property were shut down the development might never be resumed.

When our divergence of opinion threatened to make a break in what had been a very cordial friendship I suggested that they buy me out and play their own hand. They did so . . . at about one-tenth of the price I could have obtained a few months before for my one-quarter interest in the venture. Still, it was a fair price considering conditions. I didn't make a fortune out of the Miami boom, but I did get enough to keep Margaret and the family secure in our own house for a year or so while I got a start elsewhere. That was a good deal more than most people got out of it including my partners. The real beneficiary of the boom was the State of Florida which acquired a network of good roads and enough other public improvements to keep her going for the next decade. Besides, to me the mere fact of having

256

participated in such a wild episode was worth more than money. If I had had to walk out of Miami with the soles worn off my shoes I should still have been glad that I was through the boom. It was grand fun.

Ralph Chesbrough and I went up to New York together. We drove up in my car . . . thousands of people in Miami didn't have the price of even train fare northwards after the boom collapsed.

In New York I got wind of patents pending in which the mineral chromite figured largely—chromium plating was destined to replace the old nickel plating process shortly. Through Ralph's influence we got an option on the chromite deposits of Turkey—Ralph had lived in Turkey for many years and had good connections there—thus tying up the only known source of the mineral available for American control. It looked like a sitter. Such a proposition in London would not have long gone a-begging had the conditions been reversed.

But New York financiers seemed conservative. From one financial house to another we peddled our option, seeking financial backing. After some months we gave it up. Disgusted. I was still more so six months later when, after the new chromium plating process was common knowledge, the very financiers who had laughed at us were writing me in South America to reconsider their verdict. But it was too late then. Our option had expired and German interests had snapped it up. Germany now controlled the chromite deposits of Turkey and the U.S.A. was compelled to buy her ever increasing requirements from London.

Ralph went back into the American government service. This time as American Automotive Trade Commissioner for the Near East. He and Ruth left for Egypt . . . twelve years were to pass before I should see any of the Chesbrough family again.

I, too, decided to go abroad. Eight years I had spent in the United States. Full years they had been, although some of them had been irksome. In such a highly developed country I did not fit, although a generation before I should have revelled in the development of the country. But the national house was built now. Suburbia had arrived. Only one little bit of frontier had remained and—that was a source of satisfaction—I had done my bit in taming that at least. When I had pinned that shiny badge on Jamie Heddleston's chest I had left my little mark on the development of the United States.

After Ralph had gone I found myself a lodging in Eastside New York and sped the arrows from my quiver to see in which land they would fall. I took a New York directory and addressed a letter to every mining company in it that had a foreign sounding name. Those letters covered almost every country in the world.

About a hundred letters I wrote and received some twenty replies. Unfortunately most of those who replied proved on investigation to be bogus companies whose sole assets were an office in New York, a number of flashy-looking share certificates and an urge to acquire quick money. One was genuine though. A man named Fletcher owned a gold mine in Nicaragua. The name fascinated me. *La Luz y Los Angeles* Mine. The Mine of the Light and the Angels. Fletcher and I agreed on everything but the salary to be paid me and he finally engaged a man named Marshall. About a year later Marshall became famous when the rebel Sandino raided the mine and took him prisoner. Marshall disappeared with Sandino's men and was never heard of again.

About the time Marshall got the job that I had counted mine I got one more belated reply in the form of a telephone call from a downtown mining company's office. Within the hour I was interviewing their manager.

"We want a manager for our emerald mine in Colombia, South America."

"I've mined diamonds . . . but never emeralds. Don't know anything about them except that they're green."

He took off his glasses and fiddled with them. "We've already had two men running this mine. Both of them claimed to know all about emerald mining and both of them lost us money. You can't do any worse than they did."

It was not long before we had made a deal.

"When do you want me to leave?" I asked.

He consulted a shipping folder. "There's a Fruit Company boat leaving to-morrow and our man out there is in a hurry to leave. He can't go till you get there"

I walked round the desk and read the shipping folder over his shoulder.

"I see she touches in Cuba. I'll catch her in Havana. By

taking train to Florida I can squeeze in a couple of days with my family before I leave the country." They could follow later, when I had got some roots down in the country of my newest venture.

I was going southward at last. Not quite south because Colombia lies just north of the equator. Still, I should see once more the delectable lands that lie between Capricorn and Cancer. Not yet the South African *veld*. When I went back to South Africa I wanted to buy land. Land would require capital and the capital was yet to make.

THE END

INDEX

INDEX